W0255321

This series aims to report new developments in economics and mathematical systems and teaching quickly, informally and at a high level. The type of material considered for publication includes:

1. Preliminary drafts of original papers and monographs
2. Lectures on a new field, or presenting a new angle on a classical field
3. Seminar work-outs
4. Reports of meetings

Texts which are out of print but still in demand may also be considered if they fall within these categories.

The timeliness of a manuscript is more important than its form, which may be unfinished or tentative. Thus, in some instances, proofs may be merely outlined and results presented which have been or will later be published elsewhere.

Publication of *Lecture Notes* is intended as a service to the international mathematical community, in that a commercial publisher, Springer-Verlag, can offer a wider distribution to documents which would otherwise have a restricted readership. Once published and copyrighted, they can be documented in the scientific literature.

Manuscripts

Manuscripts are reproduced by a photographic process; they must therefore be typed with extreme care. Symbols not on the typewriter should be inserted by hand in indelible black ink. Corrections to the typescript should be made by sticking the amended text over the old one, or by obliterating errors with white correcting fluid. Should the text, or any part of it, have to be retyped, the author will be reimbursed upon publication of the volume. Authors receive 75 free copies.
The typescript is reduced slightly in size during reproduction; best results will not be obtained unless the text on any one page is kept within the overall limit of 18 x 26.5 cm (7 x 10½ inches). The publishers will be pleased to supply on request special stationery with the typing area outlined.
Manuscripts in English, German or French should be sent to Prof. Dr. M. Beckmann, Department of Economics, Brown University, Providence, Rhode Island 02912/USA, Prof. Dr. H. P. Künzi, Institut für Operations Research der Universität Zürich, Weinbergstraße 59. 8006 Zürich or Prof. Dr. G. Goos, Institut für Informatik, Universität Karlsruhe, 7500 Karlsruhe, Zirkel 2.

Lecture Notes in Economics and Mathematical Systems

Operations Research, Computer Science, Social Science

Edited by M. Beckmann, Providence, G. Goos, Karlsruhe, and H. P. Künzi, Zürich

75

GI

Gesellschaft für Informatik e.V.

Bericht Nr. 3

1. Fachtagung über Programmiersprachen

München, 9.–11. März 1971

Herausgegeben im Auftrag der Gesellschaft für Informatik von Hans Langmaack und Manfred Paul

Springer-Verlag

Berlin · Heidelberg · New York 1972

Prof. Dr. Hans Langmaack
Institut für Angewandte Mathematik
der Universität des Saarlandes
Prof. Dr. Manfred Paul
Gesellschaft für Informatik
Mathematisches Institut
der Technischen Universität München

AMS Subject Classifications (1970): 68 A 05, 68 A 30

ISBN-13:978-3-540-06051-2 e-ISBN-13:978-3-642-80718-3
DOI: 10.1007/978-3-642-80718-3

Vorwort

Programmiersprachen gehören seit den Anfängen der Entwicklung des Fachgebietes Informatik zu dessen innerstem Kern. Dabei faßt der Begriff "Programmiersprachen" eine Reihe von Gegenständen der Informatik zusammen, die insgesamt auf das Ziel gerichtet sind, den Benutzern von Rechenanlagen die Programmierung wesentlich zu erleichtern. Unter diesen Gegenständen finden sich vor allem:

Prinzipien für Entwurf und Entwicklung von Programmiersprachen,

Definition von Programmiersprachen,

Techniken des Übersetzerbaus für Programmiersprachen.

Wurden Programmiersprachen zu Beginn der Entwicklung hauptsächlich unter dem Gesichtspunkt des Stapelbetriebes behandelt, so erlaubt seit einigen Jahren die Ausstattung großer Rechenanlagen mit entsprechenden Betriebssystemen über Stapelbetrieb hinaus auch Dialogbetrieb. Diese Betriebsart hatte selbstverständlich Rückwirkungen auf die Untersuchungen über Programmiersprachen. Beispielsweise sind dadurch Fragen der inkrementierenden Übersetzung wieder aktuell geworden, die schon früher gelegentlich behandelt wurden. In ganz natürlicher Weise hat sich damit der Problemkreis auf Dialogbetrieb ausgedehnt, so daß der GI-Fachausschuß für Programmiersprachen auch Dialogsprachen in die Tagungsthemen einbezogen hat.

Die Aufforderung zur Einsendung von Vortragsmanuskripten zu den genannten Themen fand ein erfreulich starkes Echo. Dies war um so ermutigender, als auch die Zahl der Teilnehmer unerwartet groß war. Die lebhaften Diskussionen zeigten ein äußerst reges Interesse an den Vorträgen und den dabei angeschnittenen Fragen.

Den Vortragenden sei deshalb an dieser Stelle sehr herzlich gedankt für ihre Beiträge zur ersten Fachtagung der Gesellschaft für Informatik über Programmiersprachen. Sie waren es vor allem, die den Erfolg der Tagung ermöglicht haben. Daneben gilt unser Dank allen Teilnehmern, die durch Diskussionsbeiträge geholfen haben, die Tagung lebendig zu gestalten. Schließlich möchten wir allen Mitarbeitern danken, die die organisatorischen Arbeiten zur Vorbereitung und zur Durchführung der Tagung so erfolgreich abgewickelt haben.

München, den 1.2.1972 die Herausgeber

Inhaltsverzeichnis

AUTORENADRESSEN

K. ALBER, IBM Laboratories, Dept. 3247, 703 Boeblingen, Postfach 210.

KAREL ČULIK, Brno - Nerudova 8, Czechoslovakia.

KLAUS-DIETER GRAF, 1 Berlin 15, Uhlandstraße 29.

G. HELDMANN, Firma Siemens Systemprogrammierung SP 3.1, 8 München 25, Baierbrunnerstraße 3.

HAROLD HOEHNE, Inst. f. Nachrichtenverarbeitung, T.H. Darmstadt, Prof. Dr. Ing. R. Piloty, 61 Darmstadt, Arheilgerstraße 1.

H.-T. KRÜGER, Firma Siemens Systemprogrammierung SP 3.1, 8 München 25, Baierbrunnerstraße 3.

INGBERT KUPKA, Institut für Informatik der Universität, 2 Hamburg 13, Sedanstraße 19.

K. LAGALLY, Rechenzentrum der Technischen Universität, Arbeitsgruppe für Betriebssysteme, 8 München 2, Arcisstraße 21.

KARL-HEINZ MOHN, Rechenzentrum der Ruhr-Universität, 463 Bochum, Buscheystraße, Geb. NA.

MANFRED ROSENDAHL, Rechenzentrum der Ruhr-Universität, 463 Bochum, Buscheystraße, Geb. NA.

GERD SAPPER, Rechenzentrum der Technischen Universität München, Arbeitsgruppe für Betriebssysteme, 8 München 2, Arcisstraße 21.

R. SCHILD, Fachgruppe Computer-Wissenschaften, Eidgen. Technische Hochschule, CH-8006 Zürich, Clausiusstraße 55.

HANS ALBRECHT SCHMID, Institut für Informatik, Universität Karlsruhe, 75 Karlsruhe, Englerstraße 2.

F. SCHWENKEL, University of Notre Dame, Computer Science Department.

H. WÖSSNER, Mathematisches Institut der Technischen Universität München, 8 München 2, Arcisstraße 21.

WILLIAM A. WULF, Carnegie-Mellon University, Pittsburgh, PA/USA.

REINER ZIMMER, Siemens AG, Dv T Systemprogramme, 8 München 25, Hofmannstraße 51.

HANSPETER ZOLLER, Rechenzentrum der Ruhr-Universität, 463 Bochum. Buscheystraße, Geb. NA.

IMPLEMENTATION OF THE PROGRAMMING LANGUAGE PASCAL

by R. Schild

The programming language Pascal was developed at the Federal Institute of Technology (ETH) in Zürich by Prof. N. Wirth and implemented by his assistants U. Ammann, E. Marmier and myself. The language evolved in the course of a project for extending and generalizing Algol 60 , a project which also produced the language Algol W .

Immediately the question will be asked: Why another programming language? Isn't the confusion already large enough?

Our answer is best given by stating the goals we had set ourselves:

On the one hand we wanted to create a tool which allows the programmer to write his programs in a natural, clear, and concise way. This requirement would also make the language well suited for teaching -- not for teaching the language itself (although that is of course desirable, and unfortunately not true of many existing programming languages), but for teaching the art of programming, a quality which most languages unfortunately are lacking.

On the other hand our aim was to develop an implementation which is both reliable and efficient, efficient in the sense that the compiler should produce fast-running code, and should do so in little time.

As mentioned before, Algol 60 was used as a basis for Pascal, since it meets the demands in respect to teaching better than any other standard language. However, Algol includes certain construction principles which we did not want to incorporate in Pascal, mostly because they would have downgraded its efficiency. On the other hand, Pascal contains extensions of Algol, primarily in the domain of data structures.

The language (syntax and semantics) and its compiler were developed simultaneously. This provided us with the possibility to modify or entirely exclude constructions which could not be implemented efficiently.

Implementation

The Pascal System as it is implemented at the ETH consists of two parts: the monitor and the compiler.

The monitor (written in assembly language) is loaded into memory by the operating system. It contains routines to load the compiler, to load the compiled program, to transfer control to a loaded program, and the file handling routines.

The monitor remains in core during compilation and during execution of a program.

The compiler (written in Pascal) is loaded by the monitor and receives control from it. It then processes the user program, producing absolute (executable) code which permits faster loading. Since the compiler itself is also a Pascal program and is kept in absolute code, it, too, can be loaded very quickly.

After having returned control to the monitor, the compiler is overwritten by the user program which then receives control from the monitor.

Let us now take a closer look at the language, the compiler, and the code which it produces.

To attain high efficiency, we constructed the compiler as a one-pass-system, thereby avoiding the need for repeated input/output of scratch files. To make the syntax analysis as simple as possible we used a top-down method, representing the syntax as a set of pseudo-finite automata, and using a one-symbol-lookahead scheme. The compiler closely resembles the syntax: each automaton corresponds to a procedure.

The compiler can be divided into three distinct parts:

1) A symbol scanner, which recognizes and encodes the reserved words, reads and converts numerical constants, skips comments, and reads identifiers. It is called by the other two parts whenever the next symbol is to be read.

2) The set of procedures which process the declarations.

3) The set of procedures which process the statements.

Communication between parts 2) and 3) is acheived through a so-called context table. As soon as they are declared, all identifiers are entered there by part 2), together with their attributes. Part 3) uses this table to do type checking, to obtain information about the size of variables etc.

The context table is a list structure, with all entries for one level linked together. The attributes for each entry include pointers to other entries in the table, such as the pointer to the type of a variable, or the pointer to the component type of an array, etc. Thus part 3) actually dictates what information is to be included in the table, and part 2) enters it.

The code which is to be produced by the compiler depends on the representation of the program during execution. This representation in turn is influenced by the language itself.

Procedures in Pascal can be called recursively, recursion being an important concept in programming which should definitely be included in a language used for teaching programming. Therefore the procedure code has to be reentrant. We employed the standard manner of separating data and code, using a new data segment for each activation of the procedure. The data segments are allocated space in the run time stack and addressed viá an index register. Since the number of index registers is limited, it was natural to limit the depth of procedure nesting. This of course has no effect on the number of recursive calls of any one procedure, which is limited not by the number of index registers but by the size of the run time stack.

The data segments are linked through two chains:

- The dynamic chain, which links the segment of a called procedure to that of the calling procedure, and
- the static chain, which links the segment of a procedure with the segment of the one within which it is declared.

The base addresses in the index registers are actually a copy of the currently relevant static chain, and they must therefore be updated upon return from a procedure. However, if the called procedure is local to the calling one, updating is not necessary, and if they are both on the same level, there is only one index register to update. These are the most common cases, so the overhead is mostly negligible.

The case is slightly different with formal procedures. Here updating must take place also on entering the called procedure, since at compile time its level is not known at the point of call. It is passed as part of the procedure descriptor, along with the entry address, when a procedure is used as an actual parameter.

A Pascal program is constructed according to the following example:

```
decl
proc P1
    decl
    proc P2
        decl
        code
    proc P3
        decl
        code
    code
proc P4
    decl
    code
code
```

Since we have a one pass compiler and the declarations of the main program are processed first, it is natural that we should allocate space for these variables first (beginning with the first available address). Note that the main program is not oalled recursively, so that its data need not be in the run time stack.

Following this space we have the code for procedure P2 (code for P1 is not processed until later). As mentioned earlier, all variables local to procedures will have their space allocated in the run time stack as the procedures are called.

Next the code for P3 is processed, etc. The run time representation of the program will therefore look like this:

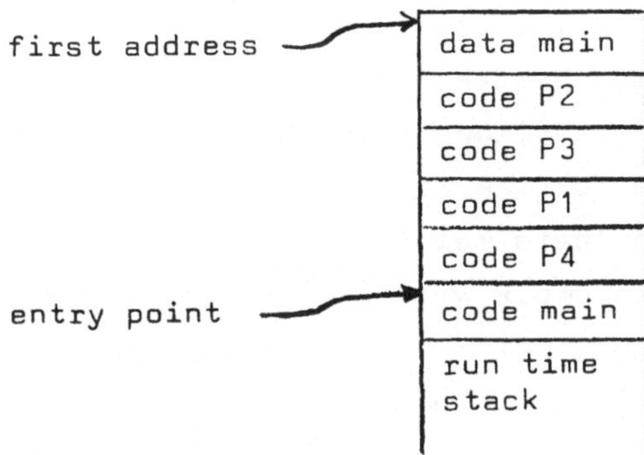

The compiled program is output onto a scratch file from which it is loaded by the monitor.

We compile the code for one procedure in a buffer and empty this buffer when the end of the procedure is encountered. This means that all storage locations addressed in this procedure must be known before its code is output. Thus we do not permit a goto-statement to lead out of a procedure, as the address of the destination would be unknown.

A similar problem occurs in two other cases:

1) if the surrounding procedure (e.g. P1) is called by an enclosed one (e.g. P2). Since we have recursion, such a call is permitted.

2) if a 'forward' declared procedure is called. The forward

declaration is desirable to allow two procedures on the same level to call each other (another form of recursion).

Ex.: <u>procedure</u> A; forward;
<u>procedure</u> B; <u>begin</u> ... A; ... <u>end</u>;
<u>procedure</u> A; <u>begin</u> ... B; ... <u>end</u>;

In both cases the address (entry point) of the called procedure is not yet known when the call is processed.

We solved this problem by compiling an indirect jump. A certain area in the execution time representation (with known address) is reserved for such jumps. While the address of a procedure is not yet known, it is assigned a 'temporary' address in this jump area. Later, when the procedure in question is compiled, a jump to the actual entry address is entered in the jump area, at the 'temporary' address.

The problem was now to reserve such an area. We chose to allocate it immediately following the data for the main program, before the code for the first compiled procedure (in our example, between 'data main' and 'code P2'). The compiled program of the example with the forward declaration will now look like this:

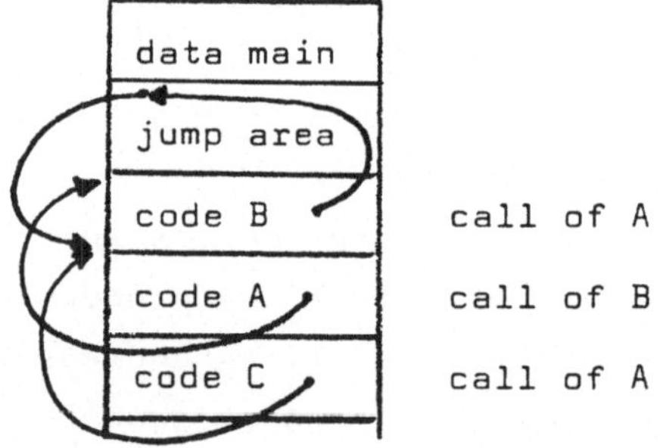

I have added a procedure C to show that if A is called from C (when its address is known) it is of course jumped to directly.

A slight disadvantage of this scheme is the fact that we have to allocate an area of fixed size, thereby limiting the number of such forward jumps. (In our implementation, the limit is 25, hardly a real restriction.)

An alternative would have been the allocation of space

at the end of the run time stack, since the field length (the amount of memory space allotted to our job) is known. This was deemed undesirable, however, because of the possibility of the run time stack's flowing into the jump table, causing difficult-to-detect run time errors.

We are now ready to take a closer look at the language itself.

One feature of Pascal makes it possible for the programmer to define his own types.

We distinguish between basic types and structured types. The basic data types are the scalar types, that is to say, they consist of an ordered set of values. The standard types, which are assumed predeclared, are all scalar : real, integer, Boolean, char, alfa. The programmer can declare new scalar types, so-called symbolic types, where the values are denoted by identifiers.

```
Ex.:    color = (red,yellow,green,blue)
        shape = (triangle,rectangle,circle)
```

A variable of type color may assume any of the four values red, yellow, green, or blue, and no other.

Internally, the symbolic constants are represented by integer values, starting at zero, but the programmer need not know this.

From the scalar types the programmer can define structured types. They are:

Array: This is a random-access structure whose components are all of the same type. The address of an element is computable from the value of one or more indices.

Ex.: <u>array</u> [1..10, red..blue] <u>of</u> integer

A multidimensional array can be thought of as a one-dimensional array whose components are arrays. Thus two-dimensional arrays are stored row by row.

Address calculation is done by shifting and adding if the component size is the form 2^m , $2^m + 2^n$, or $2^m - 2^n$.

An assignment between two arrays of the same type is permitted. It is accomplished by copying the array cell by cell.

Record: This is also a random-access structure, but the components may be of different types. Components are denoted by field names. There may be several variants of one record type, depending on the value of one or more tagfields. Thus the size of a record depends on the variant. Addresses of fields in different variants can coincide.

Ex.:

```
fig = record x,y : real;
             area : real;
          case s : shape of
        triangle:   (side : real;
                     inclination,angle1,angle2 : angle );
        rectangle:  (side1,side2 : real;
                     skew,angle3 : angle );
        circle:     (diameter : real );
      end
```

For record variables and for records as components of a structured type (except classes) the size of the maximum variant is allocated. In classes, the programmer can specify for which variant space is to be allocated.

As between arrays, assignments between two records of the same type are permitted and accomplished the same way.

Powerset: This type defines a set of values which is the powerset of its base type, which must be scalar.

Ex.: powerset 1 .. 3

A variable of this type can take on the values
[1], [2], [3], [1,2], [1,3], [2,3], [1,2,3], and [] (the empty set)

A powerset variable uses one word of memory, which in our machine consists of 60 bits. We set bit i to 1 if and only if i is a member of the particular value. E.g. the value [1,2,5,8] is represented as 00...0100100110

The operations a ∨ b (set union), a ∧ b (set intersection), and a - b (set difference) are thus easily accomplished by the logical operations a∨b, a∧b, and ¬b∧a, respectively, on the entire word.

The relation <u>in</u> (set inclusion) is also easily implemented by simply inspecting the i-th bit.

<u>File</u>: This is a sequential-access structure consisting of an unspecified number of components of the same type. A file pointer allows access to one element and can be moved forward to the next element or reset to the beginning of the file.

Files reside on external storage media. The compiler provides a buffer area which is filled by the operating system and emptied by the program (input) or vice versa (output). The programmer manipulates files through three standard procedures GET, PUT, and RESET.

The interface to the operating system consists of a file environment table which contains two pointers IN and OUT pointing into the buffer. IN always points to the location where new information can be entered into the buffer while OUT shows where information can be taken from it. One of the pointers is moved by the system, the other by the program (depending on the mode of the file) and both are inspected by system and program. With an input-file e.g., the OUT pointer is the one moved by the program.

A copy of the pointer moved by the program, located at the 'address' which was assigned to the file by the compiler, is used to access the current file element.

Taking a file named INPUT as example, this element is denoted by INPUT↑ . A call of GET(INPUT) results in this pointer being 'moved' to point to the next element. (Elements may of course be more than one word in length, such as in a file of records.) The buffer, which is treated as circular, is always an integral multiple of the file element size. Thereby any wrap-around difficulties are avoided without necessitating copying of the current file element into a work area.

If there is not enough information in the buffer, the GET-routine issues a request to the operating system for more data.

If the file is exhausted, an end-of-file flag is set which can be inspected by the programmer via the standard Boolean function EOF. The end-of-file flag is simply the sign bit of the word at file-address + 1 , and the EOF-function tests this word for < 0 .

For output files, the roles of the pointers IN and OUT as seen from the user program are reversed, but the principles remain the same. The current file element pointer is in this case moved by the procedure PUT.

The standard procedure RESET physically repositions the file to the beginning and also resets all necessary pointers.

Pascal character files (<u>file</u> <u>of</u> char) receive special treatment. Each machine word consists of ten characters. For an input file the current word is unpacked into a ten-word character buffer, and the current file element pointer (at the file address) then points into this buffer. For an output file the characters are stored in the character buffer (by the program) and then packed and put into the file buffer. This packing and unpacking is automatically done when it is necessary, by the two routines GET and PUT. For the programmer it looks as though the file pointer were moved one character each time.

Note that this character buffer is used only by the Pascal program and the standard routines; it is not seen by the system.

<u>Class</u>: This structure consists of a variable number of components of the same type (but possibly of different size, in the case of records). Elements are created or removed through standard procedures and addressed through pointer variables. Thus we are led to a new type: the <u>pointer</u>.

Each pointer type is associated with a variable of a class type (<u>not</u> with the class type itself!). Thereby we can ensure (at compile time) that pointer variables will take on only values which really point into the specified class variables, eliminating a great potential source for obscure errors.

The space for a class variable is reserved at compile

time. It is filled by the standard procedure ALLOC. With every class variable is associated a hidden pointer pointing to the next free word in the class. This pointer cannot be used directly by the programmer. A call of ALLOC(P) returns the current value of the hidden pointer in P. (Note that the name of the pointer variable suffices to indicate which class variable is meant.) At the same time, the value of the hidden pointer is increased by the size of the allocated element. If the components are variable records, the desired variant is indicated by the values of the relevant tagfields, which are written as parameters following the pointer variable in the call of ALLOC.

```
Ex.:    figure : class 100 of fig ;
        p   :  ↑ figure ;
```

Calling ALLOC(p) will increase the hidden pointer by 8 (the maximum size of the record fig), while ALLOC(p,circle) increases it by 5 (the size needed for the variant where s = circle).

The standard procedure RESET(P), where P is not a file but a pointer variable, sets the hidden pointer to the current value of P.

On entry to a procedure the hidden pointers of all local class variables are initialized so that the class appears empty.

All pointer variables may take on a value <u>nil</u> , which is a constant pointing into no class. The value <u>nil</u> is implemented in such a way that an address error results if it is used for addressing, whereupon the job is aborted by the system. An alternative would be to test for the value <u>nil</u> and to exit to a monitor error routine.

This completes our short overview of the types in Pascal and their implementation. Let us now look at some points in the compilation of code.

We introduced a few optimisations which can be done fairly easily at compile time.

Constant terms in an expression or a set of indices are evaluated at compile time.

Multiplication by an integer constant is accomplished by shifting and adding if the constant is of the form 2^m, $2^m + 2^n$, or $2^m - 2^n$ (these forms include all integers from 1 through 10). Division by 2^m is also done by shifting.

By restricting the Algol <u>for</u>-statement to the forms

<u>for</u> i := E_1 <u>to</u> E_2 or <u>for</u> i := E_1 <u>downto</u> E_2

(<u>to</u> / <u>downto</u> corresponds to <u>step</u> +1 / -1 <u>until</u> , E_1 and E_2 are expressions)

where E_2 is not allowed to change during execution of the <u>for</u>-statement (it is evaluated and stored at the beginning) we were able to produce code which is quite a bit more efficient than the corresponding Algol code.

On the other hand Pascal offers two other repetitive statements:

<u>repeat</u> S <u>until</u> B (B is a Boolean expression,
<u>while</u> B <u>do</u> S S is a statement)

which reflect the notion of executing a sequence repeatedly for an unknown number of times better than the Algol <u>for</u>-<u>while</u>-construction.

The Algol <u>switch</u> is expressed in Pascal by the <u>case</u>-statement:

<u>case</u> E <u>of</u>
v_1 : S_1 ;
v_2 : S_2 ;
⋮ ⋮
v_n : S_n ;
<u>end</u>

(E is an expression which can take on the values v_1 , v_2 , ... , v_n . if E = v_i , statement S_i is executed)

This eliminates the need for the <u>goto</u> at the end of S_i which is almost always necessary in an Algol <u>switch</u> construction. Furthermore the values v_i need not start at 1 as in Algol. Implementation of the case statement is by an indexed jump into a sequence of jump-instructions.

Parameters in procedure-calls may be accessed by reference (the address of the actual variable is stored in the appropriate field of the segment of the called procedure) or by value (the value of the actual expression is stored). We have not included the call-by-name concept because, even though it is perhaps the easiest to understand by the learner, it leads to inefficient code, which is contrary to our intentions. If the actual parameter is a procedure name (for a formal procedure) its base address (that is the static link corresponding to the level of the procedure), its entry point and an indication for each parameter (whether it is called by reference of by value) is stored. This last information is needed since the called procedure is responsible for storing the addresses or the values when the formal procedure is called.
Note by the way, that when a parameter is called by reference, the actual parameter may not be an expression. In an earlier implementation, where we did not yet have the value parameter, this had to be permitted, of course, but in this case the value of the expression was stored in a temporary cell and the address of this cell passed as the parameter. In this way we avoided things like changing the values of constants.

This covers the main points about code compilation. In conclusion I would like to mention a few points about our future plans.

The present implementation contains almost no run time checks (except for class overflow and trying to read past the end of a file). In the very near future we intend to release an implementation which will include run time index checking as well as checking for the value <u>nil</u> of a pointer. It will also include some programming aids such as frequency counts and a post mortem dump at the source level. We plan to refine our system so it becomes a valuable tool not only for the beginner but also for the expert programmer in developing good, error-free, well written programs.

A SYSTEMS PROGRAMMING LANGUAGE

by William A. Wulf *

INTRODUCTION

In the fall of 1969 Carnegie-Mellon University acquired a PDP-10 to support the research of the Computer Science Department. This research involves the production of a substantial number of large systems programs of the type which have typically been written in assembly language, e.g., compilers, interpreters, etc. In many cases it was resolved to use a higher-level language to implement these systems. This decision immediately lead to another question: which language. In turn this lead to a consideration of the characteristics, if any, which are unique to, or at least exaggerated in, the production and maintenance of systems programs. One product of these deliberations was a new language which we call Bliss. In this paper we shall deal with the design considerations which most influenced the nature of Bliss and how these considerations manifest themselves in the language.

We refer to Bliss as an "implementation language", although we admit that the term is somewhat ambiguous since presumably all computer languages are used to implement _something_. To us the phrase connotes a general-purpose, higher-level language in which the primary emphasis has been placed upon a specific application, namely the writing of large, _production_ software systems for a specific machine. We emphasize the word "production"; we are not talking about writing toy systems. Special purpose languages, for example, such as compiler-compilers, do not fit into this definition. We stress the word "implementation" in our defini-

* This work was supported by the Advanced Research Projects Agency of the Office of the Secretary of Defense (F44620-70-C-0107) and is monitored by the Air Force Office of Scientific Research.

tion and have not used words such as "design" and "documentation". We do not necessarily expect that an implementation language will be an appropriate vehicle for expressing the initial design of a large system, nor for the exclusive documentation of that system. Concepts such as machine-independence, expressing the design and implementation in the same notation, self-documentation, and others, are clearly desirable goals and are criteria by which we evaluated various languages. However, they are not implicit in our definition. There are a few extant examples of languages which fit our definition: EPL (a PL/I derivative used on MULTICS [1]), B5500 Extended Algol (Burroughs Corporation [2]), PL/360 [3], and BCPL [4].

The various arguments for and against the use of higher-level languages to write systems software have been discussed at length. We do not intend to reproduce them here in detail except to note that the skeptics argue primarily on two grounds: efficiency, and an assertion that the systems programmer must not allow anything to get between himself and the machine. The advocates argue on the grounds of production speed (and cost), maintainability, redesign and modification, understandability and correctness. The report of the NATO Conference on Software Engineering held in Garmish (October, 1968) [5] contains several discussions on these points.

It is our opinion that program efficiency, except possibly for a very small number of very small code segments, is determined by overall program design and not by locally tricky, "bit-picking" coding practices. Moreover, the critical code segments are frequently located only after the system is operational. This opinion is born out by many systems which have experienced substantial performance improvements from redesign or restructuring resulting from understanding or insight after the system has been running for some time (see, for example, David's comments, pp. 55-57 of [5]). One of the paramount design objectives of Bliss was to facilitate redesign and recoding. Since this redesign is frequently done by someone other than the program's original author, there is a corollary objective of readability. This argues for good documentation - but also for understandability of the code itself. Understandability is a function of many things, not all of which are inherent in the language in which a program is written - a programmer's individual style for example. Nevertheless, the length of a program text and the structure imposed upon that text are important factors and argue strongly for the use of a higher-level language as well as saying something about the nature of that language.

Presuming the decision to use an implementation language, which one should one choose? An argument might be made for choosing one of the existing languages, say Fortran, PL/I, or APL, and possibly extending it in some way. We have chosen to add to the tower of Babel by defining yet another new language, and some justification is required. The only valid rationale for creating a new language is that the existing ones are inappropriate to the task. What then are the special characteristics of systems programs which existing languages are inappropriate to express? (Later we shall discuss how these manifest themselves in Bliss.) The two special characteristics most frequently mentioned are efficiency and access to all hardware features of the machine. We accept these, but feel they miss the mark.

The most outstanding characteristics one observes about programming systems are their size and their rate of evolution. Programming systems are never finished so long as their host machine exists somewhere. They constantly have new features added to them and old errors repaired. The more heavily a system is used, the more rapid the rate of this evolution and repair. This situation seems inevitable. Hence, we feel that the central problem with which systems programmers, and hence systems programming languages, must deal is that of size and evolution - while retaining efficiency.

"Coping with evolution" is far too broad and vague a phrase to provide a goal from which a language designer can work. Below is a more specific list of goals which are derived from the more general one. Perhaps, of these goals the least obvious is that concerning the "representation of data structures".

All programming deals with structured information - that is, with atomic information items which not only have a value, but also bear some relation to other atomic information items. These relationships are expressed in programming languages by "data structures" such as arrays, lists, queues, stacks, etc. which are used to model the real relations which exist between data items. Most programming languages contain a fixed set of such data structures - namely, those deemed appropriate to an application area by the designers of the language. Scientific languages such as Algol and Fortran, for example, contain only arrays (as models of the mathematical vector and matrix structures). These data structures are, in turn, represented, or modeled, by the implementor of the programming system in terms of the implicit data structure of a hardware computer.

So long as the data structures required by an application area are small in number and fairly uniform over the area, as is largely the case in scientific applications, this situation is acceptable. In systems programming, however, this is decidedly not the case. All of the structures mentioned above are used, as well as many others that have no generic name. Furthermore, in the interest of efficiency, different representations of the same logical structure are used. To achieve reasonable efficiency it is imperative that a language to be used for systems programming permit the definition of the representations to be used.

When a programming system is initially built, the conscientous systems programmer devises representations to maximize the efficiency of his system. As new features are added to a system and it evolves, the original representations may no longer be the most appropriate or even remotely acceptable. To the extent to which the original representations cannot be modified, evolution requires circumventing those representations - kludges!

DESIGN GOALS IN BLISS

- space/time economy (be sure you can write a good compiler)
- access to all relevant hardware features
- object code must not depend upon elaborate run-time support (try for zero)
- control over the representation of data structures
- flexible range of control structures (notably including recursion, co-routines, and asynchronous processes)
- modularization of a system into separately compilable sub-modules
- parameterization, especially conditional compilation
- encourage program structuring for understandability } implications for control structures
- encourage program structuring for debugging } implications for control structures
- economy of concepts (involution), generality, flexibility,...
- utility as a design tool
- machine independence

Not all of the goals mentioned above are fully compatible in practice. For example, efficiency, access to machine features, and machine independence are conflicting goals. In fact the design of Bliss is not machine independent, although the underlying philosophy and much of the specific design are. The machine for which the language was being designed, the PDP-10, was constantly in the minds of the designers as the language took shape. The code to be generated for each proposed construct, or form of a construct, was considered before that construct was included in, or excluded from, the language. Thus the characteristics of the target machine pervade the language in both overt and subtle ways. This is not to say that Bliss could not be implemented for another machine; it could. It does say that Bliss is particularly well suited to implementation on the PDP-10 and that it could probably not be as efficiently implemented on another machine. We think of Bliss as a member (the only one at present) of a class of languages similar in philosophy and mirroring a similar concern for the important aspects of systems programming, but each suited to its own host machine.

As another example of the incompatibility of these goals, consider the requirement for minimal run-time support and the use of the implementation language as a design tool. In some sense a design tool should be at a higher level than the object being designed - that is, the tool should relieve the designer from concern over whichever details the designer deems appropriate only for later consideration. Any language relieves its user from concern over certain details, even assembly language frees the coder from the need to make specific address assignments. Assembly language is not a good design tool, however, precisely because the class of such facilities is small, a higher level language is better because the class is larger. There is a point, however, beyond which broadening the class of details which are handled sutomatically introduces substantial costs in run-time efficiency and requisite run-time support. The design of Bliss walks a very fine line between generality, efficiency, and minimal run-time support. At the time of this writing Bliss programs require <u>no</u> run-time support.

Let us return to the issue of the representation of data structures briefly. Two principles were followed in the design of the data structure facility of Bliss:

- The user must be able to specify the accessing algorithm for elements of a structure (which is equivalent to specifying the representation) at as low a level as he deems necessary.
- The structure definition and the algorithms which operate on the elements of a structure must be separated in such a way that either can be modified without affecting the other.

It is customary in conventional higher level programming languages to include a number of implicit data structures such as arrays, lists, strings, and so forth, as an integral part of the language. The implementor of these languages chooses a representation for these structures and the languages user has no control over them. Bliss takes an entirely different approach. The first of these principles reflects the need for flexibility and efficiency in systems programming. It also reflects my conviction that I, as the designer of Bliss, cannot - and must not try to - predict which representations a system programmer will need. Any given set of primitive structures, with or without the ability to define more complex structures from them, would be totally inappropriate. Instead, representations of structures are defined in Bliss in terms of the computational procedure, algorithm, by which elements of that structure are accessed.

Thus no decisions are made a priori by the Bliss implementation concerning the most appropriate representation of even the most elementary structures, and the user has maximal flexibility in choosing one.

The second principle reflects a concern for the modification of systems written in Bliss. So long as the representation of structures is separated from the algorithms which operate on data contained in those structures, and the representations are easily modifiable, it is possible for systems to evolve in an orderly fashion. Of course, providing such a facility does not guarantee that it will be used intelligently - but that is an educational, and possibly managerial, issue and not a technical one.

Most existing languages satisfy one or the other of the above criteria but not both. Assembly languages allow (indeed, demand) algorithmic specification of data structures since they have no implicit data structures. The specification of a structure in an assembly language program need not be localized, however, and is usually distributed to all places where an element of the structure is accessed - thus making it difficult to modify. Algol, Fortran, etc., on the other hand, localize the specification of a structure to its declaration site but do not allow its representation to be defined by the programmer.

DESCRIPTION OF BLISS

Bliss may be characterized as an Algol-PL/I derivative in the sense that it has a similar expression format and operator hierarchy, a block structure with lexically and dynamically local variables, similar conditional and looping constructs, and (potentially) recursive procedures. As may be seen from the two simple examples shown below, the general format of Bliss code is quite Algol-like; the similarity stops shortly beyond this glib comparison.

```
function factorial (n) =
   if .n leq 1 then 1 else .n*factorial (.n-1);

function QQ search (K) =
   begin register R,Q,A,E;
   E ← R ← .K/.n; Q ← .K mod .n; A ← .const;
   do if .ST[.R] eql .K
      then return .R
      else (R ← .R + .A; A ← .A + .Q)
   until .R eql .E
   end;
```

The first of these examples is the familiar recursive definition of factorial. The second example is the "quadratic quotient" hash search described by J. Bell in the February 1970 CACM.

We will now describe the features of Bliss in terms of its major aspects: (1) the underlying concept of storage, (2) control, (3) data structures, and finally mention some other miscellaneous features.

1. Storage

In order to implement the objectives set out previously concerning the representation of data structures it is first necessary to adopt precise and consistent interpretations of the concepts of "identifier", "name", and "value". The distinction between these concepts is at best fuzzy in most programming languages. The distinction we wish to make is that between an object, a name for the object, and a name of the name. In English prose if one wishes to talk about the integer just larger than five, one writes six, or 6. Six serves as a name for that particular integer, but there are many others: 6, 卌 |, VI, 5+1, etc. Now, if we wish to talk about one of these specific names of six, we enclose it in quotes; thus "6" serves as the name of a particular graphic character which, in turn, names a specific integer.

Bliss makes a similar distinction except that the objects named are *variables*, i.e., their value may change in time, represented in some storage media in the computer. The name of a variable, also called a *pointer* to the variable, is encoded as a bit pattern which itself may be manipulated. An identifier serves as the name of a name of (pointer to) a variable. To complete our analogy, then, a Bliss identifier serves the role of the quoting device in English, pointers correspond to simple names, and the objects ultimately named are variables represented in storage. The weakness in this analogy is that English provides few mechanisms for performing operations on names while in Bliss names are encoded as bit patterns and hence may be operated upon by any operator in the language (see below).

A Bliss program operates with and on a number of storage <u>segments</u>. A storage segment consists of a fixed and finite number of <u>words</u>, each of which is composed of a fixed and finite number of <u>bits</u> (36 for the PDP-10). Any contiguous set of bits within a word is called a <u>field</u>. A field may be <u>named</u>; the value of a name is called a <u>pointer</u> to that field. In particular, an entire word is a field and may be named.

In practice a segment generally contains either program or data, and if the latter, it is generally integer numbers, floating point numbers, characters, or pointers to other data. To a Bliss program, however, a field merely contains a pattern of bits on which the programmer may place any interpretation he chooses. Various specific operations are defined in Bliss and may be applied to fields and bit patterns such as fetching a bit pattern (value) from a field, storing a bit pattern into a field, integer arithmetic, comparison, boolean operations, and so on. These operations are roughly those provided by the hardware interpretations of bit patterns; from these all user-defined operations must be built. The interpretation placed upon a particular bit pattern and consequent transformation performed by an operator is an intrinsic property of that operator, and not of its operands. That is to say, there is no "type" differentation as in Algol.

Segments are introduced into a Bliss program by declarations, called "allocation declarations", for example:

```
global g;
own x,y [5], z;
local p [100];
register r1, r2 [3];
function f(a,b) = .a↑.b;
```

Each of these declarations introduces one or more segments and binds the identifiers mentioned (e.g., g, x, y, etc.) to the name of the first word of the associated segment. (The _function_ declaration also initializes the segment named 'f' to the appropriate machine code.)

The segments introduced by these declarations contain one or more words, where the size may be specified (as in "_local_ p[100]"), defaulted to one (as in "_global_ g;"), or defaulted to whatever length is necessary for initialization (as in the function declaration). The identifiers introduced by a declaration are lexically local to the block in which the declaration is made (that is, they obey the usual Algol scope rules) with one exception - namely, "global" identifiers are made available to other, separately compiled modules. Segments created by _own_, _global_, and _function_ declarations are created only once and are preserved for the duration of the execution of a program. Segments created by _local_ and _register_ declarations are created at the time of block entry and are preserved for the duration of the execution of that block. _Register_ segments differ from _local_ segments only in that they are allocated from the machine's array of 16 general purpose (fast) registers. Re-entry of a block before it is exited (by recursive function calls, for example) behaves as in Algol, that is, _local_ and _register_ segments are dynamically local to each incarnation of the block.

It is important to notice from the discussion above that identifiers are bound to names by declarations, and that the value of a name is a pointer. Thus the value of an instance of an identifier, say x, is _not_ the value of the field named by x, but rather is a pointer to x! This interpretation requires a "contents of" operator for which the symbol "." has been chosen. (Which explains the occurrence of this character in the earlier examples; this will be discussed in greater detail under the subject of data structures.) The operator "." may be applied to any expression, thus placing a "pointer" interpretation on the bit pattern which results from evaluating that expression. Thus the value of the expression "x" is the name (a pointer) of a specific variable, x, ".x" is the bit pattern stored in x, and "..x" is the value of a variable whose name is stored in x, etc.

There are two additional declarations whose effect is to bind identifiers to names, but which do not create segments; examples are:

```
external  s;
bind      y2 = y+2, pa = p+.a;
```

An external declaration binds one or more identifiers to the names represented by the same identifier declared global in another, separately compiled module. The bind declaration binds one or more identifiers to the value of an expression at block entry time. At least potentially the value of this expression may not be calculable until run-time - as in 'pa = p+.a' above. Examples of the use of bind will be found in subsequent sections.

2. Operations and Control

Bliss is an "expression language"; that is, every executable construct, including those which manifest control, is an expression and computes a value. There are no statements in the sense of Algol or PL/I. Expressions may be concatenated with semicolons to form compound expressions, where the value of a compound expression is that of its last (rightmost) component expression. Thus ";" may be thought of as a dyadic operator whose value is simply that of its righthand operand. A pair of symbols begin and end, or left and right parentheses, may be used to embrace such a compound expression and convert it into a simple expression. A block is merely a special case of this construction which happens to contain declarations, thus the value of a block is defined to be the value of its constituent expression.

The assignment operation, "←", is a dyadic operator whose left operand is interpreted as a pointer and whose right operand is an uninterpreted bit pattern. The right operand is stored into the field named by the left operand; the value of the expression is that of its right operand. Recalling the interpretation of identifiers and the "." operator, the expression

$$x \leftarrow .x+1$$

causes the value of the field named by x to be incremented by one. The value of the entire assignment expression is that of the incremented value.

There are six forms of explicit control expressions: conditional, loop, case-select, function, co-routine, and escape.

The conditional expression

$$\underline{\text{if}}\ \epsilon_1\ \underline{\text{then}}\ \epsilon_2\ \underline{\text{else}}\ \epsilon_3$$

and is defined to have the value of the expression ϵ_2 just in the case that the rightmost bit of expression ϵ_1 is a 1 and has the value of ϵ_3

otherwise. The abbreviated form "if ϵ_1 then ϵ_2" is considered to be identical to "if ϵ_1 then ϵ_2 else 0".

Where the conditional expression provides two-way branching, the case* and select* expression provide more general n-way branching:

case e of set ϵ_0; ...; ϵ_{n-1}; ϵ_n tes

select e of nset $\epsilon_0 : \epsilon_1$; $\epsilon_2 : \epsilon_3$; ...; $\epsilon_{2n} : \epsilon_{2n+1}$ tesn

The value of a case expression is ϵ_e, that is, the expression e is evaluated and this value is used as an index to select one of the expressions $\epsilon_i (0 \le i \le n)$, which then becomes the value of the entire case expression.

The select expression is somewhat similar to the case expression except that the expression e is not restricted to the range $0 \le e \le n$. Instead, after e has been evaluated its value is successively compared with the first element of each of the pairs $\epsilon_{2i} : \epsilon_{2i+1}$ in the order of increasing values of i. For each pair such that $e = \epsilon_{2i}$ the second element of the pair, ϵ_{2i+1}, is also executed and the last of these to be executed defines the value of the entire select expression.

Loop expressions imply repeated execution (possibly zero times) of an expression until a specific condition is satisfied. There are several forms:

while ϵ_1 do ϵ

do ϵ while ϵ_1

incr <id> from ϵ_1 to ϵ_2 by ϵ_3 do ϵ

---

*The symbols set-tes and nset-tesn are somewhat arbitrarily chosen bracketing devices which delimit.

In the first form the expression ϵ is repeated so long as the rightmost bit of ϵ_1 remains 1. The second form is similar except that ϵ is evaluated before ϵ_1 thus guaranteeing at least one execution of ϵ. The last form is similar to the familiar "step...until" construct of Algol, except (1) the control variable, <id>, is local to ϵ, and (2) ϵ_1, ϵ_2 and ϵ_3 are computed only once (before entry to the loop). Except for the possibility of an escape expression within ϵ (see below) the value of a loop expression is uniformly taken to be -1.

A function-call expression has the form

$$\epsilon(\epsilon_1, \epsilon_2, \ldots \epsilon_n)$$

This expression causes activation of the segment named by ϵ as a subprogram with an initialization of the formal parameters named in the declaration of the function to the values of the actual parameters $\epsilon_1, \ldots \epsilon_n$. Only call-by-value (in the Algol sense) parameters are allowed; however, call-by-reference is implicitly available since names, pointer values, may be passed. The value of a function call is that resulting from execution of the body of the function. Thus, for example, the value of the following block is 3628800.

```
begin
function factorial(n) =
   if .n leq 1 then 1 else .n*factorial(.n-1);
factorial(10)
end
```

Note that a function call need not explicitly name a function by its associated identifier; all that is required is that ϵ evaluate to the name of a segment. Thus expressions such as the following are valid and useful:

(<u>case</u>.x <u>of</u> <u>set</u> P1;P2;P3 <u>tes</u>)(.z)

Note in this example that the occurrence of a parameter list enclosed in brackets triggers a function call. An identifier by itself merely denotes a pointer to the named segment; thus P1, P2 and P3 are the names of functions (not the result of executing them) and the value of the case expression is the name of one of these functions. Function calls with no parameters are written "ϵ( )".

The body of any function may also be activated as a co-routine and/or asynchronous process. An arbitrary number of distinct incarnations of a single body are allowed; indeed, arbitrarily many simultaneous incarnations of a function body as both co-routines and subroutines may exist simultaneously. In order to permit any of several useful styles of co-routine mechanism only two primitive operations are provided directly in the language:

<u>create</u> $\epsilon(\epsilon^1,\epsilon^2,\ldots,\epsilon^n)$ <u>at</u> ϵ_2 <u>length</u> ϵ_3 <u>then</u> ϵ_4
<u>exchj</u>(ϵ_5,ϵ_6)

More complex co-routine call conventions can easily be constructed from these primitives. (Note that any of the expressions represented by ϵ's above may evaluate at execution time.)

The effect of the create expression is to establish a new, independent context (that is a stack) for the function named by ϵ with actual parameter values $\epsilon^1,\ldots,\epsilon^n$. The stack is set up beginning at the word named by ϵ_2 and is of size ϵ_3 words (to provide overflow protection). The activation point for the newly created co-routine is set to the head of the function named by ϵ. The value of the create expression is a "process name" for the new co-routine. Control then passes on to the expression following the 'create' - in particular the expression ϵ_4 is not executed at this time and the body of ϵ is not activated. When two or more such contexts have been established, control may be passed from the currently executing one to any other by executing an "exchange jump", exchj, expression. An expression "exchj(ϵ_5,ϵ_6)" will cause control to pass to the co-routine named by ϵ_5 (the value of an earlier create expression). The value ϵ_6 becomes the value of the exchj operation which last caused control to pass out of the co-routine named by ϵ_5.

The expression ϵ_4, you will note, is not executed at the time at which a co-routine is created. Instead this expression is executed only when, and if, control passes out of the body of the co-routine by a normal subroutine-type return (e.g., "falling through the end of its body"). The normal minimal action to be expected of ϵ_4 is to return the stack space used by the co-routine and to 'exchj' to some other, active, co-routine. In such a case a subroutine-type return from a co-routine corresponds to the co-routine killing its own existence.

The familiar "goto...label" form of control has not been included in Bliss. There are two reasons for this: (1) unrestricted goto's require considerable run-time support (principally due to the possibility of jumping out of functions and/or blocks), and (2) the authors feel strongly that the general goto, because of the implied violation of program structure, is a major villian in programs which are difficult to understand, modify and debug. There are "good" and "bad" ways to use a goto, and there are restrictions which could be imposed which eliminate the need for run-time support. Consideration of the nature of "good" ways, and of the restrictions necessary to eliminate run-time overhead led us to eliminate to goto altogether, and to the inclusion of conditional, looping, and case-select expressions. These alone, however, are not sufficiently general, or convenient, and consequently the 'escape' expressions were introduced. There are eight forms of the escape mechanism; one for each form of control environment:

exitblock ∈	exitcase ∈
exitcompound ∈	exitselect ∈
exitloop ∈	exit ∈
exitset ∈	return ∈

Each escape expression causes control to exit from a specified control environment (a block, a loop, or a conditional expression, for example) and defines a value (∈) for that control expression (exit exits from any form of control expression, return exits from a function). Essentially the escape mechanism provides a highly structured form of forward branch which is awkward to obtain with the other control expressions.

Consider a linked list of two word cells, the first of which contains a link (pointer) to the next cell (the last cell has link=0) and the second of which contains data. The following expression illustrates one use of an escape expression; the expression has a value which is the pointer to the first negative data item, or a value of -1 if no such item is found. The address of the head of the list is contained in a field called 'head'.

(<u>register</u> t; t ← head; <u>while</u> (t ←..t <u>neq</u> 0 do <u>if</u> .(.t+1) <u>lss</u> 0 <u>then</u> <u>exitloop</u> .t);

Note that the initialization of ('t ← head') sets the value of 't' to a pointer to 'head', not the contents of 'head'.

The concept of a "pointer" to a field (of bits within a word) was mentioned earlier. Actually in Bliss a pointer is not merely an address, but rather of: (1) a word address, (2) a field position, (3) a field size, (4) an (index) register name, and (5) an "indirect address" bit. These five quantities are encoded in a single word and as such are a manipulatable item in the language (a prerequisite of algorithmic representational specification). For simplicity we shall discuss only the first three of these quantities; the reader is referred to the Bliss reference manual [6] for more detail. The "word address", wa, field of a pointer designates the physical machine address of the word; the 'position', p, and 'size', s, designate a field within a word in terms of the number of bits to the right of and within the field.

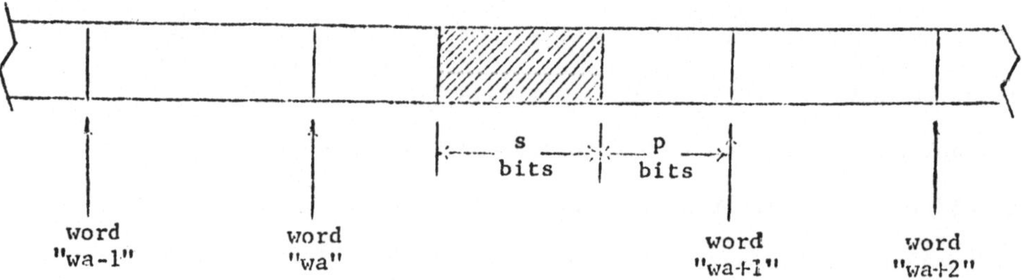

The notation used in Bliss to specify a pointer (taking only the simple wa,p,s case) is "wa<p,s>".

Assume that the declaration

$$\underline{\text{own}}\ x[100]$$

has been made. The identifier x is bound by this particular declaration to a pointer to the 36 bit field which is the first word of this 100 word segment. That is, the word address of the pointer "x" is that of the location allocated to the segment and the position and size fields have values of zero and thirty-six, respectively. If we denote the address of the segment by α_x, then an occurrence of "x" in a Bliss program is identical to an occurrence of "$\alpha_x<0,36>$". If ϵ_0, ϵ_1, and ϵ_2 are expressions, then the syntactic form

$$\epsilon_0<\epsilon_1,\epsilon_2>$$

is by definition a pointer whose word address is the value of ϵ_0 (modulo 2^{18}) and whose position and size specifications are the values of ϵ_1 and ϵ^2 (module 2^6) respectively. Thus "X<3,4>" is a pointer to a four bit field three bits from the right end of a word named X. The word address, position, and size information are encoded within a pointer in such a way that adding small integers ($<2^{18}$) to a pointer increments the word address only. Thus "X+1" is a pointer to the word following X.

3. Data Structures

In order to satisfy the objectives set out above for data strucutres it is desirable to extend the allocation declarations (global, own, local, etc.) described above. However, for exposition we shall first describe the structure mechanism in terms of the allocation declarations already available, then describe the extensions when more motivation is possible.

If you examine an array declaration in Algol, you will note that it serves at least three functions. Consider, for example, the Algol declaration

<u>real</u> <u>array</u> a[1:n, 1:m]

This declaration specifies: (1) a type (<u>real</u>), (2) the "structure" of "a" - and in particular some values to be used in the access algorithm for elements of "a", and (3) that some amount of storage must be set aside (allocated) for "a" on (each) entry to this block. In Bliss there are no implicit types, and hence no declaration of them is necessary. The other functions are split into separate declarations.

Allocation is specified by declarations of the form discussed earlier.

The definition of an accessing algorithm (that is, of a class of structures) is made by a declaration of the form:

<u>structure</u> <name>[<formal parameter list>] = ϵ

where a <name chunk> is a sequence of names separated by colons.

Consider the following example:

```
begin
    structure ary2[i,j] = (.ary2+.i*10+.j);
    own x[100], y[100], z[100];
    map ary2 x:y:z;
    :
    x[.a,.b] ← .y[.b,.a];
    :
end;
```

In this example we introduce a very simple structure, ary2, for two dimensional (10x10) arrays, declare three segments with names 'x', 'y', and 'z' bound to them, and associate the structure class 'ary2' with these names. The name forms "$x[\epsilon_1,\epsilon_2]$" and "$y[\epsilon_3,\epsilon_4]$" are valid within this block and denote evaluation of the accessing algorithm defined by the ary2-_structure_ declaration (with an appropriate substitution of actual for formal parameters).

Although they are not implemented in this way, for purposes of exposition one may think of the structure declaration as defining a function with one more formal parameter than is explicitly mentioned. For example, the structure declaration in the previous example,

```
structure ary2[i,j] = (.ary2+.i*10+.j);
```

conceptually is identical to a function declaration

```
function ary2(f0,f1,f2) = (.f0+.f1*10+.f2);
```

The expressions "x[.a,.b]" and "y[.b,a]" correspond to calls on this function, i.e., to "ary2(x,.a,.b)" and "ary2(y,.b,.a)".

Since, in a structure declaration, there is an implicit, un-named formal parameter, the name of the structure class itself is used to denote this "zero-th" parameter. This convention maintains the positional correspondence of actuals and formals. Thus, in the example above, ".ary2" denotes the value of the name of the particular segment being referenced, and 'x[.a,.b]' is equivalent to:

```
(x+.a*10+.b)
```

The value of this expression is a pointer to the designated element of the segment named by x.

In the following example the structure facility and bind declaration have been used to encode efficiently a matrix product ($z_{i,j} = \sum_{k=0}^{9} x_{ik}y_{kj}$). In the inner block the names 'xr' and 'yc' are bound to pointers to the base of a specified row of x and column of y respectively. These identifiers are then associated with structure classes which allow one-diemnsional access.

```
begin
   structure ary2[i,j] = (.ary2+.i*10+.j),
             row[i] = (.row+.i),
             col[j] = (.col+.j*10);
   own       x[100],y[100],z[100];
   map       ary2 x:y:z;
   .
   .
   .
   incr i from 0 to 9 do
      begin bind xr=x[.i,0],zr=z[.i,0]; map row xr:zr;
      incr j from 0 to 9 do

         begin
            register t; bind yc=y[0,.j]; map col yc;
            t ← 0;
            incr k from 0 to 0 do t ← .t+.xr[.k]*.yc[.k];
            zr[.j] ← .t;
         end;
      end;
   .
   .
   .
end
```

Suppose now that one wishes to alter the representation of the structure 'ary2', and access to the array is to be made through an Iliffe vector to define the relative base of each row. The major change required is to replace the current structure declaration for "ary2" by

```
own  il]10];  map row il;
structure  ary2[i,j] = (.ary2+.il[.i]+.j);
```

With this representation, the use of a special accessing algorithm (structure) for accessing columns becomes

```
structure  col[j] = (.col + .il[.j]);
```

As can be seen, these fairly simple changes to the program completely changes its representation of the data. No changes to the processing algorithm are required.

4. More on Data Structures

The example above has the disadvantage of using the size of the array explicitly in the access algorithm, so that separate strucutre declarations would be required for arrays of different size. It should be possible for obvious reasons to parameterize the dependency of the size of the information onto which the structure is going to be mapped. The required flexibility is achieved by observing that until now it only makes sense to use "dotted formals" in the access algorithm, because Bliss has a strict value substitution of parameters. Thus, if we wish (and we do so), another interpretation can be placed on the occurrence of "undotted formals" in the access algorithm. In particular, we shall use the undotted formal parameter names to denote the value of parameters associated with particular instances of a structure (as distinct from instances of accesses to that structure).

Using '{' and '}' to embrace optional syntax (i.e., "zero or one instance of") the Bliss structure declaration is of the form

structure <name>[formal parameter list>] = $\{[\epsilon_1]\}\epsilon_2$

where ϵ_2 is the accessing algorithm as before, and ϵ_1 is an expression whose value determines the size (in words) of an instance of this structure. The expressions ϵ_1 and ϵ_2 may involve undotted formals and thus be instance specific. Consider the following example, which also illustrates the extension to the allocation declarations:

```
begin
   structure ary2[i,j] = [i*j](.ary2+.i*j+.j);
   own  ary2 x:y:z[10,10];
   :
end;
```

This is essentially the same example as has already been presented of three, two-dimensional, 10×10 arrays. However, the information previously contained in a map declaration has now been included in the allocation declaration. More importantly, note that undotted formal names, which correspond to the "instance actuals: 10,10" are used to compute the size of the instances - as well as in the accessing algorithm itself. (As in Algol declarations, the instance-actuals distribute over the names to their left.) Thus the single structure declaration, 'ary2', may be used for other instances of similarly structured segments which happen to be of a size other than 10×10.

ACKNOWLEDGMENTS

I would like to express my deep gratitude to Messrs. Geschke, Wile, and Apperson (graduate students at Carnegie-Mellon University) each of whom has made valuable contributions to both the design and implementation of the language, to Dr. A. N. Habermann of Carnegie-Mellon, and D. B. Russel of SRC Atlas Laboratory (Chilton, Didcot, Berks, England) who were both involved in the initial phases of the language specification.

References

[1] EPL Reference Manual, Project MAC, April 1966.

[2] "Burroughs B5500 Extended Algol Reference Manual", Burroughs Corporation, Detroit.

[3] Wirth, N., "PL/360, A Programming Language for the 360 Computers", JACM, 15,1, Jan. 1968, p. 37.

[4] Richards, M., "BCPL: A tool for compiler writing and system programming", SJCC, 1969, p. 557.

[5] Naur, P. and Randell, B. (ed.), "Software Engineering", Scientific Affairs Division, NATO, Brussels, Belgium. (Held in January 1969 in Garmish).

[6] "Bliss Reference Manual", Computer Science Department Report, Carnegie-Mellon University, Pittsburgh, Pa., Jan. 15, 1970.

[7] "PDP-10 Reference Handbook", Digital Equipment Corporation, Maynard, Mass., 1970.

[8] Lang, Charles A., "SAL-Systems Assembly Language", SJCC, 1969, p. 543.

[9] Bell, J., "The Quadratic Quotient Method: A Hash Code Eliminating Secondary Clustering", CACM, 13, 2 February, 1970, p. 107.

THE PROGRAMMING LANGUAGE PS 440 AS A TOOL FOR IMPLEMENTING A TIMESHARING SYSTEM

by Gerd R. Sapper

The author is a member of a working group in the computing centre of the Technical University of Munich and is concerned with the development and construction of a timesharing system for a TELEFUNKEN TR 440 computer with two processors. The TR 440 is a large computer and the operating system will have to supervise batch jobs plus a satellite computer with about 50 terminals. Our storage consists of 256 k words of core storage with 0.9 μs cycletime, a 4 million word drum and a 30 million word disk. Later a mass core storage of 512 k words will be added. Every word has 48 information bits plus 2 bits each for data type and parity.

All operating systems for TELEFUNKEN computers have up to now been written in assembler languages. The development of this higher level language for developing an operating system had the following reasons.

Firstly, the majority of the programmers for this operating system have already had experience with higher level languages but have almost never programmed larger projects in assembler code. Writing in assembler would be inconvenient for these programmers.

Simple, straight forward sequences of operations, such as those in arithmetic expressions and in address calculations need complicated formulations.

Programs are not self explanatory, and are hard to follow unless they are supplemented with comments, description of intent and flow charts.

Assemblerprograms therefore often contain many trivial coding-errors, which are hard to detect since debugging aids which are both efficient and easily applied, hardly exist, and temporary changes needed during test phases are difficult to implement.

Higher level programming languages (FORTRAN, ALGOL, or PL/I) have been used with great success for the programming of basic software, but they have disadvantages too. Since their concept is machine independent, they do not allow full use of all built-in features of the computer. Performance of the programs cannot be influenced and optimised locally. The fixed data types with impicit conversions (floating point/fixed point) do not allow a value to be interpreted in a number of ways as being of different type depending on the operational context.

Efficient basic programs can only be produced if the advanced programming language used allows, to some extent, constructions which are in 1-1 correspondence with machine functions. It does not seem practical to construct a programming language which offers special constructions for all machine properties. This would make the language too difficult to learn and the programmers would finally prefer assembler coding. Also the implementation would take too much time.

With PS 440, we are not able to add the machine functions which are not directly represented in the language as procedure calls. PL 360 does it this way but in our case too many errors would be possible due to the "double"-instruction-codes and the many different kinds of address parts of the TR 440 instructions. Instead we allowed the direct insertion of TAS (TELEFUNKEN assembler language) statements in the PS 440 source, therefore demanding the existence of a TAS assembler as part of the PS 440 compiler. We take care of this, in the first run, by translating the whole program into TAS and using the TAS assembler as the second run of the PS 440 compiler implementation.

This implies that we have to use the same type of global and local range of variables as implemented in the assembler language;

otherwise we would have to give up the possiblility of using variables defined in PS 440 in the TAS insertions.

A PS 440 program therefore consists of one or more segments, leaving the simple alternative that names can either be global for the whole program or local in a segment.

The PS 440 programmer normally uses full words; the fact that such a word consists of 48 bit plus two bits for data type and two for parity is a special TR 440 property and must not be considered if the construction of machine-independant programs is intended. Doublewords, declared as long, are necessary in some cases and can contain the result of a fixed point multiplication, the dividend of an integer division, or the operand for a long shift. Since the TR 440 offers a great number of powerful halfword and index instructions, for efficiency, we have short words and index cells.

All these entities can be combined into arrays and records. Independant of the type of words the indices proceed from 0 in halfword steps as do the machine addresses; otherwise mixing assembler code and PS 440 could become hazardous. By declaring selectors it is possible to give names to parts of arrays, records or even to name any bit group in a word as we will see later and in the following examples.

full F1, F2, F3 ;	... declares three 48-bit words
short S1, S2, S3;	... declares three 24-bit words
long L1, L2. L3 ;	... declares three double words
short field G1 = [3];	... then "G1 of R1" would give the right half of the second full word in R1. R1 is a
record 6 full R1 :	record 3 full words in length
[0:53] full A1 :	... A1 is an array of 27 full words

Single bits of a full word can be accessed if we declare a selector mask (normally written as a hexadecimal constant) whose zero-bits give a "window" through which the bits will be fetched. Afterwards they will be right justified.

e.g. part field P1 = '2H FFOOOOFFFFFF' ; later referred to as:
.... P1 of ....

Note that every declaration is independant of the type of variable or constant which the declared word will contain later. Any declared quantity can be initialised - with a read only constant, by presetting when loading or by an assignment which is executed every time the program execution passes the declaration. In addition, equivalences of the following type are possible.

full H1 = R1 [I];	... everytime H1 is used I will be evaluated and the I-th element of R1 will be taken
full K1 is 1, K2 is 2 ,	... K1,K2 are names of constants and have the value 1 and 2
V2 := H1 ,	... the assignment combined with this declaration will be executed
P3 preset '3H890ABC' ;	... P3 is preset with a hexadecimal constant during loading of the program

Records and arrays can be initialised in the same way as above, but we have to write lists instead of single values on the right hand side, for example

record 6 full R2 is short (2(0),2(1),full 17) ;	... the constants are, unless otherwise indicated, written as half words

Every declaration can be preceeded by global, which extends the range over the whole programs instead of a single segment. entry will make an entity further accessible even to other PS 440 or TAS programs, which in this case have to refer to it by using spec. There are standard name for all the registers accessible to the programmer.

Now that we have illustrated types of data we will demonstrate how they can be used in formulas. For nearly all operations we use the notation, extended for our special applications, known from ALGOL. When using arithmetic operators fixed point integer operations are assumed , unless the programmer repeats the symbols for the floating point version which is rare in basic software (++ instead of +, -- instead of - etc.). Furthermore, logic operations (i.e. and, or, xor) and all kinds of shifts are provided.

The operator ref means "reference", i.e."address of", while ival, fval, sval,or lval menas, that the address of the desired index or full, short, or long word can be taken from the quantity which these operators preceed.
In the example
full X ; X := fval sval lval X ;
the statement will lead to a series of machine instructions which will take from a doubleword, whose address is in X, a new address out of the last bits, which will be the address of a half word, which again will give the address of a full word, which eventually will contain the address of the full word whose value is to be assigned to X.

We finally consider some properties of PS 440 as far as the dynamic ordering of the formulas is concerned. Formulas are normally executed in the sequence in which they are written. We requested that the use of the goto-statement should be prohibited in an advanced programming language. Although goto and labels may be used in PS 440 it is in fact possible to write PS 440 programs without any goto, if only procedures, conditional statements and do-loops are used in full extent.

Conditions are used for conditional statements and for stopping do-loops. Simple conditions can be connected with ∨∧ and ¬ and brackets are used for breaking the operator priority scheme. Besides the usual relations (<, > , ⩽ , ⩾, =, ≠), data types, sense lights, sense switches, and overflow can be checked. Every if clause has to be closed with a corresponding fi; elsf stands for else if but needs no separate fi.

A do-loop consists in the simplest form of: do ...
where the statement (or the statements enclosed between begin and end) following the do are executed continuously. It is optional to

use a variable controlling the do-loop (otherwise a hidden variable will be taken), a startvalue for this variable (otherwise 0), an increment (otherwise 1) and an endvalue (otherwise infinity). Before and after the statements within the do-loop, two conditions can be added which can terminate the loop.

If B1 and B2 are conditions and A1 and A2 are statements, then this example corresponds to the following flow-chart:

```
for LV from AW by SW to EW
    while B1   do A1
    unless B2  continue  A2 ;
```

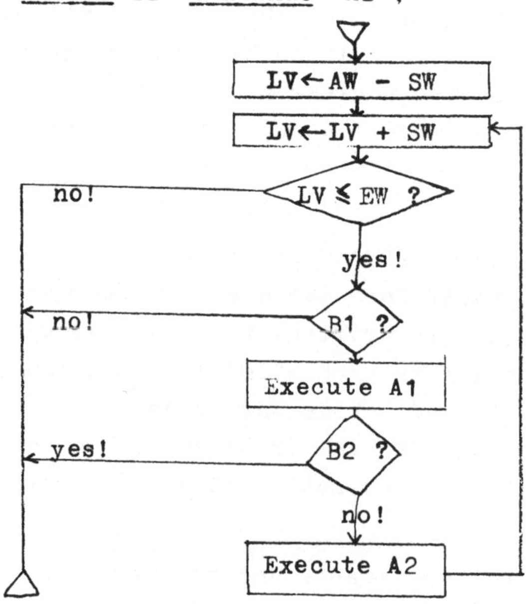

Note that by breaking the do-loop-controlled statements up into A1 and A2 we can leave the do-loop at any desired point without the otherwise necessary use of a goto.

One statement or any sequence of more than one statements enclosed between begin and end can be declared as a procedure. Procedures are called with call and a return from the procedure body, if desired before the last statement, is possible by the return -statement We have no parameter mechanism and therefore the address of a control block has to be delivered in a storage location or register known to the procedure.

The properties of PS 440 as described here are by far not complete, but, in the feeling of the author, sufficient for demonstrating how powerful PS 440 is, especially for the requirements of system programmers.

PS 440 has also been used with great success by programmers whose interests are other than the operating system. These cases concern run-time-organisations, such as input/output possibilities, storage allocation, or test facilities. These features, not normally required by the systems programmer, have been provided by adding to the PS 440 system a standard package of procedures which can be linked automatically to PS 440 programs. It gives all necessary connections to the operating system. In particular working storage can be obtained and the standard input/output media can be accessed. This package has already been used many times, notably when two compilers were written in PS 440, namely the syntax-machine which generated the greatest part of the PS 440-compiler and parts of the PS 440-compiler itself.

References

Software engineering, Report on a conference sponsored by the NATO SIENCE COMMITTEE, January 1969. 4.3.4. Higher level languages.

Niklaus Wirth: PL 360, a programming language for the 360 computers; J ACM, Vol. 15, Jan. 1968

G. Goos, K. Lagally, G. Sapper: PS 440, Eine niedere Programmiersprache. Rechenzentrum der T. U. München, Bericht 7002

G. Sapper: Die Programmiersprache PS 440. Heft 15 der Mitteilungen aus dem Leibnizrechenzentrum der Bayerischen Akademie der Wissenschaften.

GI-FACHTAGUNG "PROGRAMMIERSPRACHEN"

CODEERZEUGUNG UND CODEOPTIMIERUNG FÜR EINE MASCHINENNAHE PROGRAMMIERSPRACHE

von K. Lagally

1. Einleitung

Wenn es sinnvoll sein soll, Grundprogramme, etwa Betriebssysteme oder Sprachübersetzer, in einer höheren Programmiersprache zu schreiben, so muß gewährleistet sein, daß der Programmierer alle wesentlichen Maschineneigenschaften ausnutzen kann. Dabei sollen Sicherheit gegenüber Trivialfehlern und Bequemlichkeit bei der Formulierung des Algorithmus wesentlich höher sein als bei Verwendung einer Assemblersprache. Will man dabei nicht zuviel an Effizienz verlieren, so muß man einerseits solche Sprachmittel vermeiden, die für den Programmierer bequem sind, aber unter Umständen erheblichen versteckten Organisationsaufwand mit sich bringen (hierher gehören etwa komplizierte Indexausdrücke oder der Parametermechanismus aus ALGOL 60); andererseits lohnt es sich, bei der Codeerzeugung mehr Aufwand zu treiben, als dies gemeinhin bei höheren Programmiersprachen üblich ist, da die Übersetzungszeit bei Grundprogrammen gegenüber der Gesamtlaufzeit keine Rolle spielt.

Für die Sprache PS 440 [1, 2, 3], die am Rechenzentrum der Technischen Universität München entwickelt wurde, um Grundprogramme für einen TR 440 zu schreiben, wurde ein Übersetzer

---

[1] G. Goos, K. Lagally, G.R. Sapper:
PS 440 - eine niedere Programmiersprache
Rechenzentrum der Technischen Universität München
Bericht Nr. 7002, Mai 1970

[2] K. Lagally:
Erfahrungen mit einer Implementierungssprache für Grundprogramme
GI-Fachtagung "Rechnerstrukturen und Betriebsprogrammierung", Erlangen, Oktober 197o

[3] G.R. Sapper:
The Programming Language PS 440 as a Tool for Implementing a Time-Sharing System
GI-Fachtagung "Programmiersprachen", München, März 1971

implementiert, der gewisse lokale Codeoptimierungen durchführt. Im folgenden werden die verwendeten Verfahren sowie mögliche Erweiterungen besprochen.

2. Allgemeiner Aufbau des PS 440-Übersetzers

Der PS 440-Übersetzer besteht aus vier Teilen:

1. Ein Rahmenprogramm, das die Anschlüsse an das Betriebssystem sowie eine Reihe von organisatorischen Unterprogrammen enthält,
2. ein Leseprogramm, das die Zerlegung des Eingabestrings in Bezeichnungen, Wortsymbole, Konstanten und Sonderzeichen leistet,
3. ein Syntaxanalysator, der eine Zwischensprache aufbaut und bei Bedarf die Codeerzeugung anstößt,
4. ein Satz von Unterprogrammen zur Codeerzeugung, welche die endgültigen Befehle absetzen.

Der Übersetzer arbeitet in einem Paß und erzeugt als Zielsprache die Assemblersprache TAS. Damit ist es leicht möglich, Teile des Programms in Assemblersprache anzuschließen, etwa um an besonders kritischen Stellen die Effizienz zu steigern, oder um die in der Sprache nicht enthaltenen privilegierten Instruktionen aufzurufen. Umgekehrt bedingt diese Möglichkeit Rückwirkungen von der Struktur der Assemblersprache her, beispielsweise beim Gültigkeitsbereich von Benennungen und bei der Blockstruktur.

Codeerzeugungsroutinen werden vom Syntaxanalysator aufgerufen:

1. Zum Absetzen von Deklarationen, Konstanten und Marken,
2. zur Auswertung von Ausdrücken und Wertzuweisungen,
3. zum Erzeugen von Sprüngen und Prozeduraufrufen.

Dazu kommen noch interne Aufrufe

4. zur Adressenberechnung,
5. zur Verwaltung von Hilfszellen.

Für Alternativen, Schleifen und Fallunterscheidungen gibt es keine eigenen Routinen, da sie bereits vom Syntaxanalysator aufgelöst werden.

Im folgenden werden wir die einzelnen Routinen kurz besprechen; dabei müssen wir uns auf die grundsätzlichen Verfahren beschränken. Aufgrund der Maschinenstruktur und der verschiedenen Datentypen in PS 440 ergeben sich eine Reihe von Varianten, auf die wir nicht eingehen können.

3. Codeerzeugung

Die vom Syntaxanalysator abgelegte Eingangsinformation der Codeerzeugungsroutinen besteht aus einem Geflecht von Verbünden, die innerhalb eines kellerartig verwalteten Speicherbereichs abgelegt sind und grundsätzlich eine Baumstruktur darstellen (Figur 1a, 1b). Ein Knoten des Baumes besteht aus zwei Operanden und einem Operator. Operanden sind entweder ganze Zahlen, einfache Variablen, Registerbezeichnungen oder Verweise auf weitere Knoten, eventuell mit einem Kennzeichen, daß der Knoten eine Variable bezeichnet; in letzterem Falle entspricht ihm außer einem Wert auch eine Adresse. Das Resultat der Anwendung einer Kompilationsroutine auf einen gegebenen Baum besteht aus einem neuen, reduzierten Baum und evtl. abgesetzten Assemblerbefehlen. Die Auswertung eines Baumes ist beendet, wenn er auf einen einfachen Wert reduziert ist.

3.1 Deklarationen, Konstanten und Marken

Die hier aufgerufenen Kompilationsroutinen haben die Aufgabe, die entsprechenden Sprachelemente der Assemblersprache zu erzeugen. Wir gehen darauf nicht ein.

3.2 Ausdrücke und Wertzuweisungen

Wir nehmen vorerst an, alle vorkommenden Variablen seien einfach, d.h. ihre Adressen sind direkt auswertbar, ohne dabei Assemblerbefehle abzusetzen. Der Baum wird von seiner Wurzel her abgearbeitet; dabei werden einfache Operanden jeweils wenn möglich zurückgestellt, um mit möglichst wenig Hilfszellen auszukommen. Ergebnis der Auswertung eines Teilbaumes ist ein einfacher Wert, der in der Regel in einem Register vorliegt. Operationen mit ganzen Zahlen werden, soweit möglich, direkt ausgeführt. Bei der Festkomma-Arithmetik werden die Vorzeichenregeln, insbesondere auch im Zusammenhang mit dem unären Minus, sowie das Kommutativgesetz ausgenutzt, das Assoziativ- und Distributivgesetz dagegen nicht. Bei Bedarf werden Typenkonvertierungen, das sind in PS 440 nur Längenänderungen, eingeschoben. Die geschilderten Optimalisierungsmaßnahmen sind ausreichend, um insbesondere bei der Schleifenkontrolle, die über die normale Festkomma-Arithmetik abgehandelt wird, in der Regel optimalen Code zu gewährleisten. In Figur 2 ist dazu ein einfaches Beispiel ausgeführt.

Ist während der Reduktion des Baumes ein Teilresultat in einem Register angefallen und soll nun ein weiterer Teilbaum ausgewertet werden, so wird das Teilresultat in eine Hilfszelle gerettet. Zu diesem Zweck wird ein kleiner Keller verwendet, dessen Elemente auf Grund der einfachen Struktur der Sprache bereits zur Übersetzungszeit fest adressiert werden können. Nach Abarbeitung des Baumes sind alle Hilfszellen wieder frei.

Das angegebene Verfahren modifiziert sich, wenn die vorkommenden Variablen nicht einfach sind. Die Verwendung des Indexakkumulators BB als arithmetisches Register ist dann nur noch mit Einschränkungen möglich; insbesondere bei Wertzuweisungen ergeben sich Komplikationen, auf die hier aber nicht eingegangen werden soll.

3.3 Vergleiche und bedingte Sprünge

PS 440 kennt boolesche Ausdrücke nur in speziellen Zusammenhängen: bei Alternativen und bei der Schleifenkontrolle. In beiden Fällen werden unmittelbar bedingte Sprünge auf intern erzeugte Sprungziele abgesetzt. Die Auswertung eines booleschen Ausdrucks geschieht analog wie die eines arithmetischen Ausdrucks; jedoch ist stets noch ein Sprungziel angegeben sowie, ob bei erfüllter oder nicht erfüllter Bedingung gesprungen werden soll. Die links stehenden Operanden werden stets vor den rechtsstehenden ausgewertet; der erzeugte Code der Sprungkaskaden ist optimal.

Eine gewisse Zwitterstellung nehmen die Vergleiche ein: ihre Operanden sind arithmetische Ausdrücke, das Endresultat ist ein bedingter Sprung. Da die verschiedenen bedingten Sprungbefehle stark unterschiedliche Versorgung haben, ergeben sich oft überraschende Umformungen. Ein Beispiel ist in Figur 3 angegeben.

3.4 Adressenberechnung

Ein Knoten des Baumes kann eine Typenbezeichnung tragen; dann bezeichnet der dort beginnende Teilbaum eine Variable, deren Adresse zu bestimmen ist. Die Syntax von PS 440 ist so beschaffen, daß sich Adressen stets, wenn auch eventuell mühsam, mittels des Indexakkumulators BB allein berechnen lassen, ohne andere Registerinhalte zu zerstören. Ein besonders umständliches Beispiel ist in Figur 4 angegeben; der Code ist optimal. Die Baumreduktion verläuft sinngemäß genau so, wie oben bei der Arithmetik beschrieben wurde; jedoch arbeitet man vorzugsweise mit speziellen Maschinenbefehlen zur Adreßrechnung, den Modifizierbefehlen, die es gestatten, eine Indexgröße zu addieren, ohne dabei das Rechenwerk zu verwenden. Diese Befehle werden auch bei der Auswertung von Zeigern, beim Dereferenzieren, eingesetzt.

4. Verallgemeinerungsmöglichkeiten

Es hat sich in der Praxis gezeigt, daß die angegebenen Verfahren Code von durchaus ausreichender Qualität liefern. Nichtsdestoweniger sind an einigen Stellen Verbesserungen denkbar:

1. Zwischenresultate werden stets gerettet, wenn ein Teilbaum auszuwerten ist, unabhängig davon, ob der betroffene Registerinhalt dabei tatsächlich verändert wurde. Zur Abhilfe wäre eine Trennung der Codeerzeugung in zwei Phasen erforderlich.

2. Mehrfach vorkommende Teilausdrücke werden nicht erkannt. Ein Vorlauf zum Absuchen der Baumstruktur wäre leicht zu realisieren, lohnt jedoch kaum die zusätzliche Rechenzeit.

3. Die Registerbesetzung am Ende der Auswertung eines Ausdrucks könnte weiterverwendet werden. Hier sind merkliche Optimierungsgewinne zu erwarten, jedoch ist der Aufwand nicht unbeträchlich. Untersuchungen über Realisierungsmöglichkeiten sind im Gange.

Globale Optimierungen, wie etwa Änderungen in der Reihenfolge von Anweisungen, Vereinfachungen von Schleifen etc., wurden absichtlich nicht vorgenommen, um dem mit dem Übersetzer arbeitenden Systemprogrammierer die vollständige Übersicht über den Ablauf seines Programms zu belassen. Insbesondere in der Testphase scheinen automatische Umordnungen durchaus unerwünscht; ihr Nutzeffekt ist auch nur bei einem unzweckmäßig aufgebauten Programm erheblich.

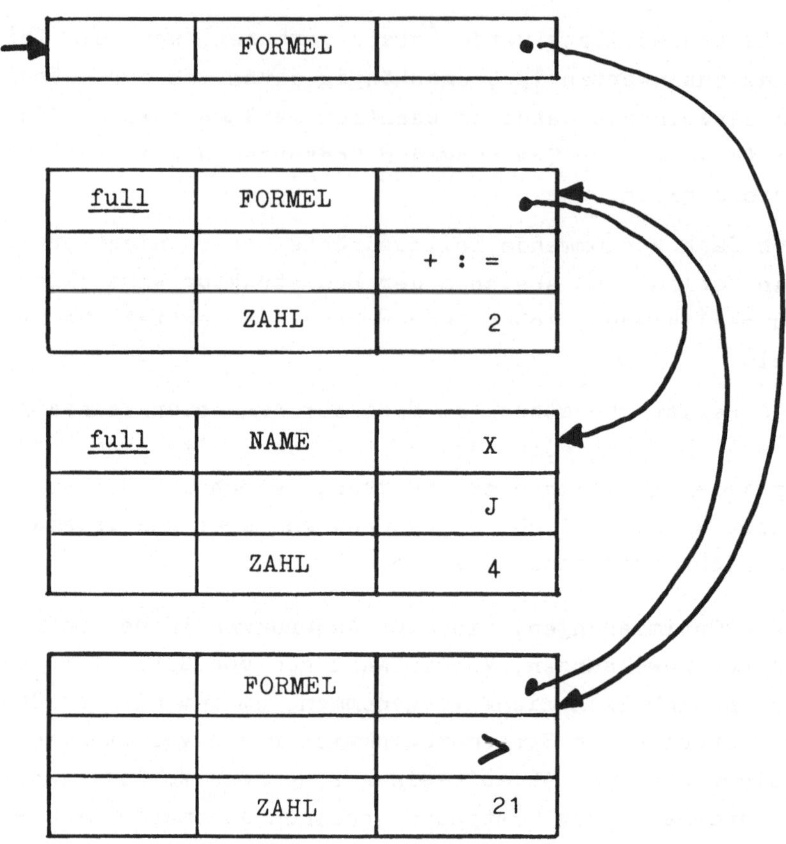

Figur 1a

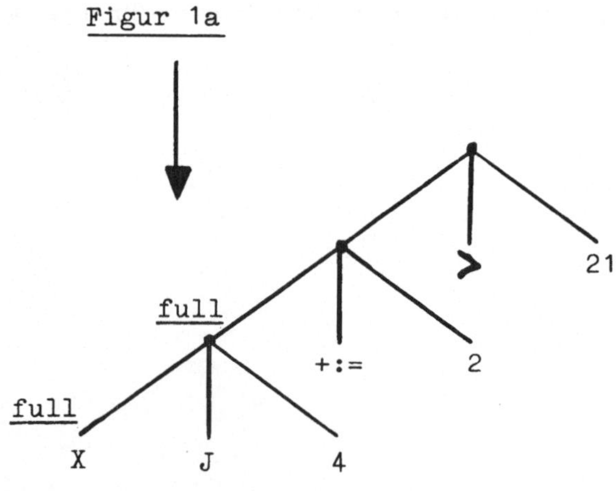

Figur 1b

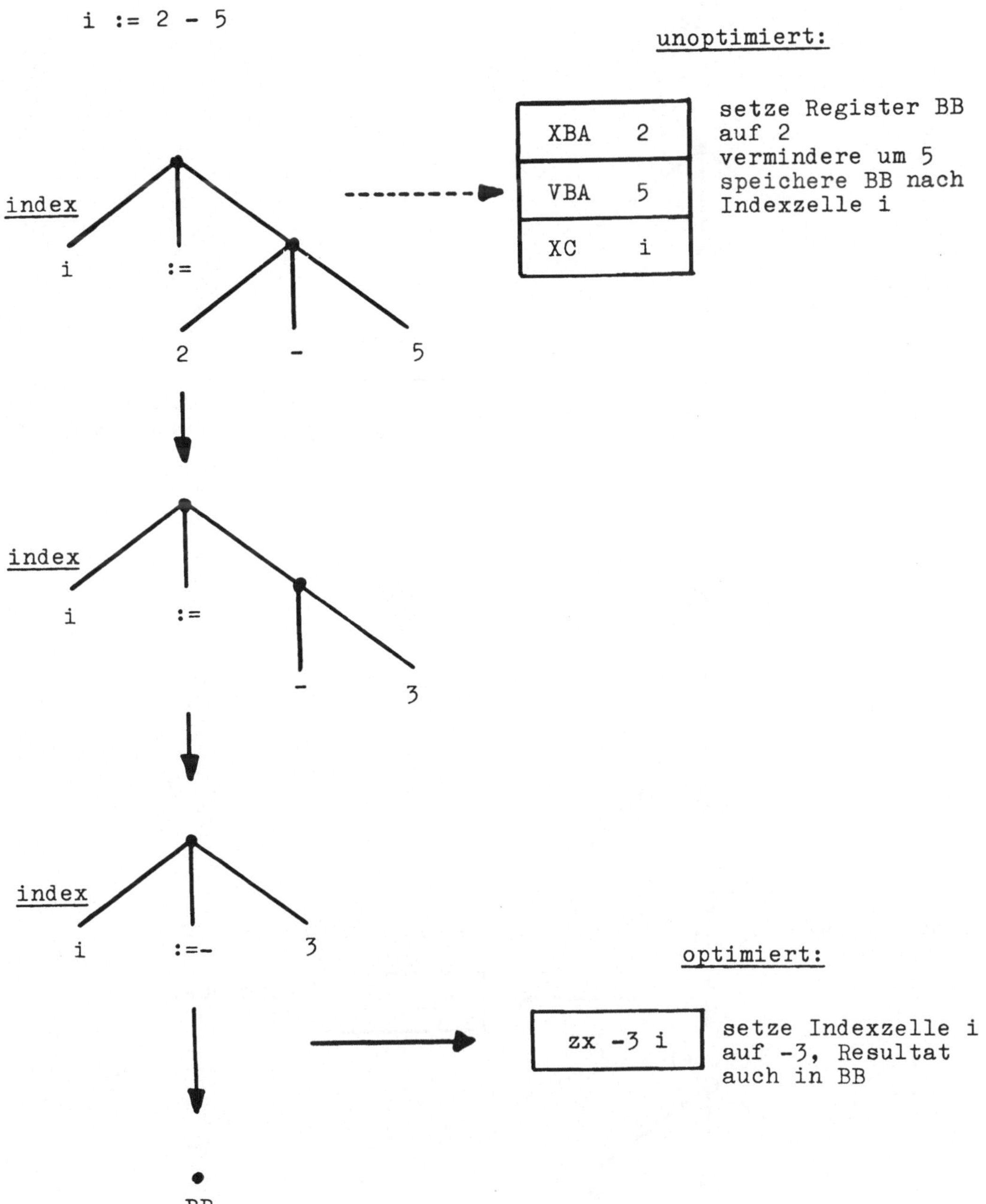

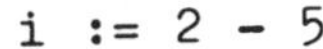

unoptimiert:

XBA	2
VBA	5
XC	i

setze Register BB
auf 2
vermindere um 5
speichere BB nach
Indexzelle i

index
i :=
2 - 5

index
i :=
- 3

index
i :=- 3

BB

optimiert:

zx -3 i

setze Indexzelle i
auf -3, Resultat
auch in BB

Figur 2

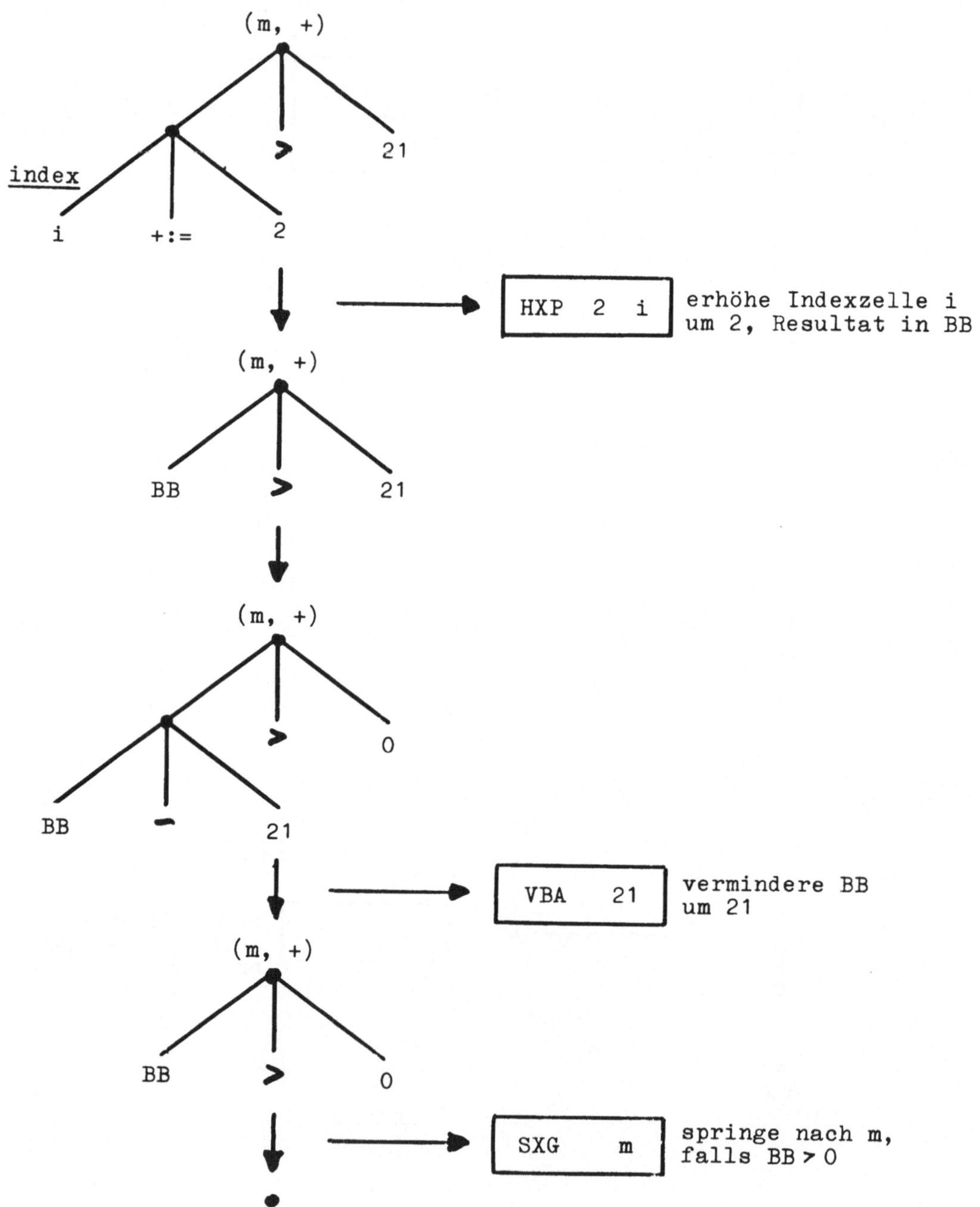
for i by 2 to 21 do ...
(m, +)
index
i
+:=
2
>
21
HXP 2 i
erhöhe Indexzelle i um 2, Resultat in BB
(m, +)
BB
>
21
(m, +)
BB
-
21
>
0
VBA 21
vermindere BB um 21
(m, +)
BB
>
0
SXG m
springe nach m, falls BB > 0

Figur 3

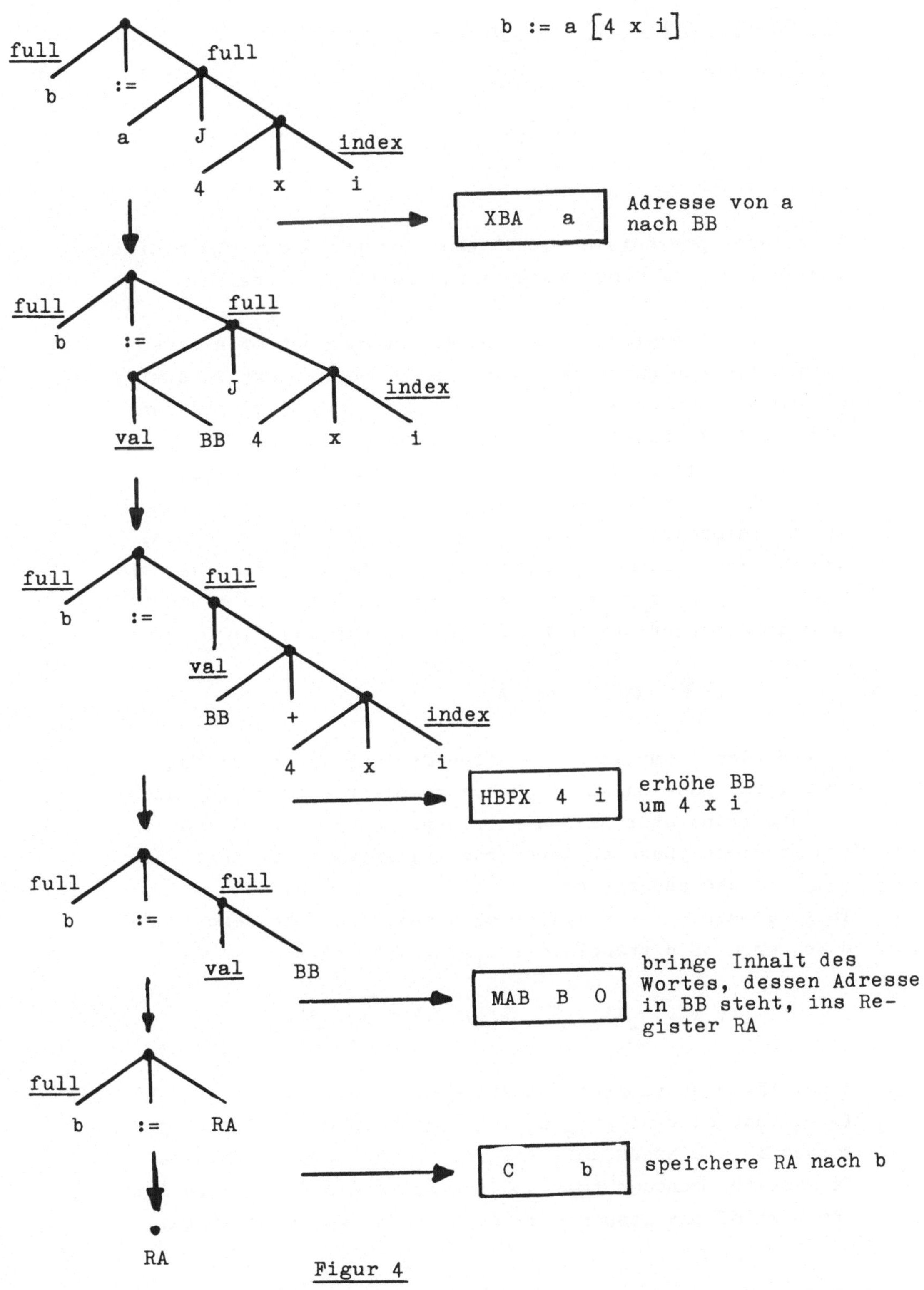

b := a [4 x i]
full
b
:=
full
a
J
index
4
x
i
XBA a
Adresse von a nach BB
full
b
:=
full
J
index
val
BB
4
x
i
full
b
:=
full
val
BB
+
index
4
x
i
HBPX 4 i
erhöhe BB um 4 x i
full
b
:=
full
val
BB
MAB B 0
bringe Inhalt des Wortes, dessen Adresse in BB steht, ins Register RA
full
b
:=
RA
C b
speichere RA nach b
RA

Figur 4

TRANSLATOR FUNCTIONS FOR COMPILER DESCRIPTION

by K. Alber

Introduction

This paper presents a formal tool for the description of the design logic of programming language translators.

A compiler translates a string of symbols out of a given alphabet - the source program text - into a certain string of symbols out of a second alphabet - the object program text -. This translation may be governed by certain system information (e.g. compiler options requiring a specific degree of optimization). Besides, the compiler may produce system information for the object program (e.g. a symbol table). Thus, formally a compiler may be viewed as an automation mapping a pair of a source state ξ and an input string α into a target state η and an output string β :

$$t(\xi, \alpha) = (\eta, \beta).$$

In practice, compilers are often designed as multi-pass compilers. Each phase of such a compiler acts as an intermediate translator having the output state and string of the previous phase as input and transforming it into another output state and string.
Thus, a multi-pass compiler of n phases can be described by a sequence of n translators $t_1, \ldots, t_n$:

$$t_n(\ldots t_2(t_1(\xi, \alpha))\ldots) = (\eta, \beta).$$

Also, the execution of a message of a conversational language (i.e. that unit of program text which is entered into the system as one executable statement) may be seen this way : It maps the message text and the current system state into the text of the response message and a successor state.

In the following, states will always be "abstract objects" as introduced by a group of the IBM-Laboratory Vienna for the formal definition of programming languages. [x]

In this paper, functions mapping pairs of a state and a string into pairs of a state and a string are called "translator functions". We will introduce a calculus for the definition of translator functions. They allow the description of both the syntactical analysis and transformation of a given program and the associated semantical actions.

This calculus is, in some way, an extension of the Backus Normal Form. It considers BNF-rules as (recursive) definitions of functions which recognize parts of an input string. Added are definitions of functions which, in a similar way, generate parts of an output string and of functions which inspect or modify a state.

In this paper, we will first present a short summary of the notion of objects as used for the states. Then we will introduce the proposed calculus of translator functions and finally we will apply it to a little example.

---

[x] See: P. Lucas, K. Walk; On the Formal Description of PL/I, in "Annual Review in Automatic Programming," Vol 6, Part 3 (1969).

Objects

In this section we will give a short overview of the notion of abstract objects as introduced and used by the IBM Vienna group for formal language definition.

An "object" represents a certain amount of information logically structured as a tree with unordered branches. The branches at each node are uniquely identified by names out of a given set S, called "selectors". The leaves (terminal nodes) carry symbols out of a given set EO, called "elemantry objects". They are special cases of objects.

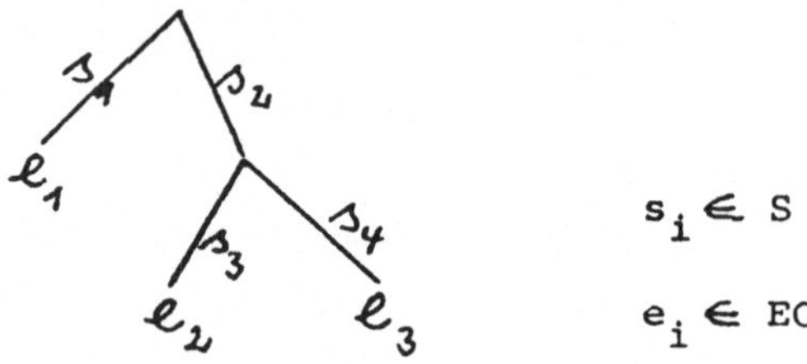

$s_i \in S$

$e_i \in EO$

The subtrees and the elementary objects at the leaves are called the "components" (and subcomponents) of an object. They are objects themselves. Each selector s naming a branch at the top node of an object identifies a component of the object, "the s-component", which is the subtree starting at the end node of the corresponding branch.

More formally, objects are defined the following way :

Given an (infinite) set S of symbols, called "selectors" and an (infinite) set EO of symbols, called "elementary objects". Then the set O of all objects generated with S over EO is given by the following definition :

An object $x \in O$ is

either an elementary object ($x \in EO$)

or a finite set of uniquely named components, where the names s_i are selectors ($s_i \in S$) and the components x_i are objects themselves ($x_i \in O$).

I.e. x is an object, $x \in O$, if and only if

either $X \in EO$

or x is a finite set of pairs of a selector and an object :

$$x = \{ \langle s_1 : x_1 \rangle, \ldots, \langle s_n : x_n \rangle \}$$

with $s_i \in S$,

s_i mutually different,

$x_i \in O$.

This definition of O is, of course, recursive. Only those sets are objects which after a finite number of steps lead to elementary objects. Also the empty set $\{ \}$ is considered to be an object, the "null object" Ω, consisting of no components.

If s is an arbitrary selector, the s-component of an object x is written in functional notation as $s(x)$. If

$$x = \{ \langle s_1 : x_1 \rangle, \ldots, \langle s_n : x_n \rangle \}$$

then $s(x)$ is defined as

$$s(x) = x_i \quad \text{if} \quad s = s_i$$
$$s(x) = \Omega \quad \text{if} \quad s \neq s_i \text{ for } i=1,\ldots,n.$$

By a composition operator $\circ$ the free semigroup S^+ with a unit element I over S is defined as

$$S^+ = \{ s_1 \circ \ldots \circ s_n \mid s_i \in S \} \cup \{ I \}.$$

The elements sel $\in S^+$ are called "composite selectors". They serve to select also the subcomponents out of an object x : If

$$sel = s_1 \circ \dots \circ s_n, \text{ then}$$

$$sel(x) = s_1(\dots s_n(x)\dots)$$

and $I(x) = x$.

We call sel(x) the sel-component of x (which may be x itself, an immediate component or a subcomponent of x).

To modify a certain component of an object x serves a function μ :
Given two objects x and y and an arbitrary (composite) selector sel. Then

$$x' = \mu(x; \langle sel:y \rangle)$$

is an object with the following properties:

1.) sel(x') = y
2.) if sel' is any selector which is "independent" from sel, then sel(x') = sel(x).

I.e. x' is received from x by just replacing the sel-component by y. This function can be used to

1.) change an existing component of a given object,
2.) add a certain component to a given object (if sel(x) = Ω),
3.) delete a certain component from a given object (if y = Ω)
4.) construct a new object (if x = Ω).

To replace more than one component the function μ is defined analogously with more than one pairs of selector sel and component object y :

$$\mu(x; \langle sel_1 : y_1 \rangle, \ldots, \langle sel_n : y_n \rangle).$$

Translator Functions

Given a finite alphabet A. Let A^* be the set of all finite strings (words) over A, including the nullstring ε. The concatenation operation in A^* is denoted by juxtaposition. Given a set of simple selectors S and a set of elementary objects EO. Let O be the set of all objects generated with S over EO as explained above.

Then a "translator function" t is a mapping from $O \times A^*$ into itself :

$$t : O \times A^* \rightarrow O \times A^* ,$$

i.e. it maps pairs (ξ , α) of an object $\xi \in O$ and a string $\alpha \in A^*$ into pairs (η , β) of an object $\eta \in O$ and a string $\beta \in A^*$:

$$t(\xi, \alpha) = (\eta, \beta)$$

To avoid complication we can, without loss of generality, assume that the input alphabet and the output alphabet of a translator function are the same.

Generally, a translator function t is defined only for a subset RS(t) of $O \times A^*$, the set of "source pairs" of t. We say that any pair (ξ , α) $\notin$ RS(t), i.e. any pair for which t(ξ , α) is not defined, is "rejected" by t. The set of all possible values of a translator function t is RT(t), the set of "target pairs" of t.

We now introduce a set of primitive translator functions and a set of operations which allow to define more complex translator functions from the primitive ones.

1.) For any $\alpha \in A^*$ there exists a <u>scan translator function</u> $\sigma(\alpha)$ which maps α into the null string ε leaving the state ξ unchanged :

$$\sigma(\alpha)(\xi, \alpha) = (\xi, \varepsilon) \text{ for any } \xi.$$

$\sigma(\alpha)$ rejects any string $\alpha' \neq \alpha$. Thus, the set of source pairs is $RS(\sigma(\alpha)) = O \times \{\alpha\}$, the set of target pairs is $RT(\sigma(\alpha)) = O \times \{\varepsilon\}$.

2.) For two translator functions t_1, t_2 there exists a <u>concatenation operation :</u>

The translator function

$$t ::= t_1 \,.\, t_2 \quad {}^*$$

is defined by :

$$t(\xi, \alpha) = (\eta, \beta)$$

if and only if there exist unique strings

$\alpha_1, \alpha_2, \beta_1, \beta_2 \in A$ and $\zeta \in O$ such that

$$\alpha = \alpha_1 \alpha_2, \; \beta = \beta_1 \beta_2,$$
$$t_1(\xi, \alpha_1) = (\zeta, \beta_1),$$
$$t_2(\zeta, \alpha_2) = (\eta, \beta_2).$$

For example, is $\sigma(\alpha_1 \alpha_2) = \sigma(\alpha_1) \,.\, \sigma(\alpha_2)$.

---

* By the symbol ::= we denote definition of the lefthand translator function name.

3.) For two translator functions t_1, t_2 with distinct set of source pairs there exists a union operation |: If $RS(t_1) \cap RS(t_2) = \{\}$ then the translator function

$$t ::= t_1 \mid t_2$$

is defined by :

$$t(\xi, \alpha) = (\eta, \beta)$$

if and only if
either $(\xi, \alpha) \in RS(t_1)$ and $t_1(\xi, \alpha) = (\eta, \beta)$
or $(\xi, \alpha) \in RS(t_2)$ and $t_2(\xi, \alpha) = (\eta, \beta)$.

Thus, the set of source pairs of t is $RS(t) = RS(t_1) \cup RS(t_2)$, the set of target pairs $RT(t) = RT(t_1) \cup RT(t_2)$.

In expressions, the concatenation operator has higher precedence than the union operator |. Both operators are associative. Thus parenthesis in expressions may be omitted.

Using thes three definitions, one can transscribe any Backus Normal Form grammar into a recursive definition of a translator function which recognizes all valid strings, transforms them into the nullstring ε, leaves the (irrelevant) state unchanged and rejects all invalid strings. E.g., the grammar :

```
expr::  = prod | expr + prod
prod::  = prim | prod * prim
prim::  = var | (expr)
var::   = letter | letter var
letter:: = A | B | ... | Z
```

may be transcribed as :

$$\underline{\text{expr}} ::= \underline{\text{prod}} \mid \underline{\text{expr}} \cdot \sigma(\text{'+'}) \cdot \underline{\text{prod}}$$
$$\underline{\text{prod}} ::= \underline{\text{prim}} \mid \underline{\text{prod}} \cdot \sigma(\text{'*'}) \cdot \underline{\text{prim}}$$
$$\underline{\text{prim}} ::= \underline{\text{var}} \mid \sigma(\text{'('}) \cdot \underline{\text{expr}} \cdot \sigma(\text{')'})$$
$$\underline{\text{var}} ::= \underline{\text{letter}} \mid \underline{\text{letter}} \cdot \underline{\text{var}}$$
$$\underline{\text{letter}} ::= \sigma(\text{'A'}) \mid \sigma(\text{'B'}) \mid \ldots \mid \sigma(\text{'Z'}).$$ *

With these definitions is $\underline{\text{expr}}(\xi, \alpha) = (\xi, \varepsilon)$ for an arbitrary object ξ if and only if α is a valid expression according to the above syntax, while $\underline{\text{expr}}(\xi, \alpha)$ is undefined if α is no valid expression.

4.) For any string $\alpha \in A^*$ there exists a <u>generate translator function</u> $\gamma(\alpha)$ which maps the null string ε into α leaving the state ξ unchanged :

$$\gamma(\alpha)(\xi, \varepsilon) = (\xi, \alpha) \quad \text{for any } \xi.$$

This translator function, which is the inverse of $\sigma(\alpha)$, rejects any string $\alpha' \neq \varepsilon$. Thus the set of source pairs is $RS(\gamma(\alpha)) = O \times \{\varepsilon\}$, the set of target pairs $RT(\gamma(\alpha)) = O \times \{\alpha\}$.

5.) For any two strings $\alpha, \beta \in A^*$ there exists a <u>transform translator function</u> $\tau(\alpha, \beta)$ which recognizes the string α only and maps it into the string β, leaving the state ξ unchanged. It is defined as

$$\tau(\alpha, \beta) ::= \sigma(\alpha) \cdot \gamma(\beta) .$$

---

* For syntactic uniqueness, we enclose explicit character strings by apostrophs. We usually denote specific translator functions by underlined names.

This function can be used in order to translate an external character string into an internal representation, e.g., τ('**', '↑') transforming the external two characters ** into an internal one character representation of a power symbol ↑.
We introduce the abbreviation :

$$\alpha ::= \tau(\alpha, \alpha)$$

for the translator function which accepts only the string α, maps it unchanged into the output string and leaves the state ξ unchanged.

6.) There exists a skip translator function which maps any string into the null string ε leaving the state unchanged :

$$\underline{\text{skip}}(\xi, \alpha) = (\xi, \varepsilon) \text{ for any } \xi \in O, \alpha \in A^* .$$

This translator function, concatenated to any other translator function may be used to skip an irrelevant rest of a source string, e.g. a comment following the last relevant character of a program.

Using the translator functions introduced so far one could describe, e.g., a prescan phase of a compiler which tests a source program for syntactical correctness and produces a target program in a compressed internal representation (omitting comments, transforming operators and keywords into single symbols and leaving other units unchanged).

7.) For two translator functions there exists a reversed concatenation operation $\times$: The translator function

$$t ::= t_1 \times t_2$$

is defined by :

$$t(\xi, \alpha) = (\eta, \beta)$$

if and only if there exist unique strings $\alpha_1, \alpha_2, \beta_1, \beta_2 \in A^*$ and $\zeta \in O$ such that

$$\alpha = \alpha_1 \alpha_2, \quad \beta = \beta_2 \beta_1,$$
$$t_1(\xi, \alpha_1) = (\zeta, \beta_1),$$
$$t_2(\xi, \alpha_2) = (\eta, \beta_2).$$

In expressions, the reversed concatenation operator $\times$ has higher precedence than the concatenation operator $\cdot$ and the union operator $|$.

Using this definition, one can e.g. describe a translator transforming expressions into reversed Polish notation:

<u>expr</u>:: = <u>prod</u> | <u>expr</u> · '+' $\times$ <u>prod</u>
<u>prod</u>:: = <u>prim</u> | <u>prod</u> · '*' $\times$ <u>prim</u>
<u>prim</u>:: = <u>var</u> | σ('(') · <u>expr</u> · σ(')')
<u>var</u>:: = <u>letter</u> | <u>letter</u> · <u>var</u>
<u>letter</u>:: = 'A' | 'B' | ... | 'Z'.

8.) In some instances the <u>null translator function</u> is needed. It transforms the null string ε into the null string and leaves the state unchanged. It may be defined as

<u>null</u>:: = $\sigma(\varepsilon)$.

It rejects any other string $\alpha \neq \varepsilon$. Thus, the set of its source and of its target pairs is RS(<u>null</u>)= RT(<u>null</u>)=$O \times \{\varepsilon\}$ This translator function is the identity with respect to the concatenation operation :

$\underline{\text{null}} \cdot t = t \cdot \underline{\text{null}} = \underline{\text{null}} \times t = t \times \underline{\text{null}} = t$

for any t.

9.) Using the null translator function, we introduce some abbreviations :

$[t] ::= t \mid \underline{\text{null}}$

meaning optional application of t, which is defined only if t rejects the null string ε.

$t\ldots ::= t \cdot [t\ldots]$

meaning iterated application of t as often as possible. E.g., the translator function var in the above examples may be defined as var:: = letter...

$t^{*} ::= [t\ldots]$

meaning application of t zero, one or more times.

The definitions introduced so far did essentially consider only the strings of the source and target pairs, while the states were left unchanged. Thus, by these notations one can define only translator functions which do syntactic analysis and transformations. The state argument ξ was irrelevant and no semantic actions describable. We now will introduce notations for state transformations, first independent from the source string, and then depending on the source string.

10.) A <u>translator function inserting a fixed object</u> into the state exists for any selector $sel \in S^+$ and any object $ob \in O$. This translator function

$$t ::= \langle sel:ob \rangle$$

is defined by :

$$t(\xi, \varepsilon) = (\mu(\xi; \langle sel:ob \rangle), \varepsilon) \text{ for any } .$$

Its set of source pairs is $R(\langle sel:ob \rangle) = O \times \{\varepsilon\}$.

Analogously a translator function modifying more than one state component simultaneously

$$t ::= (\langle sel_1:ob_1 \rangle, \ldots, \langle sel_n:ob_n \rangle)$$

is defined by

$$t(\xi, \varepsilon) = (\mu(\xi; \langle sel_1:ob_1 \rangle, \ldots, \langle sel_n:ob_n \rangle), \varepsilon).$$

11.) <u>A translator function inserting the translated source string</u> into the state is specified by the following notation : If $sel \in S^+$ is an arbitrary selector and t a translator function, then

$$t' ::= \langle sel:t \rangle$$

is a translator function defined by : If and only if

$$t(\xi, \alpha) = (\eta, \beta),$$

then

$$t'(\xi, \alpha) = (\mu(\eta; \langle sel:\beta \rangle), \varepsilon).$$

I.e. the translator function t is applied to the source pair and the resulting target string is inserted into the result state of t instead of the output string.*

12.) Finally, we introduce <u>conditional translator functions</u>. If $p_1(\xi),\dots,p_n(\xi)$ are predicates, i.e. functions of ξ having as values either T("true") or F ("false") and $t_1,\dots,t_n$ are translator functions, then

$$t::=(p_1(\xi)\rightarrow t_1,\dots,p_n(\xi)\rightarrow t_n)$$

is a translator function. It is defined the following way. If

$$p_i(\xi)=F \text{ for } i=1,\dots,k-1$$

and

$$p_k(\xi)=T,$$

then

$$t(\xi,\alpha)=t_k(\xi,\alpha)$$

If $p_i(\xi)=F$ for $i=1,\dots,n$, then the source pair (ξ,α) is rejected by t.

Using this notation one can define recursively:

$$t^n::=(n{=}0\rightarrow \underline{\text{null}},\quad n{>}0\rightarrow t\cdot t^{n-1}).$$

---

* It is assumed here, that the target strings of t are objects. We will generally make the assumption that $A^*\subset EO$. In addition we will assume $A^*\subset S$.

It should be noted that by using the notations introduced, except the last one, one can define translator functions without reference to their argument pairs (ξ,α). In the definition of conditional translator functions, however, the state argument ξ is to be mentioned explicitly. We introduce therefore the convention, that the letter ξ is reserved for the state argument in translator function definitions. We further allow, that this name ξ may also occur in any other part of a translator function definition. Example : While the translator function $\gamma(\alpha)$ generates the "constant" target string α, the translator function $\gamma(f(\xi))$ generates a target string depending on the current state ξ.

An Example

We will now demonstrate the use of the calculus of translator functions by an example. We describe the translation of expressions into an internal target language and, in parallel, the construction of a symbol table. The symbol table associates each external variable name with a number (e.g. storage address) which then occurs as the internal representation of that variable in the target language. The expression in the target language occurs in reversed Polish notation with internal representations of the operators and a load operator for each variable reference (loading at execution time the variable into a stack).

The alphabet A consists of : the external characters A, B, ..., Z, +, $\ast$, (,), all integers and the internal symbols ADD, MULT, LOAD. The set of simple selectors S consists of : all elements of A^* and the three names buf, count, symtab. The set of elementary objects EO consists of : all elements of A^* and all integers.

The states occuring in this example consist of three components :

1.) A buffer buf(ξ) containing the last identifier (variable name) read from the input string .

2.) A counter count(ξ) indicating the number of the next entry to be made into the symbol table. It is 1 in the beginning.

3.) The symbol table symtab(ξ). It is organized as an object having all those external identifiers as selectors, which have already been entered, and their associated integers as components.

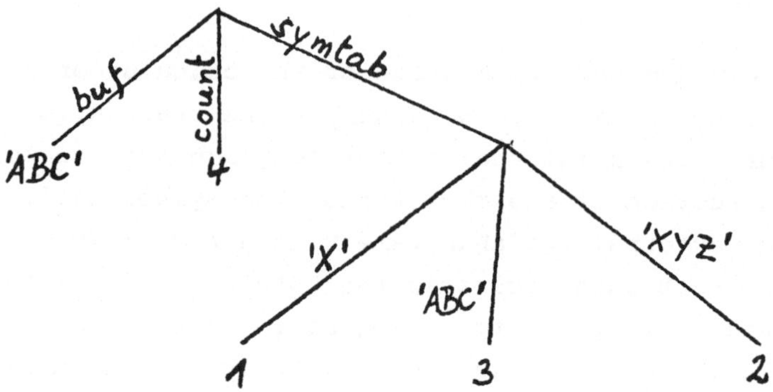

Example of a state ξ

The translation is performed by the translator function expr given by the following definitions :

expr::= prod | expr · plus × prod
prod::= prim | prod · mult × prim
prim::= var | σ('(') · expr · σ(')')
plus::= τ('+', ADD)
mult::= τ('*', MULT)
var::= read-id · test-symtab · gen-var
read-id::= <buf:id>
id::= letter...
letter::= 'A' | 'B' |...| 'Z'
test-symtab::=
    ((buf(ξ))∘symtab(ξ) = Ω → upd-symtab,
    T → null)
upd-symtab::= (<(buf(ξ))∘symtab:count(ξ)>,
    < count:count(ξ)+1>)
gen-var::= γ(LOAD) · γ((buf(ξ)) ∘ symtab(ξ))

For example, the translator function expr translates the source text

(X + XYZ) * (X + ABC)

into the target text

LOAD 1 LOAD 2 ADD LOAD 1 LOAD 3 ADD MULT

and generates the state shown in the above picture.

Conclusion

By the notation introduced in this paper, one can formally describe the design logic of a compiler. A so designed formal model of a compiler can be realized by implementing the single translator functions as recursive procedures. Some experiments have been made in the IBM Laboratories Boeblingen in a compiler project conducted by Dr. H. Schmutz, who contributed many of the ideas presented in this paper.

To gain efficiency in an implementation, one has to obey to use "deterministic" translator functions only. A translator function is deterministic if in all occuring definitions of the form $t ::= t_1 | t_2$ the decision between t_1 and t_2 depends only on the source state and the first symbol of the source string.

DESIGN OF A VERSATILE PRECEDENCE PARSING SYSTEM

by Rainer Zimmer

1. Theoretical foundations

This is more or less a status report of a project which started with some theoretical and practical investigations and will end with the implementation of a software tool, namely a system for automatic construction of parsers for common programming languages.
Firstly we shall need an introductory description of the methods used and the environment being considered.

There is up to a certain degree an alternative between the following properties of a parser construction system: On one hand a system may accept nearly every context-free language and produce parsers which are not very efficient; on the other hand a system may produce more efficient parsers but only for certain restricted classes of context-free languages. We decided to build a system of the latter type and chose the well-known precedence technique of Wirth and Weber [1]. This is a bottom-up method for context-free grammars, so it works by reducing sentences of a grammar to the starting symbol. The leftmost directly reducible phrase of a sentential form is detected by using the precedence relations, i.e. 3 binary relations $\lessdot, \doteq, \gtrdot$ defined appropriately for ordered pairs of symbols of the grammar. It is required that for every pair at most one of the 3 relations holds. Then the leftmost directly reducible phrase is always enclosed in the leftmost occurence of the relation pattern $\lessdot \doteq \ldots \doteq \gtrdot$ of adjacent symbols of the sentential form under consideration. For the method of Wirth and Weber, it is furthermore required that no different productions of the grammar have identical right parts. Thus the decision which reduction is to be made when a directly reducible phrase is found, is trivial.

<u>Figure 1:</u> Precedence method

grammar section	funct-call ::= ident (arglist) arglist ::= arg-seq arg-seq ::= arg | arg-seq , arg arg ::= expr (a) string-attr ::= CHARACTER (expr) (b) string-attr ::= CHARACTER (length) length ::= expr
leftmost directly reducible phrase of sentential form	... ident (arg-seq , arg , ...
"ambiguous" precedence relation for (a)	(≐ expr and (⋖ expr
"ambiguous" reduction for (b)	... ident (arg-seq , expr , ...

Leftmost directly reducible phrase of sentential form:

```
... ident ( arg-seq , arg , ...
   ⋖     ≐ ⋖       ≐ ≐   ⋗ ⋖
            \_____________/
                arg-seq
```

"ambiguous" reduction for (b):

```
... ident ( arg-seq , expr , ...
   ⋖     ≐ ⋖       ≐ ⋖    ⋗ ⋖
                      \__/
                        ?
```

As we have seen there are two conditions for grammars to be handled with the precedence method. The first one may be called uniqueness of precedence relations, the second one uniqueness of reductions. A grammar satisfying the first condition is a precedence grammar, a grammar satisfying both conditions is a deterministic precedence grammar.

Unfortunately most of the existing common programming languages seem to have no deterministic precedence grammars of practicable size and structure. However in our investigations we found that one can weaken the conditions in such a way that common programming languages satisfy the weaker conditions and the effectiveness of corresponding parsers is comparable to that of a deterministic precedence parser. It is well-known that every context-free grammar can be transformed to an equivalent one having unique precedence relations. Moreover, for common programming languages, one can write such grammars having a reasonable phrase structure. So we decided to weaken the second condition. This implies that a directly reducible phrase may be reduced to different symbols of the grammar and therefore requires decision facilities for corresponding parsers. The new second condition and the additional facilities must be invented together, and the condition must guarantee that the facilities work for grammars satisfying it.

Our first approach towards such a weaker second condition was the following: Given a phrase directly reducible to more than one symbol of the grammar, then the correct reduction in a bottom-up parse is determined by some reduction which precedes it. For example, let us have a programming language with an IF- and a GOTO-statement and let the phrase "identifier" reduce differently in both statements, say to "if-identifier" or "goto-identifier", respectively. Of course the correct reduction is determined by the preceding keyword which can be recognized by the parser if the grammar contains productions "if-keyword ::= IF" and "goto-keyword ::= GO TO". This is a very simple example and we have tried to formalize the new second condition in such a way that it covers more complicated

Figure 2: Weak precedence method

grammar section

```
if-stat ::= if-keyword if-ident ; then-part
if-keyword ::= IF / action: ident-state := if-ident
goto-stat ::= goto-keyword goto-ident ;
goto-keyword ::= GO TO / action: ident-state := goto-ident
ident-state ::= identifier / reduction depending on
                             preceding reduction of
                             IF or GO TO, resp.
```

cases. The result was called Weak precedence (which came out to be a somewhat unhappy naming). The corresponding parser may be taken as a deterministic precedence parser extended by a set of small finite state automata, in our example an "identifier"-automaton having an IF- and a GOTO-state. The Weak precedence parser is as effective as the deterministic precedence parser. However we found that Weak precedence normally does not apply to enough of the "ambiguous" phrases of a practical grammar but that it would apply if it contained a facility to stack its states.

So our next idea was to extend the deterministic precedence parser by a push down automaton. But a bottom-up parser already contains the parse stack and one can recognize that, in practice, the discriminating information is always located in fixed positions relative to the top of the parse stack.

The appropriate second condition depends on an integer m and says: Given a phrase directly reducible to more than one symbol of the grammar, then the correct reduction in a bottom-up parse is determined by the m parse stack elements preceding this phrase. For example, the phrase "identifier" will reduce to "if-identifier" if immediately preceded by the symbol "IF" and to "goto-identifier" if preceded by a "GO TO". (Here auxiliary reductions are not necessary.)
A context-free grammar satisfying the first condition and this second one for some m is a Soft precedence grammar.

Figure 3: Soft precedence method

grammar section 1

if-stat ::= IF if-ident ; then-part
if-ident ::= identifier / if ⟨-1⟩ $\in$ $P_1(\varepsilon)$if-ident
goto-stat ::= GO TO goto-ident ;
goto-ident ::= identifier / if ⟨-1⟩ $\in$ $P_1(\varepsilon)$goto-ident

where predecessor sets are:

$$\left.\begin{array}{l} P_1(\varepsilon)\text{if-ident} = \{\text{IF}\} \\ P_1(\varepsilon)\text{goto-ident} = \{\text{GO TO}\} \end{array}\right\} \cap = \emptyset$$

and ⟨-1⟩ is the actual immediate predecessor of the phrase

grammar section 2

funct-call ::= ident (arglist)
arglist ::= arg-seq
arg-seq ::= arg | arg-seq , arg
arg ::= expr / if ⟨-2⟩ $\in$ $P_2(J)$arg
string-attr ::= CHARACTER (length)
length ::= expr / if ⟨-2⟩ $\in$ $P_2(J)$length

where second predecessor sets are:

$$\left.\begin{array}{l} P_2(J)\text{arg} = \{\text{ident, arg-seq}\} \\ P_2(J)\text{length} = \{\text{CHARACTER}\} \end{array}\right\} \cap = \emptyset$$

and ⟨-2⟩ is the actual second predecessor of the phrase

The Soft precedence parser normally is nearly as effective as the deterministic precedence parser, and, it applies to a class of grammars wide enough for practical purposes, includes common programming languages, and it adapts to the "quality" of grammars. It can be built automatically from a Soft precedence grammar. We have a set of recursive formulas to compute if a certain symbol may precede a certain top sequence of the bottom-up parse stack.

Because of the advantages of both the Weak and the Soft precedence methods we decided to include both of them in our system.

2. Environment

The system consists of the parser frame called PP and a table program called TAPP which constructs the tables to be put in the frame. It is a component of a compiler system, other components of which also consist of construction tools and component frames. The compiler has a usual structure including a lexical analyzer, the parser, symbol table components, check and preparation components, code generation components and an error processor, all controlled by some driver component. Interfaces of the parser are to the driver, to the lexical analyzer and to successor components. They are either kept flexible or they are controlled by the table program. For example, most of the input to the parser is controlled by data passed from TAPP to the table program for the lexical analyzer. The output of the parser in the general view depends on the (easily changeable) set of actions actually included, and in particular can be programmed by the input of TAPP. TAPP also contains facilities to coordinate the parser output with other components of the compiler.

Now having the environment and the methods for the system, we shall go on with a more detailed description. We start with the important features of the parser and therefrom derive those of TAPP.

3. Features of the parser

3.1 Precedence matrix

Firstly the parser is a pure bottom-up parser. So it works by the iteration of two steps, namely: find the leftmost directly reducible phrase of the current sentential form, and replace it according to the rules of the grammar. As already mentioned the first step is done using the unique precedence relations of the grammar. Since the relations depend only on the grammar, they are computed by TAPP, which produces a corresponding table for the parser. The parser only contains the access mechanisms for the relation table.

Much of the efficiency of the parser depends on the size and representation used for this table. Normally the precedence relations form a square matrix of 2-bit information elements. For a grammar of 500 symbols its size is 62500 Bytes at 8 bits each. This seemed to be too large. Particularly so because most of the matrix elements normally are zero. So we developped condensation techniques which reduce the size of a matrix as mentioned by a factor of nearly 20. (For smaller matrices the factor may be also smaller.) Firstly we throw out rows which are copies of rows with lower index. This produces a reduction by a factor of more than 3. In the parser the rows are then accessed using a vector of pointers. Secondly we represent a row as a list of its constant subsequences, i.e., by items saying: up to column c_1 all elements are e_1, then up to column c_2 all elements are e_2, etc. To optimize the effect the columns can be sorted to obtain constant subsequences as long as possible. Doing this and taking 2 Bytes for each list item we get another reduction factor of more than 6.

The matrix format accepted by the parser is the following: There is a vector of pointers to the rows and the rows may be condensed or uncondensed. Elements of condensed rows are accessed with a binary search; elements of uncondensed rows are accessed by index.

<u>Figure 4:</u> PP precedence matrix format

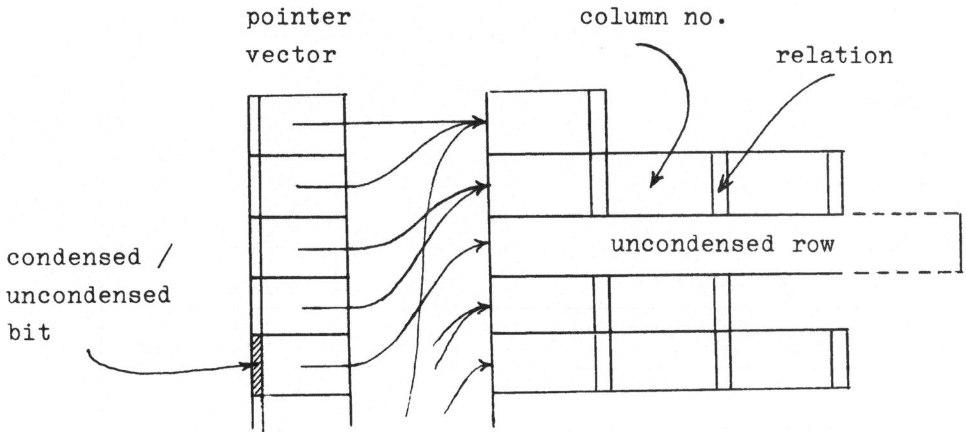

3.2 Grammar table

To do the reductions of leftmost directly reducible phrases and to do the actions belonging to the reductions, the parser contains a table of the rules of the grammar and corresponding action specifications. If a leftmost directly reducible phrase is found (using precedence relations) then the grammar table is searched for this phrase and, if present, the reduction and actions specified for it are executed. Much of the speed of the parser depends on the representation of the grammar and the corresponding search and action mechanisms. In our case all items of the grammar table, in particular the grammar symbols, are 2 Bytes long. The phrases are sorted by the symbol number of the first (leftmost) symbol, which is cut off from the phrase. Instead, phrases starting with the same symbol are chained, and they are accessed using the common number of the first symbol as an index in a vector of pointers to the phrase chains. Every phrase is followed by one or more symbols to which it can be reduced and by

Figure 5: PP grammar table format

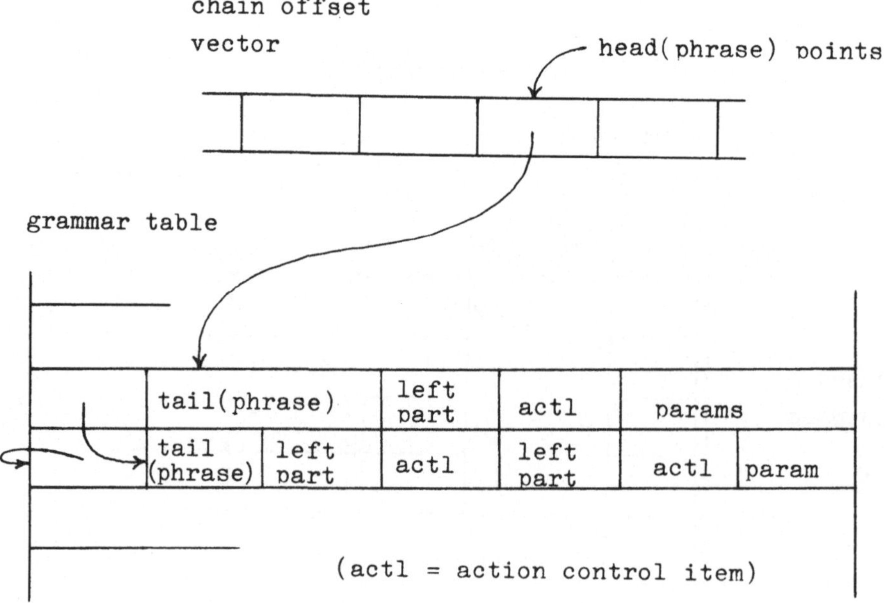

corresponding action specifications.

3.3 Actions

The action concept influences two important properties of the parser in a conflicting manner: On one hand the speed of the parser partly decreases with the overhead necessary for action calls and returns. On the other hand the versatility of the parser strongly requires a general action concept being well defined, prepared to greater changes of the action set included, and accepting generated actions. This of course implies some overhead.

In our concept actions are subroutines accessible by a transfer vector. Each action has a unique number and the n-th component of the transfer vector points to the entry of action no. n.

Figure 6: PP action concept

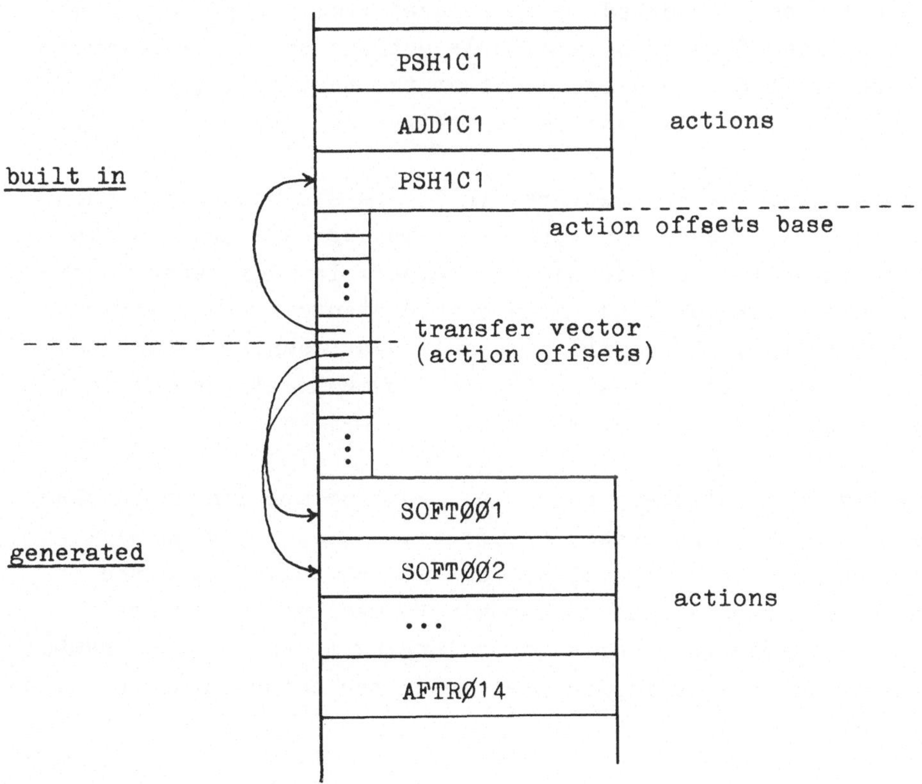

An action specification in the grammar table consists of a control item followed by a number of parameters implied by the contents of the control item. The control item itself is a small vector of bits which specify actions or action sequences supposed to occur most frequently, e.g., actions for counters or counter stacks or for output. Actions specified by these bits are always executed in a fixed sequence. For actions not covered by these bits or not fitting in this sequence there are two special bits called the BEFORE- and the AFTER-bit. They mean that there are actions to be done before or after the fixed action sequence is executed, and both of them have a parameter which is the number of an action. The actions actually to be done in the parser are programmed in the input for the table program. Every sequence of actions available in the parser can be programmed in this way, hence TAPP must assemble the control item, generate sequences of action calls which constitute the BEFORE- and AFTER-actions and also give them numbers.

So the characteristics of our action concept are that any action may be introduced to or removed from the parser, that any sequence of calls of available actions may be programmed through the table program, and that the most important action sequences are in-line and can be triggered very effectively.

There are some data structures in the parser upon which the actions work. These structures to some degree depend on the actions actually included in the parser. In many cases there will be a stack carrying names and constants in some internal representation, there will be counters or counter stacks to handle nested occurences of iterated symbols of the grammar, and there will be an output area.

Normally in a bottom-up parser all actions are linked to the reductions. For the reason of effectiveness we use an additional linking point. Special actions can be called upon the reading of symbols. So, an incoming symbol may be directly output or semantic information belonging to an incoming symbol may be read (e.g. a representation of the actual name belonging to the symbol "identifier"). These advanced actions are controlled by some vector of control items which is accessed by the incoming symbol number, and they do not require time for extra reductions or space for corresponding grammar rules.

3.4 Weak and Soft features

The Weak and Soft decision mechanisms are designed as generated actions. Hence, our parser is structured like a deterministic rather than a Weak and Soft precedence parser. In particular, for a deterministic precedence grammar our system yields a deterministic precedence parser.

The Weak features are very simple. There is a normally small state vector whose components point to the reductions just selected for possible occurences of "ambiguous" phrases. The actions set and interrogate the components of the state vector.

The Soft actions are sequences of set membership checks for constant sets of grammar symbols and of "go-ons" or "returns" according to the success of the checks. For optimization three sizes of sets can be defined. For small ones the check is a sequence of comparisons, for medium ones it is a loop of comparisons, and for big ones it is a test of a bit in a bit vector representing the set as a subset of the grammar vocabulary.

3.5 Error handling

The parser also contains a facility for automatic reporting and recovery in case of syntactical errors in the input text. It includes two types of messages, namely "illegal sequence: symbol-1 symbol-2" and "illegal phrase: symbol-1 ... symbol-m". The first one occurs when symbol-1 is followed by symbol-2 in the input text but no precedence relation holds for this pair. The second one occurs when the precedence relations indicate a leftmost directly reducible substring which is not equal to the right part of a production of the grammar. Symbol-1,...,symbol-m are the names of the symbols as used in the readable representation of the grammar. These names are passed from TAPP to the error processor which expands the coded messages of the parser. Recovery actions included in the parser are: delete a symbol, insert a symbol, assume a precedence relation, force a reduction, and overread text.

Figure 7: PP hierarchical diagram

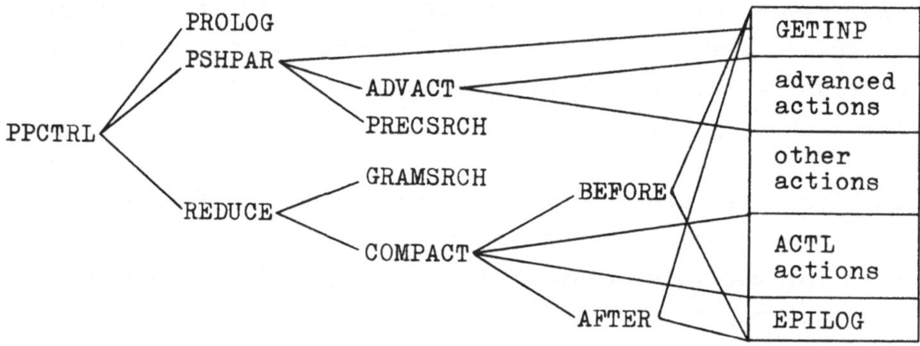

This completes the outline of the parser. It is followed by a description of the table program.

4. Features of the table program

The main functions of the table program are to read the input and therefrom to build the grammar and precedence matrix tables in the representation already described, and furthermore, to compute Soft precedence relations, to generate actions and to output some communicative data.

4.1 Input, symbol list and grammar table

The input of TAPP consists of some control data not discussed here and of the data to be included in the tables. These are symbol-specifications, productions and action-specifications. The symbol-specifications represent the vocabulary and also contain information for advanced actions. Each action-specification belongs to a production and consists of a list of action names, some with parameters. From the symbol-specifications

Figure 8: TAPP input format

```
.....
# FUNCT-CALL ::= IDENT "(" ARGLIST ")" @ TERMK(FCLL)
# ARGLIST ::= ARG-SEQ @ TERMK1(ARGL)
# ARG-SEQ ::= ARG @ PSH1C1
# ARG-SEQ ::= ARG-SEQ "," ARG @ ADD1C1
# ARG ::= EXPR @ TERMK(ARG)
# STRING-ATTR ::= "CHARACTER" "(" LENGTH ")"
$ "CHARACTER" CHAR LOC REC<
# LENGTH ::= EXPR @ TERMK(LGTH)
.....
```

a list of the symbols is built which, among other purposes, serves to translate the symbols within the productions into the internal symbol numbers. The grammar table of TAPP is a list of fixed length entries, one for each production, so it can easily be sorted. Each entry also contains space for an action control item and the fixed maximum number of parameters which may be associated with it. From the corresponding action-specification three sequences of actions are assembled, one fitting into the control item, and, if necessary, one BEFORE- and one AFTER-sequence. The latter ones are given numbers and

Figure 9: TAPP table formats

symbol list

```
1 SYMLIST (MAXSYMNO),
  2 CHAIN BIT(16),
  2 ADVACT BIT(16),
  2 SYMOUT BIT(16),
  2 ABBRSYM CHAR(4),
  2 SYMTYPE CHAR(1),
  2 SYMLGTH BIT(8),
  2 SYMTEXT CHAR(MAXSYM);
```

grammar table

```
1 GRAMTAB (MAXRULENO),
  2 PHRLGTH BIT(16),
  2 PHRASE (MAXPHR) BIT(16),
  2 LEFTPART BIT(16),
  2 ACTL BIT(16),
  2 ACTLPARAMS,
    3 WPCOMP BIT(16),
    3 BEFORE BIT(16),
    3 KEY BIT(16),
    3 AFTER BIT(16);
```

stored somewhere for later generation. The numbers are made parameters of the control item. TAPP contains a list of action names to translate those occuring in action-specifications into internal numbers.

4.2 Precedence matrix computation

For the computation of the precedence relations the method of D.F.Martin [2] is used. To keep it effective, at least two memory resident relation matrices are necessary. If one has three resident matrices one does not need external storage. The logic of the computation is very simple. It consists of several runs through the grammar, transpositions, transitive closings and multiplications of square bit matrices. The condensation is done using row comparisons and transpositions. The sort of the rows for optimizing the condensation effect makes necessary a renumbering of the symbols in the symbol list and the grammar table. After this both the symbol list and the grammar table are sorted according to the new final numbers.

4.3 Computation of Soft actions

The requirements concerning memory space and matrix operations for the precedence computations also hold for the computation of the Soft relations. But, to obtain the final Soft actions, one needs additional features: an evaluation mechanism for Soft relations already computed, a control mechanism to determine which relations are to be computed next, and an editor. The Soft components constitute the most logically complex section of TAPP.

The control part has a buffer where the groups of reductions having the same right part are stored together with some information saying which are yet to be handled and where the soft actions are stored and can be continued. It also has an intersection stack which contains intersections of Soft sets, i.e. matrix rows, already computed and reflects the fact that to compute sequences of possible parse stack predecessors one has to follow a tree. Using these two facilities the control part determines the sequence of Soft relations computed.

The evaluation part, on the other hand, computes intersections of Soft sets useful for the decisions in the parser, stores them, and also stores the corresponding decisions in a coded form. The sequence of all coded decisions of a group of reductions constitutes a skeleton of the corresponding Soft action.

Finally the editor part generates the Soft actions from the skeletons and from the sets produced by the evaluation part.

Figure 10: Generated Soft actions

```
*ACTION #Ø49
SOFTØ49  EQU   *                        set membership checks:
         SPCKS 1,SETØ16,3               S = small set
         SPCKM 1,SETØ17,12,169Ø         M = medium set
         SPCKL 1,SETØ18,1698            L = long set
         SPCKD 1,4Ø9,SØ49Ø1
         SPCKM 2,SETØ19,8
         SPRET 1698
SØ49Ø1   EQU   *
         SPCKL 2,SETØ2Ø
         SPCKM 2,SETØ21,9,169Ø
         SPRET 1698
SETØ16   EQU   *       S,P1()SYM1
         ...
SETØ17   EQU   *       M,P1()SYM3
         ...
         ...
SETØ21   EQU   *       M,P2(SYM4)SYM2
         ...
*END OF ACTION #Ø49
```

4.4 Output

With exception of the precedence matrix and some listings, all output of TAPP is done in this last section. This includes output of the generated sequences of action calls for BEFORE- and AFTER-actions, output of the generated Soft actions, output of the grammar table and the symbol list, and output of a cross reference list and some statistical data. An extra grammar table and symbol list are passed to the generator program for the lexical analyzer and another symbol list is passed to the error processor.

Figure 11: TAPP hierarchical diagram

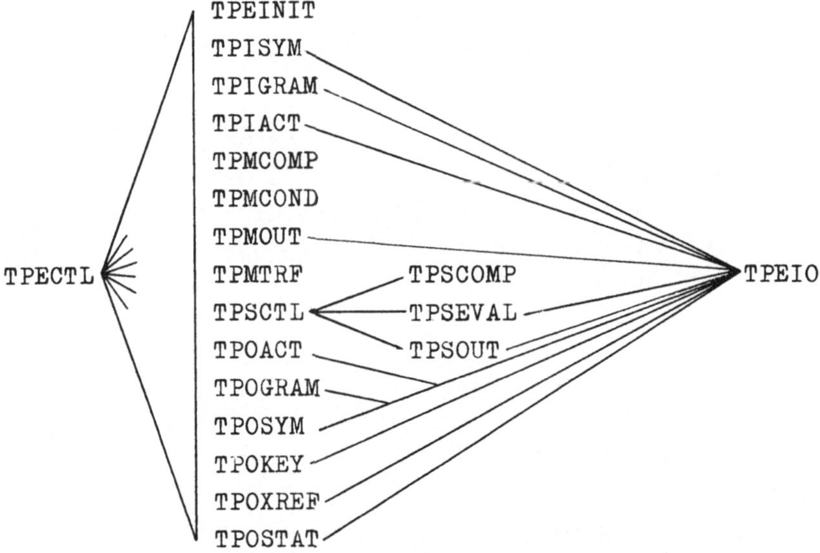

5. Implementation aspects

Having the large design of our system we shall now look at some practical considerations and discuss the most important implementation aspects.

Since the system shall be used in large commercial compilers for common programming languages, initially for PL/I, we have strong size and speed conditions, and therefore we decided to write both the parser and the table program in assembly language using as an implementation tool our powerful macro processor GPSP. The system is implemented in a static linkage environment. Accordingly, the precedence and grammar tables are output as relocatable modules to save assembly time, but all other data are, for individual reasons, output as macros or simply stream data. In particular actions are generated on a macro level and output as a macro.

For the parser the stronger restriction was the size. But, using our condensation methods for the precedence matrix, we save about 50 kB for PL/I and the parser for this language is estimated to require 35 kB of memory, which fits very well into a 65 kB environment. We do not have an estimation of the speed of the parser, but the design contains some facilities optimizing the speed, e.g. advanced actions, action control items, mixed representation of matrix rows allowing uncondensed rows and thus quickest access for the most frequent symbols, the indexed chain technique for the search of phrases in the grammar table, and the distinguished handling of Soft sets of different sizes.

For TAPP both size and speed are to be considered. Given a grammar having 500 symbols and 750 productions with right parts of up to 6 symbols the grammar table of TAPP, which is larger than that of the parser, will take 18 kB, the symbol list will take 15 kB, and the two boolean matrices necessary for the computation of precedence and Soft relations will take 31 kB each, i.e. all together 95 kB. The code of TAPP may take 40 or 50 kB. Hence to fit into an 131 kB environment, as may be sensible, one will have to use an overlay technique. This does not seriously affect the speed of TAPP, because TAPP works by a sequence of about 20 non-recursive functions, some of which need most of the time of TAPP, and therefore these functions are realized as overlays. The functions which take most of the time of TAPP are the precedence computation and the Soft computation. On our Siemens 4004/45, the precedence computation for PL/I, including condensation, may take 10 - 15 minutes, and the Soft computation may take 120 - 150 minutes. These data are not representative and they should be considered as extremal.

Implementation times may be 3 or more man-month for the parser and 5 or more for the table program.

6. Summary

We have had a look at the design of a parser writing system based on the precedence technique, but extended to cover existing common programming languages. In this sense it is a versatile system. Moreover a parser produced by the system is to some degree tailored to its language. We have seen some theoretical foundations of the system and what its facilities may be like in a certain envir_onment and under certain restrictions. The final properties of the system may be reported when it is ready and in use.

References

1. Wirth,N. and Weber,H., EULER: A generalization of ALGOL and its formal definition: Part I. Comm.ACM 9 (1966) 13-25
2. Martin,D.F., Boolean Matrix-Methods for the Detection of Simple Precedence Grammars. Comm.ACM 11 (1968) 685-687
3. Zimmer,R., Weak Precedence, Proc. of the ICS 70 / ACM Europe, Part II (1970) 576-587
4. Zimmer,R., Soft Precedence (to be published).

AIDA, EIN DIALOGSYSTEM UND SEINE IMPLEMENTIERUNG IN ALGOL

von K.-H. Mohn, M. Rosendahl und H.P. Zoller

0. Zusammenfassung

Es wird die im Rechenzentrum der Ruhr-Universität Bochum entwickelte Dialogsprache AIDA (An Interpreter for direct Access oder An Interpreter for Dialogue Algol) und ihre Implementierung mittels ALGOL 60 beschrieben. Die Sprache ist ein Dialekt von Algol, d.h. bis auf wenige Elemente enthält sie Algol 60. Dazu enthält sie Operationen auf Vektoren und Arrays, Listenoperationen ähnlich wie in LISP und Tischrechnerfunktionen. Falls man diese zusätzlichen Eigenschaften der Sprache nicht benutzt, ist es möglich, aus einem in dieser Dialogsprache entwickelten Programm ein Algolprogramm zu erzeugen.

Die Implementierung der Arrayoperationen, insbesondere der Operationen Reduktion, Neustrukturierung usw. erfolgt durch in ALGOL geschriebene LISP-Programme. Der Quellentext wird vom Interpreterprogramm mittels eines Variablen- und Operatorenkellers interpretiert, dadurch ist es möglich, bei Austesten des Programms nach Programmänderung an der Unterbrechungsstelle fortzufahren. Dadurch werden Neuübersetzungs- und Montierzeiten eingespart.

1. Ziele des Systemkonzepts

1.1. Direkter Eingriff in den Programmlauf

Beim Arbeiten an einem Computer im open-shop Betrieb und mit Maschinen-Code war es möglich, nach dem Programmstart den Lauf evtl. schrittweise zu verfolgen und an bestimmten Stellen zu unterbrechen. Man konnte das Programm verändern und anschließend weiterlaufen lassen.

Mit dem Übergang zum closed-shop kam eine völlig neue Bearbeitungsmethode:

(a) An die Stelle des Maschinen-codes traten benutzerorientierte Programmiersprachen wie FORTRAN, ALGOL.

(b) Die Steuerung des Programmablaufs übernahm nun das Betriebssystem. Ein Monitor erzeugte automatisch die Folge Übersetzung, Montage, Objektlauf, ohne Eingriffsmöglichkeit des Benutzers.

Mit dem Übergang zu Time-sharing-System hat man wieder den direkten Zugriff zum Computer, allerdings zunächst nur "hardware"-seitig.
"Software"-seitig arbeitet man immer noch in der Folge Übersetzung-Montage-Lauf - evtl. Dump. Nach Rekonstruktion der Fehlerursache muß ein Programm jeweils neu übersetzt und montiert werden.

Um auch "software"-seitig wieder "open-shop" Möglichkeiten zu schaffen, gibt es 2 Wege:

(1) Incremental compiling

d.h. bei Änderung der Quelle wird nur der geänderte Teil neu übersetzt. Hierbei kann jedoch nicht im Objektlauf fortgefahren werden.

(2) Interpretation

Das Quellenprogramm wird nicht übersetzt, sondern beim Lauf des Programms wird die Quelle jeweils in der dynamischen Folge interpretiert.
Hierbei kann man den Programmlauf anhalten, sowohl Quelle als auch die Belegung von Variablen ändern und dennoch den Lauf an der Unterbrechungsstelle fortsetzen. Nachteil des Interpretierens ist eine längere Programmlaufzeit.

Beim vorliegenden System wurde die Interpretation gewählt. Der Benutzer, der sein Problem auch mit ALGOL oder FORTRAN lösen kann, müßte nun die Vorteile der schnelleren Programmentwicklung gegen die Nachteile längerer Produktionsläufe abwägen. Daher wurde die AIDA Sprache sehr stark an ALGOL 60 [1] angeglichen, um bei der Programmentwicklung Compilations- und Interpretationstechnik mischen zu können. Wenn man die zusätzlichen Sprachelemente, die über ALGOL hinausgehen nicht benutzt, läßt sich aus einem AIDA-Programm leicht ein lauffähiges ALGOL-Programm erzeugen. Dies hat auch den Vorteil, daß für die Benutzung des Systems keine neue Sprache zu erlernen ist. Andererseit kann man vorhandene Algolprogramme im System benutzen.

1.2. Komplexe Operationen und Datenstrukturen

Für ein Dialogsystem ist es wünschenswert, mit möglichst kurzem Quellentext wirkungsvolle komplexe Anweisungen an das System zu geben. Einige Ansätze hierzu sind die Matrixoperationen von BASIC [4] und APL [2,3] ;
Beim AIDA-System wurden diese verallgemeinert und mittels der vom LISP übernommenen Datenstruktur sehr einfach durch rekursive Programme verwirklicht.
Durch diese Darstellung der Variablen mittels Atoms und Listen, wie in LISP [7], kann man LISP-Funktionen formulieren und erhält dadurch Möglichkeiten wie in LISP2 [9] .

Diese Darstellung erlaubt es auch, ähnlich wie die <u>modes</u> in ALGOL 68 [8], neue Datenstrukturen und Operationen auf diesen zu definieren, z.B. Systeme zum Rechnen mit komplexen Zahlen oder mit mehrfacher Genauigkeit.
Eine weitere für die Zukunft vielleicht bedeutende Möglichkeit dieser Datenstruktur liegt in der Darstellung mehrdimensionaler Objekte. So steht für Dialogsysteme mit graphischer Ein- und Ausgabe eine Programmiersprache zur Implementierung zur Verfügung.

1.3. Implementierung mittels einer formalen Sprache

AIDA ist ganz in Algol geschrieben, wodurch sich folgende Vorteile ergeben:

(1) Unabhängigkeit der Implementierung vom Maschinentyp.

Bisher werden zur Implementierung u.a. rekursive Unterprogramme benutzt. Dies ist nur bei wenigen Algol-Compilern möglich. Man kann aber die rekursiven Aufrufe in Sprünge umwandeln und die Parameter mit einem Keller übergeben. Dann läßt sich das System mit jedem Algol-Compiler übersetzen.

(2) Leichte Systempflege und Änderung der Systemoperationen.

In einem Algolprogramm sind Änderungen und Verbesserungen leichter durchzuführen als in einem Assemblerprogramm. Die einzelnen Systemoperationen sind integer procedures, die nach einem einheitlichen Schema über Verteiler angesprungen werden.
So können diese procedures leicht variiert oder korrigiert werden, ohne daß dies Auswirkungen auf andere Systemteile hat. Insgesamt kann man sagen, daß die Implementierung in einer formalen Sprache zu einem modularen Aufbau mit klaren Schnittstellen führt. Insbesondere nutzen wir hier die Vorteile des procedure-Konzepts und der Blockstruktur von Algol 60 aus.

(3) Kurze Implementierungszeit und leichteres Erkennen von Systemfehlern.

2. Datenstruktur

Die Variablenwerte werden intern auf 2 Arrays CAR und CDR gespeichert. Der Speicherraum wird wie in LISP durch einen Freispeichervermerk verwaltet und durch Garbage-collection bereinigt.
Die Variablen sind wie in LISP entweder Atoms oder S-Expression bzw. Listen.
Die Atoms haben CAR ≤ 0, die Listen CAR > 0.
Bei den Atoms gibt der CAR-Wert den Typ und CDR den Wert an.
Die Listen haben die gleiche Struktur wie in LISP.

Eindimensionale Arrays sind Listen, z.B.: <u>array</u> a [1:3] ;

Wie bei EULER [5,6] braucht ein Array nicht rechtwinklig zu sein, sondern es kann etwa a [1] wieder ein Array, a [2] dagegen eine einfache Variable sein. So lassen sich beliebig strukturierte Listen aufbauen, mit denen auch Graphen, Bäume usw. beschrieben werden können.

In AIDA sind auf diesen Listen Operationen erklärt, die in ALGOL nur auf einfachen Variablen erklärt sind.

Das Programm, das dies z.B. für dyadische Operationen ausführt, ist:

```
dop (op, a, b) : =
if CAR [a] < 0 and CAR [b] < 0 then op (a,b)
else if CAR [a] > 0 and CAR [b] > 0 then
     cons (dop(op, CAR [a] , CAR [b] ), dop(op,CDR [a] , CDR [b])
else if CAR [a] < 0 and CAR [b] > 0 then
     cons (dop(op,a,CAR [b] ), dop(op,a,CDR [b] ))
else if CAR [a] > 0 and CAR [b] < 0 then
     cons (dop(op,CAR [a] , b), dop(op,CDR [a] , b))
else 0;
```

Falls a und b die gleiche Dimension haben, wird jeweils elementweise verknüpft, solange a und b ein Element besitzen. Das <u>array</u> a [1:n, 1:m] verknüpft mit b [1:u, 1:v] ergibt ein <u>array</u> c [1:min(n,u), 1:min(m,v)] ;
Bei Listen ergibt diese Operation eine Liste, deren Struktur der Durchschnitt der beiden Listen ist.

Falls die Dimensionen von a und b nicht übereinstimmen, wird nach dem Distributivgesetz verfahren. Es sei a ein Skalar und b ein Vektor $(b_1, b_2, \ldots, b_n)$, dann ist:

$$\text{dop}\ (\text{op},a,b) = (\text{op}(a,b_1),\ \text{op}(a,b_2),\ \ldots,\ \text{op}(a,b_b)).$$

Zwei zu verknüpfende Listen brauchen also weder in Dimensionen noch in den Längen übereinstimmen.
Ein ähnlich aufgebautes Programm mop wendet monadische Operatoren auf eine beliebige Liste an. Über die so erweiterten ALGOL-Operationen und Standardfunktionen hinaus gibt es folgende Operationen:

A,B (catenate): verknüpft zwei Atoms oder Listen zu einer Liste (ähnlich <u>append</u> bei LISP)
⊛/A (Reduktion): Es wird A [1] ⊛ A [2] ⊛...⊛ A [n] gebildet (ähnlich wie bei APL).
& A (size): Es wird der Dimensionsvektor von A gebildet.
A & B (reshape): Die Liste B wird auf Grund des Dimensionsvektors A neustrukturiert.
A$⊛_1$ $⊛_2$ = B (inner produkt): Es wird das innere Produkt gebildet. Z.B.: A+ ∗ = B ist die Matrizenmultiplikation.
A⊛.!B (outer produkt): Es wird jedes Element von A mit jedem Element von B entsprechend ⊛ verknüpft.
, A (ravel): Aus jedem Atom oder jeder Liste wird ein Vektor gemacht.
! A (jota): Es wird der Vektor (1,2,3,...,A) erzeugt.
[B] A (transpose): Die Liste A wird so umstrukturiert, daß die B-te Dimension die erste wird.

Dazu gibt es noch die LISP-Operationen CONS, CAR, CDR; für CONS (AB) kann man auch A.B schreiben. So kann man wie in LISP sowohl Listen als auch S-Expression in AIDA schreiben.

A [B] (index): Aus der Liste A wird das B-te Element genommen. Falls B ein Vektor B:= $(b_1, b_2, \ldots, b_n)$ ist, wird zunächst das b_1-te, von diesem das b_2-te usw. genommen. Dadurch, und durch die Definition von catenate, ist die Notation der Indexausdrücke die gleiche wie in ALGOL. Falls die Anzahl der Elemente in B kleiner ist als die Dimension von A, ergibt A [B] nicht ein einzelnes Element, sondern eine Unterliste bzw. ein Teilarray.

Als Beispiel für die einfache Beschreibung dieser Operationen mittels der hier verwendeten Datenstruktur und rekursiven Programme soll die Operation für das innere Produkt gebracht werden:

```
    integer procedure inner (plus, mal a, b);
    begin
    integer procedure inner2 (x,y);
(1) inner2:= if x = 0 then 0
(2) else if CAR [CAR [x]] < 0 then red (plus, dop (mal,x,y))
(3) else cons (inner2 (CAR [x] , y), inner2 (CDR [x] , y));
    inner:= inner2 (a,b);
    end;
```

Das Programm inner2 hat nur den Zweck, unnötige Parameterübergaben zu ersparen. An einem kurzen Beispiel soll das Programm erklärt werden. Es sei folgendes Matrizenprodukt zu bilden:

$$\begin{pmatrix} a_{11} & a_{12} \\ a_{21} & a_{22} \end{pmatrix} \times \begin{pmatrix} b_{11} & b_{12} \\ b_{21} & b_{22} \end{pmatrix}$$

Nach Zeile (3):

$$\left((a_{11}, a_{12}) \times \begin{pmatrix} b_{11} & b_{12} \\ b_{21} & b_{22} \end{pmatrix} , (a_{21}, a_{22}) \times \begin{pmatrix} b_{11} & b_{12} \\ b_{21} & b_{22} \end{pmatrix} \right)$$

Nach Zeile (2):

$$\begin{pmatrix} a_{11} & b_{11} + a_{12} & b_{21} & & a_{11} & b_{12} + a_{12} & b_{22} \\ a_{21} & b_{11} + a_{22} & b_{21} & & a_{21} & b_{12} + a_{22} & b_{22} \end{pmatrix}.$$

Falls die Größen der Felder nicht im Sinne eines Matrixprodukts kompatibel sind, wird bei dieser Definition von dop kein Fehler bei inner gemeldet. Durch Änderung von dop (nur noch gleichlange Felder werden verarbeitet) ist es aber einfach möglich, ohne inner zu ändern, in solchen Fällen eine Fehlermeldung zu erhalten.

Die übrigen Operationen wie outerprodukt, index usw. sind durch ähnliche rekursive Proceduren realisiert.

Beim index-Programm erhält man automatisch eine Fehlermeldung, falls der Index über die obere Grenze hinausläuft. Dadurch ist eine dynamische Kontrolle gegeben. Auch die übrigen dynamischen Kontrollen (undefinierte Variablen, Parameteranzahl) lassen sich leicht realisieren. Um undefinierte Variablen zu erkennen, braucht nur jeder neu auftretenden Variablen ein Atom zugeordnet werden, deren CAR undefiniert bedeutet. Bei den einzelnen Operationen kann ein solches Atom erkannt werden. Falls man Deklarationen wünscht, lassen sich mittels CAR auch nicht deklarierte Variablen erkennen.

Zusammenfassend läßt sich sagen, daß gewünschte Varianten jeweils lediglich eine Änderung an einzelnen Unterprogrammen erfordern. Die Änderungen haben keine Rückwirkung auf andere Teile, etwa die syntaktische Analyse.

Auch neue Systemoperationen lassen sich als integer-procedure leicht in das System einfügen. Dabei ist die Verschlüsselung der Operation in AIDA von der Operationsdefinition unabhängig. So läßt sich aus einer Bibliothek von ALGOL-Unterprogrammen leicht ein spezielles System zusammenstellen, dessen Notation in AIDA frei gewählt werden kann.

3. Arbeitsweise an Hand eines Beispiels

Den Aufbau des Systems zeigt das grobe Blockdiagramm in Abbildung 1:

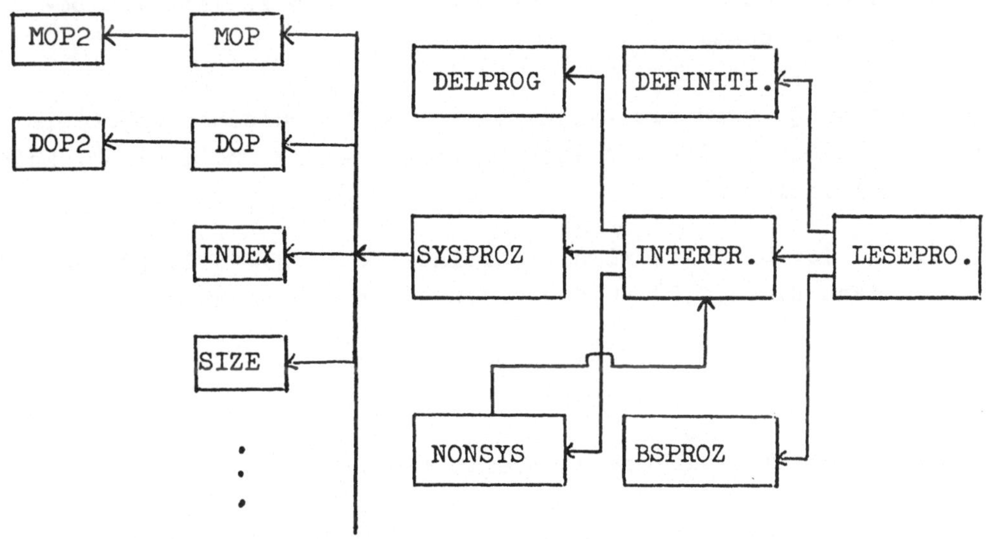

Abb. 1

An Hand des Beispiels (Berechnung von Binomialkoeffizienten) soll kurz ein Dialog in AIDA beschrieben werden.

```
(1)   □: ]'BIN A; B I;
(2)         B:=1;
(3)         for I:=1 until A do
(4)         B:= (B,0) + (0,B);
(5)         :=B;
(6)       ]
(7)         BIN 3; □.
(8)         1  3  3  1
(9)   □:
```

Beim TR440 Konsol-Betriebssystem [13]
wird durch □: der Teilnehmer zu einer Eingabe aufgefordert, die er mit □. beendet.

Die Eingabe des Benutzers von AIDA soll nun zeilenweise besprochen werden.

(1): Mit]' wird die Definition eines monadischen Operators BIN eingeleitet. A ist der Parameter, B und I sind lokale Variablen.

(4): In der Schleife wird B fortlaufend zu B:=(1,0)+(0,1)=(1,1) dann B:=(1,1,0)+(0,1,1)=(1,2,1) usw. berechnet.

(5): Durch den monadischen Zuweisungsoperator wird B als Funktionswert übergeben.

(6):] beendet die Operatordefinition.

Der so definierte Operator wird in einem Interpretationsspeicher eingetragen. Die Anfangsadresse und der Operatorname dieser Eintragung kommen in das Operatorenverzeichnis, siehe Abb. 2.

(7): Die nun eingegebenen Anweisungen werden direkt ausgeführt. Das Leseprogramm ruft den Interpreter auf, sobald Eingabeende (□.) gegeben wird und man sich nicht in der Definitionsphase befindet. Kommt in einer Anweisung keine Wertzuweisung (:=) vor, so wird der errechnete Wert ausgedruckt (Zeile (8)).

Eine Korrektur im Programm läßt sich durch folgende Eingaben erreichen:

a)]'BIN 3.5 inf.
   fügt eine Zeile mit der Zeilennummer 3.5 zwischen den Zeilen 3 und 4 ein.

b)]'BIN 5/3 inf.
   ändert in Zeile 5 ab dem dritten Zeichen.

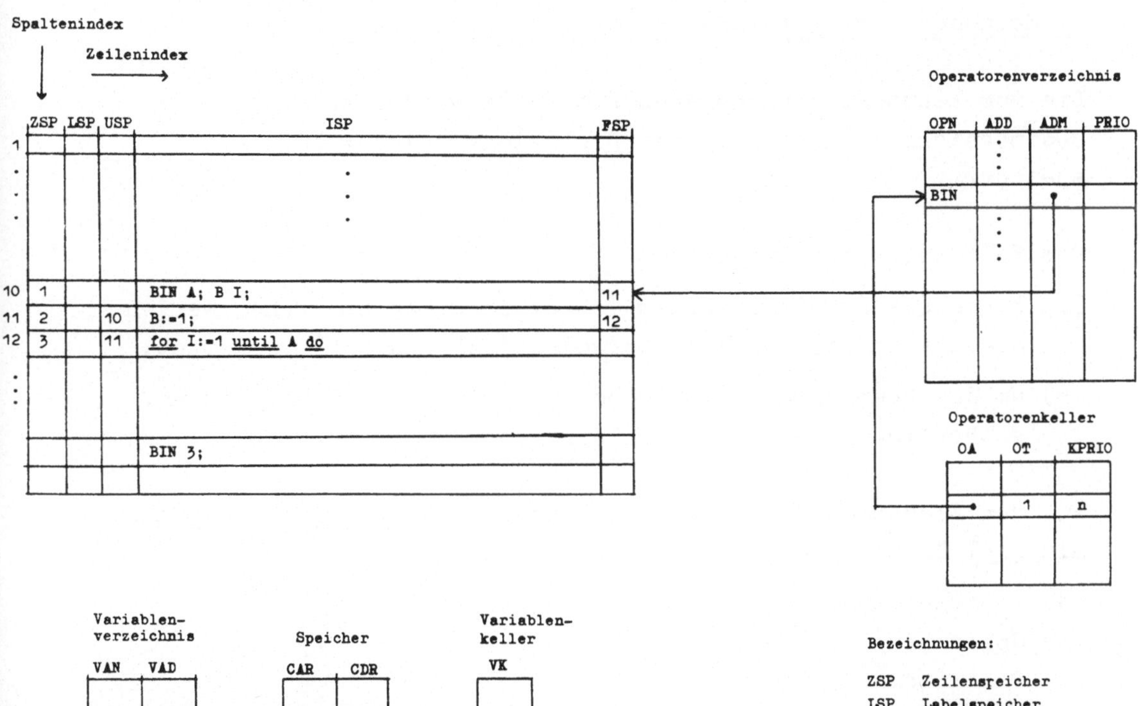

Abb. 2

Bezeichnungen:

ZSP	Zeilenspeicher
LSP	Labelspeicher
USP	Ursprungsspeicher
ISP	Interpretationsspeicher
FSP	Folgespeicher
OPN	Operatornamenspeicher
ADD	Adresse dyadisch
ADM	Adresse monadisch
PRIO	Priorität
OA	Operatoradresse
OT	Operatorryp
KPRIO	Kellerpriorität
VAN	Variablenname
VAD	Variablenadresse

4. Methoden der Syntaxanalyse beim Interpretieren

Die vom Benutzer eingegebenen Programme werden auf einem 2-dimensionalen Feld dem Interpretationsspeicher ISP abgespeichert.

Das Feld ist 2-dimensional um

(a) Einschübe in ein Programm leichter zu machen. Daher werden die Zeilen des ISP über Verweise (FSP und USP) verkettet.

(b) Um das Überschlagen von "compound statements" und das Aufsuchen von Labels zu beschleunigen.

Auf den Elementen dieses Feldes werden die syntaktischen Einheiten als real Größen abgespeichert. Das sind:

(1) nichtnegative Zahlen
(2) Operatoren und Variablen
(3) Delimiter
(4) Stringadressen.

Die Zahlen werden ≥ 0, alle anderen < 0 gesetzt. Durch das Leseprogramm wird sichergestellt, daß die Delimiter begin und end immer in der 1. Spalte stehen. Dies ermöglicht es, daß beim Überschlagen von "compound statements" lediglich in der 1. Spalte gesucht werden muß. Labels werden in einer zusätzlichen Spalte (LSP) gesondert abgelegt. (siehe Abb. 2) Dies erlaubt ein schnelles Auffinden der Labels bei Sprüngen.

Die syntaktische Analyse erfolgt nun nach der Methode der sequentiellen Formelverarbeitung von Bauer-Samelson [10] mit Operatoren- und Operandenkeller. Im Vektor OA des Operatorenkellers (Abb. 2) befindet sich der Index, wo die Operation im Operatorenverzeichnis zu finden ist. Der Typ (monadisch, dyadisch) steht in OT, die Kellerpriorität in KPRIO. Im Operandenkeller wird die Adresse der Variablen, d.h. wo das Atom oder der Listenkopf in CAR und CDR steht, gespeichert.

Falls im Interpretationsspeicher ein Element gefunden wird, das eine Variable oder einen Operator bedeutet, wird zunächst im Operatorenverzeichnis (in OPN) nachgesehen, ob es ein Operator ist, andernfalls wird das Element als Variable interpretiert. Bei Variablen wird im Variablenverzeichnis (VAN) geprüft, ob der Name bereits aufgetreten ist. Wenn ja, wird die Adresse (VAD) in den Variablenkeller (VK) gebracht, andernfalls wird ein neues Atom erzeugt, dessen CAR ein Indikator für undefinert ist und dessen Adresse nach VK und VAD gebracht wird. Der Variablenname kommt nach VAN.

Auf eine Variable folgt ein dyadischer Operator und dann eventuell beliebig viele monadische Operatoren. Die monadischen Operatoren haben die höchste Priorität und werden von rechts nach links abgearbeitet. Die dyadischen Operatoren haben Prioritäten wie in Algol und werden bei gleicher Priorität von links nach rechts abgearbeitet. Von diesen Regeln gibt es keine Ausnahme, um die Interpretation nicht zu verlangsamen. Dies bedingt zwei Unterschiede zu Algol:

(1) - a power b   in ALGOL - (a <u>power</u> b)
                  in AIDA   (-a) <u>power</u> b

Das gleiche gilt für <u>not</u>.

(2) Eine mehrfache Zuweisung ist nicht möglich, da a:=b:=c bedeuten würde: a:=b danach b:=c;

Falls ein Operator ein im Interpretationsspeicher abgelegtes Programm ist, wird dies aufgerufen. Die Parameter werden, falls sie Variablen sind, aus dem Operandenkeller, falls sie Operatoren sind, aus dem Operatorenkeller übernommen. Dann wird der Interpreter neu aufgerufen.

Beispiel: Im Interpretationsspeicher abgelegtes Programm.

```
]FUN ++ A B;
 :
]
```

Aufruf: A:= + FUN 3 4;

```
Operatorenkeller:   :     Operandenkeller   :
                    :=                      A
                    +                       3
                   FUN                      4
```

Nun wird + ⟶ ++
3 ⟶ A
4 ⟶ B

übergeben. Diese Möglichkeiten der Parameterübergabe weichen von Algol ab.

Zusätzlich gibt es eine procedure-Form mit Parameterübergabe wie in Algol.

Beispiel: procedure - Definition:

```
]MAX (A,B);
 :
]
```

Aufruf: A:= MAX (C!D);

Der Operator ! verknüpft die Parameter zu einem Operanden, dieser wird übergeben und wieder in A und B zerlegt. Da die Adressen in CAR, CDR übergeben werden, ist bei Variablen ein "call by name" möglich. Aber auch ein "call by value" ist möglich, dann muß bei der Definition]MAX (value A, value B); geschrieben werden.

Falls das oberste Element im Operatorenkeller und das zuletzt eingelesene syntaktische Element im Interpretationsspeicher ein Delimiter ist, wird das Programm DELPROG aufgerufen, das für jede Kombination einen besonderen Programmteil startet oder bei unzulässigen Kombinationen einen syntaktischen Fehler meldet.

5. Systemkommandos

Der gesamte Zustand des Systems wird im Interpretationsspeicher (ISP), Variablenverzeichnis, Operatorenverzeichnis und den Speichern CAR, CDR festgehalten. Dies sind Algol-arrays. Durch einfache Algol-EA Prozeduren ist es möglich, diese auf einen Hintergrundspeicher zu bringen und bei einer neuen Sitzung wieder zu erreichen. So kann nach einer Unterbrechung an einem System lückenlos weitergearbeitet werden.

Auch ist es möglich, gewisse vorrätige Programme oder Programmpakete vom Hintergrund in das System einzuschleusen.

Diese Transporte werden durch bestimmte Systemkommandos veranlaßt.

6. Schlußbemerkungen

Bei der Entwicklung von AIDA wurde das Hauptgewicht auf maximalen Komfort für den Benutzer und leichte Implementierung gelegt, weniger dagegen auf Programmeffektivität. Über die Programmlaufzeit eines AIDA-Programms verglichen mit etwa einem ALGOL-Programm liegen z.Z. noch nicht genügend Erfahrungen vor.

Zur Beschleunigung des Programms könnte man gewisse Suchroutinen in Feldern durch spezielle Maschinenbefehle ersetzen. Eine zweite Möglichkeit wäre, statt ALGOL eine zur Software-Implementierung spezieller konzipierte Sprache, etwa BCPL [11] oder PS440 [12] zu benutzen.

Literatur

[1] Nauer, P. (Ed.:)
Revised Report on the Algorithmic Language ALGOL 60
Numer. Mathematik 4(1963) S. 420-453 oder Commun. ACM 6 (1963) S. 1-17.

[2] Iverson, K.E.:
A Programming Language, Wiley, New York 1962.

[3] Falkhoff, A.D., Iverson, K.E.:
The APL 360 Terminal System in "ACM Symposium on Experimental Systems for Applied Mathematics", Academic Press 1968.

[4] Kemeny, J.G. and Kurtz, T.E.:
Basic Programming. Wiley & Sons, New York 1967.

[5] Wirth, N. and Weber, H.:
EULER: A Generalization of ALGOL and its Formal Definition: Comm. ACM 9(1966) S. 13-25, 89-99.

[6] Goos, G.:
EULER TR4, Programmbeschreibung AEG-Telefunken N 31 1.2.09 (1968).

[7] Mc. Carthy, I. u.a.:
LISP 1.5 Programmer's Manual MIT-Press 1962.

[8] A.v. Wijngaarden (Ed.):
Report on the Algorithmic Language Algol 68,
Numer. Mathematik 14 (1969) S. 79-218.

[9] Abrahams, P.W. u.a.:
The LISP2 programming language and System in Proc. AFIPS (1966) Fall Joint Computer Conf. S. 661-676.

[10] Bauer, F.L. und Samelson, K.:
Sequential Formula Translation, Comm. ACM 3 (1960)
S. 76-83.

[11] Richards, M.:
BCPL: A tool for compiler writing and system programming.
Proc. AFIPS (1969) Spring Joint Computer Conf. S. 557-566.

[12] Goos, G.,Lagally, K. und Sapper, G.:
PS 440, eine niedere Programmiersprache, Rechenzentrum
der Technischen Universität München, Bericht 7002 (1970).

[13] TR440, Teilnehmerbetriebssystem BS 3,
AEG-Telefunken, Fachbereich Informationstechnik N 31 (1970).

PARTITIONED GRAMMARS AND SYNTAX ANALYZERS

by F. Schwenkel

Abstract

Context-free grammars of programming languages can frequently be partitioned in a natural way, such that:

- in a well-defined sense, each subgrammar is complete, and

- each subgrammar possesses its own separate syntax analyzer.

The idea is worked out in detail in the case that all subgrammars are simple precedence grammars. Sufficient conditions are derived for the existence of a simple coordinating mechanism for the separate syntax analyzers of the subgrammars. It is shown that partitioned precedence grammars define a wider class of languages than simple precedence grammars. Some practical applications are discussed.

Introduction

Anyone trying to formalize a nontrivial programming language by a simple precedence grammar [1] very likely will encounter considerable difficulties:

- Precedence conflicts are sometimes impossible to eliminate without serious concessions in the form of the grammar, or (worse) in the notation of the language under design.

- Productions with identical right parts are forbidden, which is unfortunate since these tend to come up quite naturally when the same kind of construct is used for different purposes (examples: names used to identify both variables and labels;

arithmetic expressions occurring as dimension limits, subscripts, and function arguments).

It is known [2] that the two kinds of difficulties can be traded for each other:

- Every context-free grammar can be (equivalently) transformed such that it has no precedence conflicts (in which case it will, in general, contain productions with identical right parts).

- Every context-free grammar can be (equivalently) transformed such that the right parts of the productions are unique (in which case it will, in general, have precedence conflicts).

Sometimes one of the transformations can be applied without making concessions on the other side [3]. It should be kept in mind, however, that in practical applications, grammar transformations are frequently undesirable since they tend to conflict with the semantics ordinarily associated with the productions.

Finally, even if these problems have been overcome, there is still the problem of

- the <u>size of the precedence tables</u> which, although hardly prohibitive for use on medium-size computers, cannot be neglected. Roughly, the space required goes with the square of the total number of symbols (terminal and nonterminal) of the grammar.

Partitioned grammars

Since precedence techniques, if applicable, are quite satisfactory, it is not surprising that several extensions of the simple precedence technique have been used [4, 5, 6]. The extension discussed in this paper, although developed in detail for use with precedence syntax analyzers, is more general since it can be applied equally well with other types of bottom-up syntactic analyzers.

The basic idea is to divide up the original grammar (without any change in the productions) such that each subgrammar can be dealt with separately. Clearly, this should have beneficial effects with respect to all three problems discussed above:

- A small subgrammar is much less likely to contain precedence conflicts.
- The prohibition of productions with identical right parts now applies only to each of the subgrammars separately, but no longer to the grammar as a whole.
- The total size of the tables is much reduced, to roughly the sum of the squares of the size of the subalphabets. To give a crude example: original grammar with 100 symbols and a precedence table of 10,000 entries on one side; on the other side 10 subgrammars with 10 symbols each, and a total of 1000 table entries.

Since we want to perform syntactic analysis for each subgrammar separately, the following conditions for proper partitioning are plausible:

(I) Each subgrammar completely defines all its nonterminal symbols, i. e. none of its nonterminals is also a nonterminal of some other subgrammar.

(II) Cross-references between subgrammars occur through their start symbols only. In other words, the start symbol of a subgrammar is the only one of its nonterminal symbols allowed to occur in other subgrammars.

According to (I), any such occurrence would have to be as a terminal symbol, i.e. on the right side of a production. (Note that, from now on, unless said otherwise, we will take attributes like "terminal", "nonterminal", "start symbol" as being relative to the subgrammar under consideration.)

Consider this example of a partitioned grammar for nested lists of integers:

Part 1: integer

digit → 0 / 1 / 2 / ... / 9

integer → digit / integer digit

Part 2: list

listhead → (/ (constant / listhead , constant

list → listhead)

Part 3: constant

constant → integer / list

Start 3

Note the way in which start symbols of subgrammars are shown. This grammar is properly partitioned: the nonterminal sets of the subgrammars don't overlap, and cross-references are through start symbols only. "Start 3" is meant to indicate that the language we want to define is the set of "constants" (consisting of both integers, and lists of integers). In other words, there is a start subgrammar (Part 3) whose start symbol (constant) is also the start symbol of the whole grammar.

Note that mutual (recursive) cross-references are allowed, such as the ones between Part2 and 3 in the example.

Partitioned syntax analyzers

Consider a context-free grammar G, partitioned into subgrammars G_i with start symbols S_i, one of them designated as start subgrammar G_s with start symbol S_s. Now assume that for each of the subgrammars a separate, deterministic, left-to-right, bottom-up syntax analyzer R_i (the local analyzer for G_i) with a look-ahead of one source character is available. Then an analyzer for the whole grammar could operate as follows.

First, the local analyzer R_s of the start subgrammar is activated. After reducing some initial (maybe empty) segment of the input string, it may reach a segment generated by another subgrammar G_j. At this point, a forward switch should occur, suspending the current analyzer R_i (initially R_s), preserving its current configuration, and activating the local analyzer R_j.

After reducing the substring that caused the forward switch, a back switch to G_i should occur, re-activating R_i in the configuration in which it was suspended, with the distinguished symbol S_j of G_j as its next input.

While R_j is in control, more forward and back switches may become necessary. These in turn may trigger other switches (before control reverts to R_j), arising from nested cross-references between subgrammars. It is possible that fresh copies of R_j are started (and run to termination) before control returns to the suspended copy of R_j.

For the sample grammar above, and the input string (5, (6)) , we get the following sequence of steps:

→ R3 (start R3)

R3 → R2 (forward switch to R2)
input "("
R2 → R3

R3 → R1

input "5"

reduce "5" to <u>integer</u>

R3 ← R1 (back switch to R3), input <u>integer</u>

reduce <u>integer</u> to <u>constant</u>

R2 ← R3 , input <u>constant</u>

reduce "(<u>constant</u>" to <u>listhead</u>

input ","

R2 → R3

R3 → R2

input "("

R2 → R3

R3 → R1

input "6"

reduce "6" to <u>integer</u>

R3 ← R1 , input <u>integer</u>

reduce <u>integer</u> to <u>constant</u>

R2 ← R3 , input <u>constant</u>

reduce "(<u>constant</u>" to <u>listhead</u>

input ")"

reduce "<u>listhead</u>)" to <u>list</u>

R3 ← R2 , input <u>list</u>

reduce *list* to *constant*

R2 ← R3 , input *constant*

reduce "*listhead* , *constant*" to *listhead*

input ")"

reduce "*listhead*)" to *list*

R3 ← R2 , input *list*

reduce *list* to *constant*

← R3 (stop)

Ignoring the grammar switches, the sequence of reductions performed by the local analyzers constitutes a complete bottom-up parse of the source string.

Switch mechanism

Clearly, the switch mechanism which is to control the forward and back switches will have to be recursive.

A forward switch amounts to a prediction as to what subgrammar is appropriate to reduce the next segment of the source string. Hence such a partitioned analyzer, although all its local analyzers have been assumed to operate bottom-up, may go through an intricate pattern of top-down and bottom-up analysis steps.

The switch mechanism, in principle, must have the authority to start, suspend, and re-start the local analyzers, and to control the input to the local analyzers. Aside from that, it may be considered as being completely separated from the local analyzers. This is what one would do for theoretical work on partitioned analyzers. It implies that the switch mechanism has to have its own complete decision-making machinery.

In practice, however, one would try to integrate the decision-making machinery of the switch mechanism with that of the local analyzers. Put differently, we may try to have the local analyzers themselves make switch decisions, so that the switch mechanism may become rather rudimentary. In order to pursue this path we have to become more specific about the local analyzers.

(1,1)-context controlled switch mechanism

Consider a grammar G that has been partitioned into simple precedence subgrammars G_i, so that we may assume the local analyzers R_i to be simple precedence analyzers. We reproduce the algorithm of such an analyzer [1] in a form suited for our specific purpose.

```
      Note initial stack level ( ≥ 0 )
  ┌─> If stack at initial level, or stack top symbol ≤ next source symbol:
  ├──    Stack source symbol; Repeat
  │   If source string exhausted, or stack top symbol ⋗ next source sy.:
  │      Find left end of handle (located at stack top)
  │      (stop at initial stack level)
  └──    If found: Reduce handle; Repeat
      Terminate (no precedence relation between a pair of symbols,
      or irreducible stack)
```

If the analyzer terminates properly, it will have cleaned up its stack, leaving its start symbol as the only contents. Hence we may as well let all local analyzers share the same stack.

Note that forward switches always occur while examining the next source character. To preserve the configuration of a local analyzer at the moment of suspension, all we have to do is to record its initial stack level for later reference (after control returns to the analyzer).

Upon re-activation of a suspended analyzer, its next input, i. e. the start symbol left behind by the terminating analyzer, is already in the place where it belongs, at the top of the common stack.

From now on, by "the stack", or "the stack of a local analyzer" we always refer to the common stack. [1)]

---

1) Incidentally, this stack can also be shared by the switch mechanism since its activities are sandwiched between those of the local analyzers. For simplicity, we will neglect stack use by the switch mechanism, i. e. consider only stack entries made by local analyzers.

We will now discuss the <u>forward switch problem</u>. The decision about a forward switch has to be made when examining the next source character: it could be the input to the current analyzer, or it could be the input to some other analyzer (including the case of a fresh copy of the current analyzer) reached by one or more forward switches. The left context of this source symbol, in condensed form, is available on the stack. Hence it is plausible to try to make forward switch decisions on the basis of pairs:

(stack top symbol a , next source symbol b) .

Accordingly, we assume there exist <u>forward switch functions</u>:

$$f_i(a,b) = \begin{cases} j & \text{if a forward switch from } R_i \text{ to } R_j \text{ is to occur when } a \text{ is at the stack top of } R_i \text{, and } b \text{ is the next source symbol} \\ 0 & \text{otherwise} \end{cases}$$

We can write this also in the form of a relation:

$$a \underset{i}{\textcircled{j}} b \quad \text{if and only if} \quad f_i(a,b) = j$$

It is appropriate to speak of <u>(1,1)-context controlled switch functions (relations)</u>, since we examine one stack symbol and one source symbol only.

To include the special case of a local analyzer just getting started, with its stack still empty, we allow a to be the empty string, ε .

Clearly, additional context of a and b could be considered, as well as the chain of suspended analyzers. But, just as in the case of ordinary (non-partitioned) syntactic analysis, these extensions are not particularly attractive, and shall not be considered here.

Forward switch relations with $a \nmid \varepsilon$ originate from adjacent symbols in productions:

Let $U \underset{i}{\triangleq} V$ if G_i contains a production with right side ...UV...

Further, consider <u>local left and right sets</u>:

$$V' \in \mathcal{L}_i(V) \quad \text{if} \quad V \underset{i}{\overset{*}{\Rightarrow}} V' \ldots \; ,$$

meaning that V generates a string starting with V' in one or more steps, using productions in G_i only;

$$U' \in \mathcal{R}_i(V) \quad \text{if} \quad U \underset{i}{\overset{*}{\Rightarrow}} \ldots U' \; ,$$

meaning that U generates a string ending with U' in one or more steps, using productions in G_i only.

Let $\mathcal{L}(V)$, $\mathcal{R}(U)$ denote left and right sets in the ordinary (non-local) sense [1], defined without regard to subgrammars.

Note that, if $U \underset{i}{\doteq} V$, and U is at the stack top of R_i , then we may expect any source symbol in $\{V\} \cup \mathcal{L}(V)$. In particular, if V implies a cross-reference to G_j $(i \neq j)$, i. e. if

$$S_j \in \{V\} \cup \mathcal{L}_i(V)$$

then source symbols in $\mathcal{L}(S_j)$ should trigger a forward switch:

$$U \underset{i}{\textcircled{j}} b \quad \text{for all} \quad b \in \mathcal{L}(S_j) \cap T \; ,$$

where T denotes the set of terminals of G .

In order to have uniquely defined forward switch relations, multiple cross-references:

$$S_j \, , \, S_k \in \{V\} \cup \mathcal{L}_i(V) \qquad (i,j \neq k)$$

must not interfere with each other:

$$\mathcal{L}(S_j) \cap \mathcal{L}(S_k) \cap T = \emptyset$$

Moreover, there must be no conflicts between $\underset{i}{①}$ relations and ordinary precedence relations $\underset{i}{\doteq}$ and $\underset{i}{\lessdot}$.

Conversely, if these conditions are satisfied, the forward switch problem for $a \neq \varepsilon$ is solved.

If $a = \varepsilon$, the forward switch decision must be made on the basis of the source symbol b alone. If $b \in \mathcal{L}_i(S_i)$, then R_i should move it to its stack. If not, consider the cross-reference

$$S_j \in \mathcal{L}_i(S_i) \quad (i \neq j) \; ^{1)} .$$

If $b \in \mathcal{L}(S_j)$, a forward switch to R_j should occur. Note that we have to require

$$\mathcal{L}_i(S_i) \cap \mathcal{L}(S_j) \cap T = \emptyset .$$

Again, in the case of multiple cross-references:

$$S_j , S_k \in \mathcal{L}_i(S_i) \quad (i,j \neq k) ,$$

we have to require:

$$\mathcal{L}(S_j) \cap \mathcal{L}(S_k) \cap T = \emptyset .$$

Conversely, if these conditions are satisfied, the forward switch problem for $a = \varepsilon$ is solved.

---

1) We don't have to consider $S_j \in \{S_i\} \cup \mathcal{L}_i(S_i)$ since $S_j \neq S_i$ according to partitioning condition (I).

Our augmented <u>local analyzer algorithm</u> is now:

→ **If** stack top symbol (maybe ε) $\overset{\textcircled{j}}{i}$ next source symbol:
Request forward switch to R_j

If stack at initial level, and next source character in local left set of subgrammar, or if stack top symbol $\overset{\lessdot}{=}$ next source character: Stack source character; Repeat

If source string exhausted, or next source symbol is not a symbol of the subgrammar, or stack top symbol ⋗ next source symbol:
Find left end of handle (stop at initial stack level)

If found: Reduce handle; Repeat

Request back switch (see below)

As an illustration, take our previous sample grammar:

Part 1: integer

digit → 0 / ... / 9

integer → digit / integer digit

No cross-references.

Part 2: list

listhead → (/ (constant / listhead , constant

list → listhead)

If newly started, R_2 will pick up an opening parenthesis. Will request a forw. switch to R_3 if "(" or "," is at the stack top, and the next source char. is in $\mathcal{L}(\text{constant}) \cap T = \{0, \ldots, 9, (\}$.

Part 3: constant

constant → integer / list

Will not pick up any source character. Switches to R_1 on digits, and to R_2 on opening parentheses.

Note that the opening list parenthesis "(" is not causing any trouble in R_3 (although it occurs in both $\mathcal{L}(\text{constant})$ and $\mathcal{L}(\text{list})$), since it is not in the local left set $\mathcal{L}_3(\text{constant})$.

We come now to the back switch problem which we shall try to solve with the following simple strategy: a back switch (from R_j to R_i) occurs when the current local analyzer (R_j) runs out of reductions. This is in line with our philosophy of delegating switch decisions to the local analyzers.

As a first step, we adopt the common restriction that R_j cannot directly reduce its start symbol S_j. In other words, we allow S_j to occur in the right part of productions of G_j, but not as the only symbol. Hence if, for some reason, R_j is unable to pick up the next source symbol, it will eventually run out of reductions. If this happens at the end of an S_j-phrase (source substring generated by S_j), then R_j will run out of reductions at the moment when its stack has been reduced to its start symbol S_j.

To prevent R_j from picking up any source symbol b which may follow the S_j-phrase in the source string, we will make sure that $\gtrdot b$ relations hold for all symbols that may occupy the stack top at the moment of the back switch. Consider two adjacent symbols U , V in G_i, i. e. $U \doteq_i V$, and assume we are just finishing analyzing a U-phrase that ends on an S_j-phrase. In other words, let

$$S_j \in \{U\} \cup \mathcal{R}_i(U) \quad (i \neq j) \quad ,$$

so that the analysis of the U-phrase will have triggered a forward switch to R_j from which we now have to recover before entering the V-phrase which comes next in the source string, starting with some terminal symbol $b \in \{V\} \cup \mathcal{L}(V)$.

We have to prevent R_j , and all other analyzers which may have in turn been triggered by R_j , from picking up b . Possible stack top symbols at this moment are S_j , and symbols in the right set of S_j, belonging to subgrammars G_k with $S_k \in \mathcal{R}(S_j)$ $(j \neq k)$. Hence possible stack top symbols are those in

$$(\{S_j\} \cup \mathcal{R}(S_j)) \cap A_k \ , \quad \text{for all } k \text{ with } S_k \in \{S_j\} \cup \mathcal{R}(S_j) \ ,$$

where A_k denotes the alphabet (set of symbols) of G_k . We introduce $\gtrdot$ relations for all possible combinations of these stack top symbols and next source symbols. In formulas:

$$(\{S_j\} \cup \mathcal{R}(S_j)) \cap A_k \underset{k}{\gtrdot} (\{V\} \dot{\cup} \mathcal{L}(V)) \cap T_k \ ,$$

$$\text{for all } k \text{ with } S_k \in \{S_j\} \cup \mathcal{R}(S_j) \ ,$$

where T_k denotes the set of terminals of G_k .

If none of these $\gtrdot$ relations conflicts with any of the other precedence relations and forward switch relations of the subgrammars, the desired back switches will indeed occur, and the back switch problem is solved.

In our previous sample grammar, none of the more tricky back switch cases arise:

Part 1: *integer* *digit* → 0 / ... / 9 *integer* → *digit* / *integer* *digit*	R_1 switches back after reaching the end of the string of digits which it was called in to reduce, since it cannot pick up non-digits.
Part 2: *list* listhead → (/ (constant / *listhead* , *constant*	The relation *list* $\gtrdot_2$) forces R_2 to switch back after forming *list* on its stack.
Part 3: *constant* *constant* → *integer* / *list*	R_3 switches back after every reduction.

As we have seen, considerable effort is needed to put partitioned grammars to work. Hence it may be appropriate to show that they actually define a larger class of languages than simple precedence grammars:

> The family of partitioned precedence languages is closed under union of languages with disjoint left terminal sets.

In other words, if partitioned precedence languages L(G) and L(G') are given with $\mathcal{L}(S_s) \cap \mathcal{L}(S'_{s'}) \cap T \cap T' = \emptyset$, then $L(G) \cup L(G')$ is also a partitioned precedence language: Clearly, we can put given partitioned analyzers for L(G) and L(G') together such that the new analyzer, in the very first step of a syntactic analysis, will switch forward to the appropriate one of the original analyzers.

It is known that this closure property does not hold for the class of simple precedence languages. In fact, the only published example of a non-precedence language [7] is such a union of simple precedence languages with disjoint left sets.

Implementation considerations

We try to assess the cost of analyzer switching, both in time and space. Our sample syntax analysis (given above) shows that there are about as many grammar switches as reductions. Fortunately, switches are quite straightforward (involving a few stack operations only), and can probably be neglected in comparison to the more complex operations involved in a reduction.

The storage requirements of the switch mechanism are much more critical; as it stands, they would offset much of the gains made by partitioning the precedence matrix. For each local analyzer, we need a matrix of $|A_i| * |T|$ entries to represent its switch function f_i. In addition, the local analyzers have to be interfaced. Presumably, each local analyzer has a local code table of $|T|$ entries to relate source characters to its local precedence table. Moreover, start symbols left on the stack upon a back switch have to be recoded, e.g. with the assistance of a matrix with one row and one column per subgrammar. These interfacing tables, however, are negligible in comparison to the forward switch matrices. Fortunately, the latter can be drastically reduced in practice, since switch decisions can frequently be based directly on the left terminal sets $\mathcal{L}(S_i) \cap T$ $(i=1,\ldots,n)$ of the subgrammars, representable as one $n * |T|$ matrix. There is a variety of more or less refined space-saving switch schemes based on this idea; we briefly describe one that has actually been implemented [12] .

It employs several additional tables, defined as follows:

one <u>global switch table</u> of size $n * |T|$:

$$GS(i,b) = \begin{cases} j & \text{if all forward switches from } R_i \\ & \text{upon source character } b \text{ lead to } R_j \\ 0 & \text{otherwise} \end{cases}$$

n <u>local switch vectors</u> of size $|A_i|$:

$$LV_i(a) = \begin{cases} j & \text{if stack symbol } a \text{ has only one kind} \\ & \text{of switch relations, } a \underset{i}{\textcircled{j}} \text{ (but no} \\ & \text{relations } a \underset{i}{\textcircled{k}},\ j \neq k \text{)} \\ 0 & \text{otherwise} \end{cases}$$

n <u>local switch tables</u> of size $n * A_i$:

$$LT_i(a,j) = \begin{cases} \underline{\text{true}} & \text{if a forward switch } R_i \rightarrow R_j \text{ is} \\ & \text{to occur with } a \text{ at the stack top,} \\ & \text{and next source character } b \in \mathcal{L}(S_j) \\ \underline{\text{false}} & \text{otherwise} \end{cases}$$

also written as: $a \underset{i}{\circledast} S_j$ if and only if $LT_i(a,j) = \underline{\text{true}}$.

Suppose analyzer R_i has no precedence relation for its current stack top symbol a, and the next source character b. This is a potential (forward or back) switch situation; it can be resolved as follows:

<u>If</u> $LV_i(a) = j$ and $b \in \mathcal{L}(S_j)$, or if
$GS(i,b) = j$ and $a \circledast_i S_j$: Forward switch to R_j

<u>Else</u> attempt to reduce the stack; if this is impossible: Back switch .

Of course, not all partitioned precedence grammars can be handled by this scheme. However, the additional restrictions have turned out to be rarely noticeable in practical applications.

To give some idea of the effectiveness of this particular space-saving scheme; the EULER grammar [1] was processed twice, first in one piece, and then in 10 parts, with a reduction of 2.5 : 1 in the total table space required.

Related work

Conway [8] seems to have been first to use the idea of grammar partitioning (although he didn't describe it in grammatical terms), in connection with finite state subgrammars. It was rediscovered by Tixier whose thesis [9] is a formalization of [8] . Woods [10] applies Conway's method to natural language analysis. Korenjak [11] uses grammar partitioning as an intermediate step in the construction of LR(k) analyzers; the analyzer itself is not partitioned. It remains to be seen whether partitioned (or otherwise extended) precedence analyzers can compete with the more recent SLR(1) analyzers [13, 14] .

References

[1] N. Wirth and H. Weber. EULER: a generalization of ALGOL, and its formal definition: Part I. Comm. ACM 9 (1966), 11 - 23, 25.

[2] J. N. Gray and M. A. Harrison. Single pass precedence analysis. IEEE Conference Record of 1969 Tenth Annual Symposium on Switching and Automata Theory, 106 - 117.

[3] A. Learner and A. L. Lim. A note on transforming context-free grammars to Wirth-Weber precedence form. Computer J. 13 (1970), 142 - 144.

[4] W. M. McKeeman, J. J. Horning, and D. B. Wortman. A Compiler Generator. Prentice-Hall, 1970.

[5] J. D. Ichbiah and S. P. Morse. A technique for generating almost optimal Floyd-Evans productions for precedence grammars. Comm. ACM 13 (1970), 501 - 508.

[6] R. Zimmer. Soft precedence. Technical Report, Siemens AG, Munich, 1970.

[7] M. J. Fischer. Some properties of precedence languages. ACM Symposium on Theory of Computing, 1969, 181 - 190.

[8] M. E. Conway. Design of a separable transition-diagram compiler. Comm. ACM 6 (1963), 395 - 408.

[9] V. Tixier. Recursive functions of regular expressions in language analysis. Technical Report No. 58, Stanford Computer Science Department, 1967.

[10] W. A. Woods. Transition network grammars for natural language analysis. Comm. ACM 13 (1970), 591 - 606.

[11] A. J. Korenjak. A practical method for constructing LR(k) processors. Comm. ACM 12 (1969), 613 - 623.

[12] F. Schwenkel. Precedence syntax directed processor system. User's Manual. University of Notre Dame, Computer Science Department, 1969.

[13] F. L. DeRemer. Simple LR(k) grammars: definition and implementation. Computer Evolution Project Report, Vol. 2, No. 4, University of California at Santa Cruz, 1970.

[14] J. J. Horning and W. R. Lalonde. Empirical comparison of LR(k) and precedence parsers. SIGPLAN Notices 5, 11 (Nov. 1970), 10 - 24.

ÜBERBLICK ÜBER DIE ALGOL 68-IMPLEMENTIERUNG AN DER TU MÜNCHEN

von H. Scheidig und H. Wössner

Zusammenfassung: Es wird der Aufbau eines ALGOL 68-Übersetzers skizziert, der zur Zeit an der Technischen Universität München für den Rechner Telefunken TR 4 erstellt wird. Dabei werden insbesondere diejenigen Probleme hervorgehoben, die bei der Übersetzung der bisher bekannten Programmiersprachen nicht oder zumindest nicht im gleichen Umfang auftreten. Als Beispiele für solche Probleme seien erwähnt: die Syntaxanalyse für ALGOL 68 (als nicht kontextbeschränkte Sprache), die Art- und Lebensdauerprüfung ("mode" und "scope" check) und Fragen der Laufzeitorganisation.

Einführung

Bei der Übersetzung eines ALGOL 68-Programms stehen gewisse Aufgaben, das Quellenprogramm umzuformen oder Informationen daraus in Listen zusammenzustellen, in einer Folgerelation, derart daß jeweils eine solche Aufgabe erst nach vollständiger Durchführung der anderen bearbeitet werden kann. Definiert man einen "Lauf" eines Übersetzers als einen Programm-Modul, der mit einem sequentiellen Durchgang durch das Quellenprogramm verbunden ist, so ergibt sich, daß zwei derartige Aufgaben nicht in einem einzigen Lauf erledigt werden können. Neben diesen Folgerelationen - sofern sie nicht durch geeignete Spracheinschränkungen aufgehoben werden - sind bei der Zusammenfassung aller Übersetzeraufgaben zu verschiedenen Läufen eines konkreten Übersetzers aber auch technische Gesichtspunkte zu berücksichtigen, beispielsweise die Größe des verfügbaren Arbeitsspeichers und die Logik des Programmaufbaus.

Der an der Technischen Universität München für den Rechner Telefunken TR 4 entstehende ALGOL 68-Übersetzer umfaßt (ohne das abschließende Ladeprogramm) fünf Läufe, deren wesentliche Tätigkeiten im folgenden kurz beschrieben werden sollen. Im Rahmen dieses Vortrags sollen jedoch vor allem Probleme erläutert werden, die etwa im Vergleich zur Übersetzung von ALGOL 60 neu sind (weitere Einzelheiten finden sich in

[2] - [6]). Abgesehen von dem maschinenbedingten Verzicht auf Parallelverarbeitung (und die Synchronisieroperationen) werden bei dieser Implementierung keine schwerwiegenden Abstriche an der Sprache [1] gemacht.

Lauf 1 (Syntaxanalyse und Listenerzeugung)

Die spezifischen Schwierigkeiten der ALGOL 68-Übersetzung beginnen bereits bei der (artunabhängigen) Syntaxanalyse, für die die bei ALGOL 60 übliche Matrixmethode nicht geeignet ist. Im Falle von ALGOL 68 kann nämlich der zur Analyse einer syntaktischen Konstruktion benötigte Kontext beliebig lang sein; für gewisse, sogenannte "alternative" Konstruktionen ist eine definitive Interpretation zunächst sogar ausgeschlossen.

Wir setzen zur Syntaxanalyse ein in Floyd-Evans Production Language (FEPL) geschriebenes Programm ein [4]. Der Vorteil dieser Methode liegt einmal darin, daß beliebig langer Kontext in Betracht gezogen werden kann, und zum anderen in einer weitgehenden "Selbstdokumentation" des Analysators. Ein FEPL-Programm besteht aus einer geordneten Menge von Produktionen, die in unserem Beispiel die Syntax von ALGOL 68 bzw. die Analyse von ALGOL 68-Programmen beschreibt und darüberhinaus mit dem Analysevorgang die Aufrufe "semantischer Routinen" verknüpft. Diese Semantikroutinen sind hierbei in Assemblersprache geschriebene Unterprogramme, während bei anderen Anwendungen der Floyd-Evans Production Language zu ihrer Formulierung die von Feldman entwickelte "Formal Semantic Language" FSL benutzt wird.

Unser Analysator umfaßt mit etwa 1250 Produktionen mehr als das Doppelte eines entsprechenden Programms, das an der University of Texas für einen ALGOL 60-Übersetzer geschrieben wurde. Für den ~~viel~~ höheren Schwierigkeitsgrad der Syntaxanalyse von ALGOL 68 im Vergleich zu ALGOL 60 sind vor allem zwei Gründe zu nennen:

1. die geringe Redundanz der Sprache und
2. das Vorkommen der (schon erwähnten) alternativen Konstruktionen.

Dabei bezeichnen wir nur solche Konstruktionen als alternativ, die einen Indikanten (d. h. ein frei gewähltes Wortsymbol) als Bestandteil enthalten und je nachdem, ob dieser eine Art oder einen Operator bezeichnet, als Vereinbarungen (oder Generatoren) bzw. als Formeln (oder Operatoren) zu interpretieren sind. So ist z. B.

p(x)

nicht (in diesem Sinne) alternativ, obwohl erst die zugehörige Deklaration von p Aufschluß darüber gibt, ob es sich um eine Indizierung oder einen Prozeduraufruf handelt. Dagegen ist etwa die Konstruktion

(1 : a + b) x y;

alternativ: Existiert für den konstituierenden Indikanten x eine Artvereinbarung, so handelt es sich hier um die Identitätsvereinbarung einer Feldvariablen y (der Deutlichkeit halber stelle man sich in diesem Falle eckige Klammern anstelle der runden vor). Besteht jedoch für x eine Operationsvereinbarung, so liegt eine Formel vor, in der der Operator x auf den Klammerausdruck (mit der Marke 1) als ersten und auf y als zweiten Operanden angewandt wird. In keinem der beiden Fälle muß die Definition von x der Anwendung, also dem Auftreten dieser Konstruktion, vorangehen.

In diesen Beispielen wurde zugleich gezeigt, daß eckige Klammern ganz allgemein durch runde ersetzt werden können; darüberhinaus können runde Klammern auch für begin - end, if - fi usw. stehen. Diese Überladung der runden Klammern und die Möglichkeit alternativer Konstruktionen erschweren nicht nur unmittelbar die Syntaxanalyse, sondern belasten den Übersetzer auch noch nach dieser Phase. Beispielsweise ist es im Gegensatz zu ALGOL 60 während der Syntaxanalyse nicht möglich, für jeden Klammerausdruck zu unterscheiden, ob er ein "Block" ist (also Vereinbarungen enthält) oder nicht.

Parallel zur Syntaxanalyse werden mittels der Semantikroutinen des FEPL-Programms die im weiteren benötigten Listen aufgebaut; die wichtigsten sind:

die Liste IDLIST, in die Identifikatoren und Wortsymbole eingetragen werden,

die "Deklaratorenliste" DK, in der alle in dem jeweiligen Programm vorkommenden Arten in geeigneter Weise dargestellt werden, und

die "Verkettungsliste" VK, deren Einträge den Vereinbarungen (und formalen Parametern), Generatoren und Markendefinitionen zugeordnet sind; die VK-Einträge enthalten neben Verweisen auf die zugehörigen Einträge in IDLIST und DK die Informationen, welche die aus den genannten Gründen vorläufige Blockstruktur des Programms charakterisieren.

Außerdem wird während der Syntaxanalyse das Quellenprogramm in eine (erste) Zwischensprache übersetzt. Dabei wird insbesondere jede Konstruktion, die zu einem Eintrag in VK Anlaß gibt, durch den Verweis auf diesen Eintrag repräsentiert. Die übrigen Symbole des Quellenprogramms werden in interner Form dargestellt. Alternative Konstruktionen werden grundsätzlich wie Vereinbarungen (bzw. Generatoren) behandelt; jedoch werden in einer "Modifizierungsliste" ML zusätzliche Informationen gehalten, die eine eventuell nötige spätere Korrektur ermöglichen.

Nach der Syntaxanalyse liegen die genannten Listen zwar komplett vor; sie müssen nun in einer "nachsyntaktischen" Phase aber umgruppiert und ergänzt werden. (Eine analoge Situation ergibt sich am Ende von Lauf 2.) Diese Listenmanipulationen sind einesteils technisch bedingt und andernteils mit der Prüfung von Kontextbedingungen ([1], Kap. 4) verbunden. Insgesamt erfordern sie einen wesentlich höheren Aufwand als die Erzeugung und Verarbeitung der jeweiligen Zwischensprache. Da die meisten dieser Prozesse aber nicht ohne eine genaue Angabe der Listenstrukturen beschrieben werden können, beschränken wir uns darauf, bei der folgenden Erläuterung von Lauf 2 auf ein repräsentatives Beispiel einzugehen.

Lauf 2 (Identifizierungs- und Artvergleichsprozesse)

Lauf 2 besteht aus drei Teilen mit folgenden Aufgaben:

1. Verarbeitung der Zwischensprache: Das Quellenprogramm wird mit gewissen im weiteren benötigten Zusatzinformationen versehen; insbesondere werden die angewandten Identifikatoren identifiziert. Ferner können jetzt die alternativen Konstruktionen richtig interpretiert werden, nachdem sämtliche Art- und Operatorvereinbarungen in VK aufgelistet sind; danach wird die Liste ML nicht mehr benötigt.

2. Beschaffung von DK-Informationen über nicht im Programm definierte Größen aus Bibliotheken: Dazu gehören z. B. sämtliche Standardoperationen und -prozeduren. Darüberhinaus hat der Programmierer die Möglichkeit, eigene vorübersetzte Prozeduren in Bibliotheken einzutragen.

3. Weitere Listenmanipulationen:
   Eine wesentliche Tätigkeit von Lauf 2 ist die Prüfung weiterer Kontextbedingungen. Diese Prozesse verwenden ausschließlich die Listen DK und VK. Dabei sind vielfach Vergleiche von Arten durchzuführen; beispielsweise muß erkannt werden, daß die folgenden Arten $\underline{x}$, $\underline{y}$ und $\underline{z}$ identisch sind:

   $\underline{x}$ = $\underline{\text{struct}}$ ($\underline{\text{int}}$ a, $\underline{\text{ref}}$ $\underline{u}$ b)
   $\underline{y}$ = $\underline{\text{struct}}$ ($\underline{\text{int}}$ a, $\underline{\text{ref}}$ $\underline{v}$ b)
   $\underline{z}$ = $\underline{\text{struct}}$ ($\underline{\text{int}}$ a, $\underline{\text{ref}}$ $\underline{\text{struct}}$ ($\underline{\text{int}}$ a, $\underline{\text{ref}}$ $\underline{w}$ b) b),

   wobei $\underline{u}$, $\underline{v}$ und $\underline{w}$ beliebige Elemente der Menge $\{\underline{x}, \underline{y}, \underline{z}\}$ sind.

Die allgemeine Prüfung der Identität von Arten ist keineswegs trivial, da unter Verwendung von Verbund-, Vereinigungs-, Feld- und Prozedurarten beliebig lange und insbesondere zyklische Arten definiert werden können. Der folgende formal beschriebene Algorithmus zur Lösung dieses Problems geht bei der Realisierung selbstverständlich von den DK-Einträgen aus.

Zunächst wird jeder Art m eine (abbrechende) "Charakteristik" $\chi(m)$ nach folgenden Regeln zugeordnet:

a) $\chi(m) = s(\chi(m_1)\, i_1, \ldots, \chi(m_r)\, i_r)$,
falls m = <u>struct</u> $(m_1 i_1, \ldots, m_r i_r)$, $r \geqslant 1$

b) $\chi(m) = u(\chi(m_1), \ldots, \chi(m_r))$,
falls m = <u>union</u> $(m_1, \ldots, m_r)$, $r \geqslant 2$

c) $\chi(m) = p(\chi(m_1), \ldots, \chi(m_r))$,
falls m = <u>proc</u> $(m_1, \ldots, m_{r-1})\, m_r$, $r \geqslant 1$

d) $\chi(m) = r\,(\underline{row}(n)\, \chi(\overline{m}))$,
falls[1] $m = \underline{row}(n)\, \overline{m}$

e) $\chi(m) = \underline{ref}(n)\, \chi(\overline{m})$ bzw. $\underline{long}(n)\, \chi(\overline{m})$,
falls $m = \underline{ref}(n)\, \overline{m}$ oder $\underline{long}(n)\, \overline{m}$

f) $\chi(m) = z(m)$,
falls m eine sonstige ("primitive") Art ist; dabei sei z(m) eine ganze Zahl, die m eineindeutig zugeordnet ist.

---

1) <u>row</u> wird als Symbol für den Protobegriff "row of" eingeführt. <u>row</u>(n) sei eine Sequenz von n Symbolen <u>row</u>; Sequenzen von <u>ref</u>, <u>long</u> usw. werden im folgenden ebenso zusammengefaßt.

g) Ist m eine nichtprimitive Art mit Komponenten- bzw. Teilarten m_i, $i = 1, \ldots, r$, und verläuft die Bestimmung von $\chi(m)$ nach a - f zyklisch, so wird in $\chi(m)$ für jedes m_i, das Beginn eines bereits durchlaufenen Zyklus ist, $\chi(m_i) = 0$ gesetzt.

Im obigen Beispiel der Arten $\underline{x}$, $\underline{y}$, $\underline{z}$ mit $\underline{u} = \underline{v} = \underline{x}$ und $\underline{w} = \underline{z}$ ergeben sich danach die folgenden Charakteristiken:

$\chi(\underline{x})$ = s(z(<u>int</u>) a, <u>ref</u> 0 b)

$\chi(\underline{y})$ =

$\chi(\underline{z})$ = s(z(<u>int</u>) a, <u>ref</u> s(z(<u>int</u>) a, <u>ref</u> 0 b) b)

Das Ziel, das mit der Einführung von Charakteristiken verfolgt wird, ist es, den Vergleich von Arten zurückzuführen auf den einfacheren Vergleich von Charakteristiken. Das Beispiel zeigt, daß zwar die Charakteristiken von $\underline{y}$ und $\underline{z}$ gleich sind, aber nicht die von $\underline{x}$ und $\underline{y}$. Der Unterschied zwischen $\chi(\underline{x})$ und $\chi(\underline{y})$ beruht darauf, daß die angegebenen Regeln das mehrfache Durchlaufen eines Zyklus noch nicht vollständig ausschließen. Um diesen Unterschied zu beseitigen, definieren wir schließlich die "Verkürzung" einer Charakteristik:

1. $\chi = \chi(m)$ sei die Charakteristik einer Art m. Dann werden χ selbst und jeder darin enthaltene Klammerausdruck $\alpha(\ldots)$, $\alpha \in \{s, u, p, r\}$, als Komponenten von χ bezeichnet.

2. χ_1 und χ_2 seien Komponenten von χ, und χ_2 sei in χ_1 enthalten. $\overline{\chi}_1$ sei aus χ_1 durch Substitution von 0 für χ_2 gebildet. Gilt dann $\overline{\chi}_1 = \chi_2$, so stimmen χ_1 und χ_2 bis auf mehrfaches Durchlaufen des gleichen Zyklus überein. In diesem Fall ist χ_1 in χ durch $\overline{\chi}_1$ zu ersetzen; χ heißt dann eine "verkürzte" Charakteristik. (Ein derartiger Verkürzungsschritt bedingt i. a. rekursiv ablaufende Operationen, da innerhalb von χ_1 und χ_2 weitere unterschiedlich oft durchlaufene Zyklen auftreten können.)

3. Wurden in einer Charakteristik χ sämtliche möglichen Verkürzungsschritte ausgeführt, so heißt χ eine "minimale" Charakteristik.

Damit gilt nun: Zwei Arten m_1 und m_2 sind genau dann gleich, wenn ihre minimalen Charakteristiken gleich sind. Der Vergleich von $\chi(m_1)$ und $\chi(m_2)$ ist dabei eine im wesentlichen lineare Operation.

Lauf 3 (Art- und Lebensdauerprüfungen)

Der anschließende Lauf 3 setzt sich aus zwei Phasen zusammen, von denen die erste das Quellenprogramm in Postfixform überführt und weitere für die zweite Phase benötigte Informationen auflistet. In der zweiten Phase werden dann außer dem statischen Teil der Lebensdauerprüfung der Anpassungsprozeß und die Operatoridentifizierung durchgeführt; da diese Artprüfungsprozesse einen zentralen Teil des Übersetzers bilden, soll darauf wenigstens kurz eingegangen werden.

Für die Wertzuweisung x := 1 an eine reelle Variable x wird in ALGOL 68 ebenso wie in ALGOL 60 eine automatische, nicht explizit angegebene Konvertierung des Wertes von 1 in den entsprechenden reellen Wert vorgenommen. Derartige implizite Artübergänge werden in ALGOL 68 als "Anpassungen" (coercions) bezeichnet. Sie beschränken sich jedoch nicht auf die in ALGOL 60 oder FORTRAN vorgesehenen Konvertierungen, sondern sind entsprechend der größeren Zahl verfügbarer Datenarten weitaus vielseitiger und komplexer. Die entsprechenden Vorschriften sind - im Gegensatz zu ALGOL 60 - durch die Syntax von ALGOL 68 fixiert.

Jede Anpassung C eines Objekts σ führt dessen "Eigenart" (a priori mode) m in eine "Zielart" (a posteriori mode) über, ohne die syntaktische Struktur von σ zu verändern. Dabei ist $C = c_1 \ldots c_n$ eine

Sequenz elementarer Anpassungsoperationen c_i, von denen es die folgenden acht gibt:

Anpassungsoperation	Bedeutung
dr	Dereferenzieren ("dereferencing")
dp	Deprozedurieren ("deproceduring")
pr	Prozedurieren ("proceduring")
rw	Dimensionieren ("rowing")
un	Vereinigen ("uniting")
wd	Ausweiten ("widening")
	z. B. wd_{ir} : <u>int</u> → <u>real</u>,
	wd_{rc}: <u>real</u> → <u>compl</u>
co	Koordinieren ("hipping")
vd	Entwerten ("voiding")

Beispiel: <u>real</u> x := 1.0; <u>compl</u> y := x

Hier ist in der zweiten Vereinbarung auf x die Anpassungssequenz

$$C = wd_{rc}\ dr$$

anzuwenden, wobei die Eigenart <u>ref</u> <u>real</u> von x durch Nacheinanderausführung von dr und wd_{rc} in die Zielart <u>compl</u> überführt wird.

Es erhebt sich nun die Frage, wodurch Anpassungen ausgelöst werden. Dies geschieht durch die folgenden "Anpassungsinstruktionen" :

1. "Internoperatoren" $\alpha \in \{$:=, :=:, :≠:, ::, ::=, =, :, <u>of</u>$\}$,
2. Symbole $\alpha \in P_i = \{$<u>for</u>, <u>from</u>, <u>by</u>, <u>to</u>, <u>case</u>$\}$
   bzw. $\alpha \in P_b = \{$<u>if</u>, <u>thef</u>, <u>elsf</u>, <u>while</u>$\}$,
3. Indizierungen und Aufrufe von Prozeduren (mit Parametern) α,
4. Operatoren α.

Diese Anpassungsinstruktionen legen gleichzeitig fest, welche der elementaren Anpassungsoperationen für die Anpassungen der betroffenen Objekte verfügbar sind. Hierzu sind die elementaren Anpassungsoperationen in vier verschiedene Klassen von "strong" (s-), "firm" (f-), " weak" (w-) und "soft" (t-) Operationen eingeteilt. Die Zuordnung einer solchen Klasse von γ-Operationen, $\gamma \in \{s, f, w, t\}$, zu einem Objekt schreibt dann vor, daß dessen Anpassung ausschließlich aus γ-Operationen besteht, d.h. eine "γ-Anpassung" ist. In der folgenden Abbildung sind alle möglichen Anpassungen durch ein "Anpassungsdiagramm" dargestellt:

Jeder in Pfeilrichtung durchlaufene Weg, der von dem Eingang "m" nacheinander über Operationen c_n^γ, c_{n-1}^γ, ..., c_1^γ zu einem Ausgang "m^γ " führt, entspricht einer γ-Anpassung

$$C^\gamma = c_1^\gamma \dots c_n^\gamma ,$$

die eine Eigenart m in eine Zielart m^γ überführt (und umgekehrt).

Kommen in einem Ausdruck mehrere Anpassungsinstruktionen vor, so verläuft deren Abarbeitung in analoger Weise wie die Auswertung dieses Ausdrucks von innen nach außen. In dem Beispiel

$$x := y + z$$

werden zunächst durch den Operator "+" f-Anpassungen der Operanden y und z (an die Parameterarten der zugehörigen Operationsvereinbarung) ausgelöst; anschließend veranlaßt die Instruktion ":=" eine t-Anpassung von x und eine s-Anpassung der rechten Seite, deren Eigenart die Ergebnisart der Operation + ist.

Dieses Beispiel führt auf ein zusätzliches Problem, das durch die in ALGOL 68 eingeführte "Überladung" von Operatoren entsteht. Ein Operator kann nämlich gleichzeitig (d.h. im gleichen Gültigkeitsbereich) als Bezeichnung für verschiedene Operationen vereinbart werden.

Abb. 1. Anpassungsdiagramm

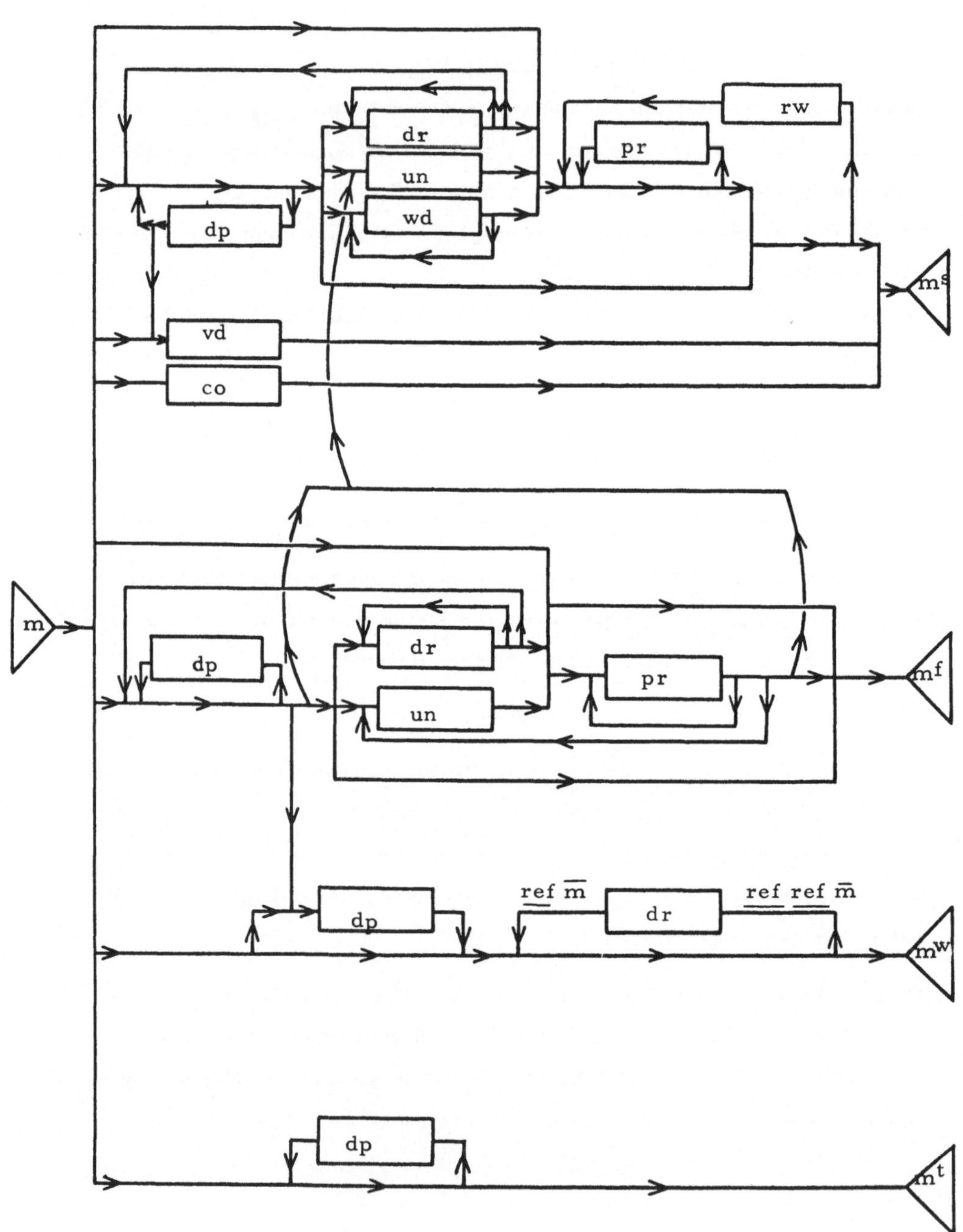

Bei jeder Anwendung eines Operators muß daher (mit Hilfe des Anpassungsprozesses) zuerst festgestellt werden, welche aus der Reihe der für diesen Operator gültigen Vereinbarungen tatsächlich zuständig ist, d.h. welche Parameterarten der in Frage kommenden Operationen als Zielarten der jeweiligen Operanden erreichbar sind. Diese Tätigkeit wird als Operatoridentifizierung bezeichnet. Von ihren speziellen Problemen sowie von der in ALGOL 68 vorgeschriebenen "Balance" der Komponentenarten zusammengesetzter Ausdrücke sei im weiteren abgesehen.

Mit diesen Bemerkungen sollte gezeigt werden, welches Ausmaß der Anpassungsprozeß in ALGOL 68 annimmt. Das Verfahren, das für die Bestimmung der nötigen Anpassungen eingesetzt wird, hat damit für die Übersetzung von ALGOL 68 eine mit der Syntaxanalyse vergleichbare Bedeutung. Die Effizienz des in diesem Übersetzer verwendeten Verfahrens, das nun kurz charakterisiert werden soll, beruht auf der Verwendung der Matrixtechnik, die wir für die Syntaxanalyse ausschließen mußten.

Für jede Anpassungsinstruktion α, die auf Objekte σ_i mit den Eigenarten m_i wirkt ($i \leq 2$), definieren wir eine "Anpassungsfunktion"

$$A(\alpha, m_1) \text{ bzw. } A(\alpha, m_1, m_2),$$

die als Ergebnis die Anpassungssequenzen für σ_i liefert.
Es stellt sich heraus, daß sich alle Anpassungsfunktionen, ausgenommen diejenigen für Operatoren, auf die zu $\sigma_1 := \sigma_2$ gehörige Funktion

$$A(:=, m_1, m_2)$$

zurückführen lassen; am einfachsten ist das am Beispiel der Funktionen

$$A(\alpha, m) = A(:=, \underline{\text{ref}}\ \underline{\text{int}}, m),\ \alpha \in P_i, \text{ und}$$
$$A(\alpha, m) = A(:=, \underline{\text{ref}}\ \underline{\text{bool}}, m),\ \alpha \in P_b,$$

zu sehen. Beschränken wir zunächst die Arten m_i ($i = 1, 2$) auf

$$m_i = \underline{\text{ref}}\,(n_i)\,\overline{m}_i, \quad \overline{m}_i \in \{\underline{\text{int}}, \underline{\text{real}}, \underline{\text{compl}}\},$$

und setzen

$$A = A(:=, m_1, m_2) = (C_1, C_2),$$

wobei C_i die Anpassungssequenzen für σ_i seien, so kann diese Funktion A durch die folgende "Anpassungsmatrix" $\mathfrak{A}$ definiert werden:

$\overline{m}_1$ \ $\overline{m}_2$	<u>int</u>	<u>real</u>	<u>compl</u>
<u>int</u>	$(\emptyset, dr(n_2 - n_1+1))$	undef.	undef.
<u>real</u>	$(\emptyset, wd_{ir} dr(n_2))$	$(\emptyset, dr(n_2 - n_1+1))$	undef.
<u>compl</u>	$(\emptyset, wd_{rc}\ wd_{ir}\ dr(n_2))$	$(\emptyset, wd_{rc} dr(n_2))$	$(\emptyset, dr(n_2 - n_1 + 1))$

Dabei müssen für die Matrixelemente $\mathfrak{A}_{ii}$ bzw. $\mathfrak{A}_{ij}$, $i \neq j$, die Nebenbedingungen

$$n_2 \geqslant n_1 - 1 \geqslant 0 \text{ bzw. } n_1 = 1$$

erfüllt sein.

Dieser einfache Ausschnitt unterscheidet sich vom allgemeinen Fall vor allem dadurch, daß sämtliche Anpassungen nicht-rekursiv bestimmt werden. Das ändert sich, sobald Arten hinzugenommen werden, die Prozedur-, Feld- oder Vereinigungsarten sind oder enthalten. Im Falle der allgemeinen Anpassungsmatrix $\mathfrak{A}$ greift die Funktion A wiederholt auf Elemente von $\mathfrak{A}$ zu, wobei die eventuell rekursive Abfolge dieser Zugriffe durch $\mathfrak{A}$ selbst gesteuert wird. Diese Matrix $\mathfrak{A}$ ist etwa von der Größe 15 x 15 ; ihre Zeilen- und Spalteneingänge werden von den Bestandteilen gebildet, aus denen sich Arten zusammensetzen (abgesehen von <u>ref</u> und <u>long</u>). $\mathfrak{A}$ ist somit programmunabhängig und insbesondere unabhängig von der internen Darstellung der Arten. Neben der effizienten Bestimmung der Anpassungssequenzen bietet diese Methode auch eine übersichtliche Beschreibung des Anpassungsprozesses.

Zum Abschluß dieses Abschnitts sei noch angedeutet, was mit dem statischen Teil der Lebensdauerprüfung gemeint ist. Damit die für die Laufzeitorganisation benötigte statische Schachtelung von Prozeduren und von Blöcken relativ zu Prozeduren festgelegt werden kann, muß zunächst die Lebensdauer von Prozeduren bestimmt werden. Dies ist erst zu diesem Zeitpunkt möglich, da beispielsweise parameterlose Prozeduren als prozedurierte Ausdrücke vorliegen und somit erst durch den Anpassungsprozeß erkannt werden. Zur Motivierung der nächsten Aufgabe betrachten wir das folgende Programmbeispiel:

```
begin ref int xx;
      begin int x; xx := x end;
      val xx := 1 end
```

Hier wird durch die Wertzuweisung xx := x der Namensvariablen xx als Wert der durch x bezeichnete Name n zugewiesen. Durch <u>val</u> xx := 1 (<u>val</u> stellt eine Dereferenzieroperation dar), soll dann diesem Namen, auf den xx verweist, der Wert 1 zugewiesen werden; dies ist aber nicht möglich, da n in dem äußeren Block nicht mehr am Leben ist. Derartige unzulässige Verwendungen von Namen (oder Prozeduren) werden durch die Lebensdauerbedingung 8.3.1.2.c. Step 1 von [1] verboten. Die Prüfung dieser Bedingung ist i.a. erst zur Laufzeit eines Programms möglich. Aufgrund einer geeigneten Klassifizierung kann jedoch ein Teil dieser Prüfungen bereits zur Übersetzungszeit erledigt werden. Schließlich werden die noch übrigen (dynamisch durchzuführenden) Prüfoperationen bestimmt.

<u>Lauf 4 (lineare Adreßfortschaltung)</u>

Die in Lauf 3 gewonnenen Anpassungssequenzen werden in Lauf 4 an die entsprechenden Stellen des Quellenprogramms abgesetzt. Die Hauptaufgabe dieses vierten Laufs ist jedoch die lineare Adreßfortschaltung bei indizierten Größen in Laufanweisungen.

Diese Optimierung ist von ALGOL 60 her bekannt, wenngleich die Bedingungen dafür in ALGOL 68 komplizierter sind (s. [3]).

Lauf 5 (Laufzeitorganisation)

Der fünfte Lauf bereitet schließlich die Laufzeitorganisation vor und erzeugt Code. Wir beschränken uns hier auf einige Bemerkungen zur Speicherverwaltung.

Zur Ausführung eines ALGOL 68-Programms wird wie bei einem ALGOL 60-Programm ein Speicherbereich benötigt, der den Keller aufnimmt. Abgesehen von einer einfacheren Parameterübergabe bei Prozeduraufrufen kann der Keller zur Laufzeit auch in derselben Weise verwaltet werden wie bei ALGOL 60. Bei unserer Implementierung ist er "prozedurweise" organisiert:
Bei Eintritt in eine Prozedur P wird Speicher reserviert für alle in P durch Identitätsvereinbarungen erklärten (lokalen) Größen, sofern der aktuelle Parameter der jeweiligen Vereinbarung ein (eventuell initialisierter) lokaler Generator ist. Bei Feldern bedeutet das nur die Speicherreservierung für den Deskriptor; der Speicher für das eigentliche Feld wird bei "festen" Feldern (bei denen alle Indexstatus gleich 1 sind) wie in ALGOL 60 bei Abarbeitung der Vereinbarung reserviert, "flexible" Felder (bei denen mindestens ein Indexstatus gleich 0 ist) erfordern eine Sonderbehandlung (s. u.). Zusätzlich wird Platz reserviert für etwaige Hilfsgrößen, für die organisatorischen Informationen über die statische und dynamische Prozedurschachtelung und für Blockleitzellen. Der zu diesen Zwecken reservierte Speicher, dessen Länge statisch bestimmbar ist, wird als "Festspeicher" der Prozedur P bezeichnet. Er wird bei Verlassen von P (nach entsprechender Auswertung der organisatorischen Informationen) freigegeben. Im Anschluß an den Festspeicher von P wird der "dynamische Speicher" mit Hilfe der Blockleitzellen "blockweise" reserviert.

Eine ähnliche Reservierung des für globale Generatoren und für flexible Felder benötigten Platzes im Keller würde diese Kellerstruktur zerstören; insbesondere wäre dann die Freigabe des gesamten für P reservierten Speichers bei Verlassen von P nicht mehr zulässig. Deshalb wird der zur Verfügung stehende Speicher folgendermaßen verwendet: Vom unteren Ende her wird der Keller aufgebaut; vom oberen Ende her wird Platz reserviert für globale Generatoren, flexible Felder und sonstige Größen, die bei Verlassen des Blocks, in dem sie erzeugt werden nicht gelöscht werden dürfen (z. B. auch Felder, die als aktuelle Werte von Größen mit Vereinigungsarten auftreten).

In diesen zweiten Speicherbereich, der "Halde" (heap), sind Freigaben nur aufgrund von "Speicherbereinigung" (garbage collection) möglich. Ein entsprechendes Unterprogramm wird automatisch aufgerufen, wenn der Zwischenbereich für eine notwendige Verlängerung des Kellers oder der Halde nicht mehr ausreicht.

Literatur

[1] A. van Wijngaarden (Ed.), B. J. Mailloux, J. E. L. Peck and C. H. A. Koster, Report on the Algorithmic Language ALGOL 68. Num. Math., 14, 79 - 218 (1969).

[2] G. Goos, Eine Implementierung von ALGOL 68. Bericht Nr. 6906, Rechenzentrum der TU München, 1969.

[3] U. Hill, Automatische rekursive Adressenberechnung für höhere Programmiersprachen, insbesondere für ALGOL 68. Dissertation, TU München, 1969.

[4] H. Scheidig, FEPLA: Ein Assembler für die Floyd-Evans Production Language. Bericht Nr. 6801, Rechenzentrum der TU München, 1968.

[5] H. Scheidig, Anpassungsoperationen in ALGOL 68. Dissertation, TU München, 1970.

[6] H. Wössner, Operatoridentifizierung in ALGOL 68. Dissertation, TU München, 1970.

A STRUCTURAL MODEL FOR DIALOG LANGUAGES

by Ingbert Kupka

1. Motivation and preliminaries

The following ideas have come up in connection with a research project APL-440 which is still in operation. The aim of the research group (at present the author of this paper and his co-worker N. Wilsing) is to study practical and theoretical aspects of dialog languages by means of a special model.
Language and system APL-440 are made up of both a dialect of K. E. Iverson's language APL (Iverson[2]) and an implementation on a TR440/TR86-System at the Rechenzentrum of the Hamburg University. An implementation of APL already existing is APL\360.
There is no common opinion about what dialog languages should be (see Klerer, Reinfelds[3] and Sammet[4]). On the other hand it is necessary for a task like the above-mentioned project to select some possibilities from many others for a first verification.
Simply speaking, a dialog language is a linguistic medium for interactive communication between computers and human users or programmers. A computer hereby is to be seen as a program-controlled digital computer.
Let us consider the three semiotical aspects in a sense explained by Carracciolo di Forino[1], i. e. syntax, semantics, and pragmatics, and begin to discuss the latter two. Considering the semantics, the problems of the user are relevant, whereas the functional capabilities of the computer are relevant to the pragmatics. Since existing computers are far from being General Problem Solvers we have the alternative of making simple, and transparent too, either the pragmatics or the semantics of the linguistic elements. In the first case an operational character aiming at computer operations is attributed to the linguistic elements, in the second case it is a declaring and problem-defining one. Thus we call

$$x = - a/2 - \sqrt{(a^2/4 - b)}$$

'operational', and

x is the smaller root of $x^2 + ax + b$

'problem-defining'. We prefer the simpler pragmatics and hence the operational linguistic elements.

The kind of interactivity has to be defined, too. To begin with, we may say that both computer and programmer produce a sequence of characters each. In this connection 'characters' for the moment have to be regarded as physical states like 'input of character A' or 'dark display unit'. The computer shall be regarded as deterministic and the programmer as independently acting. Consequently there is a one-sided dependence between the two sequences of characters. The sequences running simultaneously

$a_1 \; a_2 \; a_3 \; a_4 \; \ldots.$ (produced by the programmer),

$r_1 \; r_2 \; r_3 \; r_4 \; \ldots.$ (produced by the computer)

shall be further restricted, at first to finite sequences and secondly to those at which temporal overlaps of characters among and between the sequences are excluded. This may be for instance illustrated by

$$\begin{array}{lllllllllll} a_1 & & & & a_2 & a_3 & & \ldots & & \ldots a_n & \\ & r_1 & r_2 & r_3 & & & r_4 & \ldots & & & \ldots r_m \; . \end{array}$$

2. States of the computer as background of the dialog

The above restrictions allow a representation of dialogs like

$$A_1R_1 \; A_2R_2 \; A_3R_3 \; \ldots. \; A_nR_n \quad .$$

Here, A_1, A_2, ... are sequences (of characters) with limited length, produced by the programmer and with characters from a finite alphabet Γ_a, whereas R_1, R_2, ... are sequences with limited length, produced by the computer and with characters from a finite alphabet Γ_r. The R_j may be empty sequences. The A_i are called 'statements', the R_j 'results'. On the premises the results are dependent on the statements. A dependence of the kind $R_i = f(A_i)$, however, is by no means general enough as it does not admit any connected dialog with more than one statement. We call a dialog with this property a 'primitive dialog'. In general a dependence

$$R_i = f(A_1, A_2, \; \ldots \; , A_i)$$

is necessary. From the pragmatic point of view the introduction of a sequence Z_o, Z_1, Z_2, ... , Z_n of 'internal states' and the formulation of the dependence by

$$R_i = f(Z_{i-1}, A_i), \quad i = 1, 2, \ldots, n,$$
$$Z_i = g(Z_{i-1}, A_i), \quad i = 1, 2, \ldots, n,$$

are preferable.
The Z_i shall be members of a finite set Ψ of states Y_j. In addition, a finite set Φ of 'transitions' α shall exist. Let each $\alpha \in \Phi$ be associated with a set of ordered pairs Y_j, Y_k such that all Y_j in the first position are different from each other. We mark the association with a single pair by

$$Y_j \xrightarrow{\alpha} Y_k$$

The states $Y \in \Psi$ indicate the essential information in certain registers and in the storage, whereas $\alpha \in \Phi$ indicates executions of the instructions. A more accurate definition of these terms is possible, but quite complicated and unnecessary for the following. The existence of pairs Y_j, Y_k related to $\alpha \in \Phi$ and Y_k, Y_l related to $\beta \in \Phi$ and so on causes the introduction of chains of states:

$$Y_j \xrightarrow{\alpha} Y_k \xrightarrow{\beta} Y_l \xrightarrow{\delta} \ldots\ldots \xrightarrow{\omega} Y_p$$

For the states Z_j we demand: For each pair Z_{i-1}, Z_i and for $i = 1, 2, \ldots., n$, there is at least one chain of states which leads from Z_{i-1} to Z_i :

$$Z_{i-1} = Y_j \xrightarrow{\alpha} Y_k \xrightarrow{\beta} \ldots\ldots \xrightarrow{\omega} Y_p = Z_i,$$

and this chain is uniquely defined by A_i and Z_{i-1}.
Certain parts of this chain can be related to the result R_i, or precisely speaking to the generation of that sequence of characters.

3. Main features of simple operational dialog languages

The next step consists of developing a rough definition for especially simple operational dialog languages. A first demand for it reads:
Already in the initial state Z_0 dialogs must be possible which immediately aim at certain, mainly basic, user problems without the dialog creating the linguistic form for it previously.

Hence it follows: at least in the beginning of a dialog the semantic meaning of certain characters or sequences of characters must be fixed. The possibility of changing or modifying such fixations at a later state of the dialog shall be included. The same method is also applied to FORTRAN, for example, where implicit declarations do exist which can be overruled by explicit ones. For the fixation of implicit meanings we suggest the following proceeding:
The set Φ of transitions which may be regarded as basic computer operations shall be divided into two parts, $\Phi_{external}$ and $\Phi_{internal}$, whose former, $\Phi_{external}$, contains operations directly relevant to the programmer, and whose latter, $\Phi_{internal}$, contains the operations with mainly internal meaning. Arithmetic and relational operations would belong to $\Phi_{external}$ and instructions for address modification to $\Phi_{internal}$. Let $\sigma \in \Gamma_A$, i. e. a character, or let σ be a sequence of characters from Γ_A, and let $\alpha \in \Phi$. We say α is generated by σ if:

σ is part of $A_1 \Longrightarrow \alpha$ occurs in the chain from Z_0 to Z_1

Correspondingly, in most programming languages the character '+' generates the instruction for addition. Here all cases are excluded in which a character has to be interpreted differently, even if there is a main interpretation. For this reason we define:

α is generated by σ with the probability $\rho(\sigma,\alpha)$ if:

σ is part of $A_1 \Longrightarrow \alpha$ occurs with the probability $\rho(\sigma,\alpha)$ in the chain from Z_0 to Z_1

Since Γ_A is finite and the length of A_1 limited, $\rho(\sigma,\alpha)$ is uniquely declared as a relative frequency. This definition is still unsatisfactory because the possibility of 'syntactically incorrect' statements A_1 diminishes the probabilities $\rho(\sigma,\alpha)$. Therefore we assume that there is a distinction between syntactically regular statements and syntactically irregular ones and we confine the statements A_1 for the definition of the probability $\rho(\sigma,\alpha)$ to the syntactically regular ones. The following demand may be regarded as a characteristic of

the simplicity of a dialog language:
To each $\alpha \in \Phi_{external}$ exactly belongs one sequence σ of characters which generates α with a probability near to 1.

In addition to this direct generation of an operation by a character or a sequence of characters one has to consider an indirect generation, too. Let us assume that a function could be defined at the state Z_o similarly to defining a Statement Function in FORTRAN. A '+' -mark occuring in it only would lead to an addition when the function shall be called in a later statement. A general explanation of this indirect generation does already imply details of the syntax; that is the reason why it is not made here.
A further demand on dialog languages which shall get the attribute 'simple' concerns the use of names. In an operational language there must occur 'objects' and 'operations' with objects. Operations may also be objects. The demand for simplicity reads:

The naming of an object with a name occuring for the first time is possible within a single statement.

This demand excludes the compulsion to declaration as occuring in ALGOL, for instance. The possibility of naming fields immediately and without preceding declaration, for example is given in APL and AMTRAN (see[3],[4]).

4. Dialog characteristics of the internal states

The initial state Z_o may be regarded as the total of the implicit fixations. One can assume that in the case of a single implicit fixation there are several possibilities none of which exceeds the others. This leads to a model with several states Z_o', Z_o'', ... , which are formally equivalent to the initial state Z_o. The user may choose one of them by means of a suitable statement like $Z_1 = Z_o'$. The dialog language hence splits into several 'sublanguages' each of which belongs to Z_o or to one of the states equivalent to Z_o. In order to render precise these facts we consider the states $Z \in \Psi$ appearing in sequences Z_o, Z_1, Z_2, ... of dialogs.
Let Z be divided into components. One component, named G, may

contain the implied fixations related to a sublanguage:

$$Z = (G, \ldots\ldots)$$

G is called the basic state characterizing the sublanguage. Further components are obtained as carriers of information with a specified meaning:
A list N may consist of all objects respectively of their descriptions generated during the dialog. Thereby it is useful to allow cancellations. N is called a 'namelist'. This means that an object will be filed with a name and called by this name.
Let a 'record' of the dialog be another component P of Z. Thus we get

$$Z = (G, N, P, \ldots).$$

These components are still sufficient for a formal description of the model. If we regard the real computer states, however, as we have done to define relations between characters and transitions, we have to provide an internal component I. So we have

$$Z = (G, N, P, I).$$

Especially the initial state is

$$Z_o = (G_o, \emptyset, \emptyset, I_o).$$

For Z_i we write

$$Z_i = (G_i, N_i, P_i, I_i).$$

Structural details for G_i, N_i, and P_i, are explained as follows:
There is a finite set of basic states one of which actually is G_i. A formal description of G_i demands a syntax of the sublanguage. G_i is recursively defined by

$$G_i = h'(G_{i-1}, A_i) = \begin{cases} G_{i-1} & \text{if } h(A_i) = \emptyset \\ h(A_i) & \text{if } h(A_i) \neq \emptyset \end{cases},$$

with a certain mapping h.
N_i is empty or N_i contains elements n of the form

$$n = \{\text{name, type of the object, description of the object}\}.$$

This does not indicate the method of storing the information but the logical structure of N_i. As a special name the empty name, symbol ε, is allowed. An object may be filed with this name, without explicit command, for a call in the next or a later statement. See the following example:

$$N_o = \emptyset$$

A_1: 2+4
R_1: 6

$$N_1 = \{n\},\quad n = \{\varepsilon,\ \text{INTEGER},\ 6\}$$

A_2: /2
R_2: 3

$$N_2 = \{n\},\quad n = \{\varepsilon,\ \text{INTEGER},\ 3\}$$

Furthermore internal names are permitted for use by the system itself if there are objects to be filed. An example:

$$N_o = \emptyset$$

A_1: x = 2+y
R_1: ? y =

$$N_1 = \{n\},\quad n = \{?,\ \text{'incomplete statement'},\ y(x = 2+y)\}$$

A_2: 4

The namelists are defined recursively by

$$N_i = (N_{i-1} - l(G_{i-1},N_{i-1},A_i)) \cup k(G_{i-1},N_{i-1},A_i)$$

where

$k(G_{i-1},N_{i-1},A_i)$ is the increase of the list,

$l(G_{i-1},N_{i-1},A_i)$ is the part of the list which is to delete,

$l(G_{i-1},N_{i-1},A_i) \subset N_{i-1}$.

The record P_i is empty or it contains elements

$$p_j = \begin{cases} \{j,A_j,R_j\} \\ \{j,A_j\} \end{cases},$$

which we call complete and incomplete entries. The recursion formula for P_i corresponds to that for N_i:

$$P_i = (P_{i-1} - q(G_{i-1},P_{i-1},A_i)) \cup r(G_{i-1},A_i),$$

where

$$r(G_{i-1},A_i) = \begin{cases} \emptyset \\ \{\{i,A_i\}\} \\ \{\{i,A_i,R_i\}\} \end{cases}$$ is the set containing the actual entry,

$q(G_{i-1},P_{i-1},A_i)$ is the part of P_i which is to delete,

$q(G_{i-1},P_{i-1},A_i) \subset P_{i-1}$.

It is noteworthy that a later alteration of entries is impossible. Altered entries only may be filed as objects in the namelist.
In order to get completeness we add

$$I_i = s(G_{i-1},N_{i-1},P_{i-1},I_{i-1},A_i)$$

without further details. By this way the mapping g in $Z_i = g(Z_{i-1},A_i)$ is completely described by h, k, l, q, r, s.
The component I_i is of no importance for the mapping f, thus

$$R_i = f(G_{i-1},N_{i-1},P_{i-1},A_i).$$

5. Types of statements

We can classify the statements related to three regularity types giving a disjoint partition and related to nine further types which need not give a disjoint partition.

Type FI: Formally irregular statements

Type AI: Actually irregular statements

Type AR: Actually regular statements

Statements of the types AI and AR are called formally regular. The exact definition of these types requires a syntax. The definition of the types may also be considered as demand on the syntax. Examples:

A_1: $x = 2\cdot(3+4$, formally irregular,

A_1: $x = y\cdot(3+4)$, actually irregular (y undefined),

A_1: $x = 2\cdot(3+4)$, actually regular.

A formally irregular A_i corresponds to a syntactically incorrect program in programming languages, a formally regular A_i to a syntactically correct program if the syntax does not refer to the namelist or the record.
The affiliation with type FI depends on G_{i-1} but not on N_{i-1}, P_{i-1}, I_{i-1}. The affiliation with the types AI, AR depends on G_{i-1}, N_{i-1}, P_{i-1}. The following equivalence must be valid:

A_i is of the type AI $\Longleftrightarrow$ A_i is not of the type FI and there exist N'_{i-1}, P'_{i-1} such that A_i is of the type AR with respect to G_{i-1}, N'_{i-1}, P'_{i-1}

The following 6 types refer to the mapping g. The dependence on the state components is evident.

Type 0: Passive statements; these leave basic state, namelist, record unaltered; characteristic:
$h(A_i)$, $l(G_{i-1},N'_{i-1},A_i)$, $k(G_{i-1},N'_{i-1},A_i)$, $r(G_{i-1},A_i)$, $q(G_{i-1},P'_{i-1},A_i)$ $= \emptyset$
for all $N'_{i-1} \supset N_{i-1}$, $P'_{i-1} \supset P_{i-1}$.

Type 1: Sublanguage statements, altering the implied fixations; characteristic: $h(A_i) \neq \emptyset$.

Type 2: Name statements with cancelling effect; characteristic: $\exists\, N'_{i-1} \supset N_{i-1}$ with $l(G_{i-1},N'_{i-1},A_i) \neq \emptyset$.

Type 3: Name statements with storing effect; characteristic: $\exists\, N'_{i-1} \supset N_{i-1}$ with $k(G_{i-1},N'_{i-1},A_i) \neq \emptyset$.

Type 4: Record statements with cancelling effect; characteristic: $\exists\, P'_{i-1} \supset P_{i-1}$ with $q(G_{i-1},P'_{i-1},A_i) \neq \emptyset$.

Type 5: Record statements with storing effect; characteristic: $r(G_{i-1},A_i) \neq \emptyset$.

Examples for type 2 and type 3 are the following JOSS statements:

Set x = 1 .	(type 3)
Set y = 3 + x .	(type 3)
Delete x .	(type 2)
Delete all values .	(type 2)

Three further types refer to the mapping f, for which we now formulate a condition: In

$$R_i = f(G_{i-1},N_{i-1},P_{i-1},A_i)$$

should N_{i-1} and P_{i-1} be replaceable by sublists $\tilde{N}_{i-1}$, $\tilde{P}_{i-1}$, which exactly contain respectively the objects or the entries essential for the result R_i. Naturally $\tilde{N}_{i-1} = \emptyset$ or $\tilde{N}_{i-1} = N_{i-1}$ may occur, likewise $\tilde{P}_{i-1}$. We demand the existence of sublists $\tilde{N}_{i-1}$, $\tilde{P}_{i-1}$ with those properties and that $\tilde{N}_{i-1}$ and $\tilde{P}_{i-1}$ do not depend on each other. Thus we can write

$$\tilde{N}_{i-1} = u(G_{i-1},N_{i-1},A_i),$$

$$\tilde{P}_{i-1} = v(G_{i-1},P_{i-1},A_i).$$

This definition of $\tilde{N}_{i-1}$, $\tilde{P}_{i-1}$ depends on the syntax of the system. Now we can declare:

Type 6: Statements referring to the namelist, characteristic: $u(G_{i-1},N_{i-1},A_i) \neq \emptyset$.

Type 7: Statements referring to the record, characteristic: $v(G_{i-1},P_{i-1},A_i) \neq \emptyset$.

Type 8: Statements not referring to the namelist nor to the record, characteristic:
$u(G_{i-1},N_{i-1},A_i) = \emptyset$, $v(G_{i-1},P_{i-1},A_i) = \emptyset$.

The language may permit statements belonging to more than one type. The statement

$$x = x + 1 ,$$

for example, belongs to type 2 and type 3.
The structure of the dialog language implies a structure for each dialog. Let us consider a dialog represented by

$$\{Z_i\}_{i=o,1,\dots,n},\ \{A_i\}_{i=1,2,\dots,n},\ \{R_i\}_{i=1,2,\dots,n}\ .$$

We say the pair (A_i,R_i) leads directly to the pair (A_j,R_j), $j > i$, and write

$$(A_i,R_i) \longrightarrow (A_j,R_j) ,$$

if at least one of the following conditions is valid:

1. A_i belongs to type 1, A_{i+1} does not belong to type 1, and $j = i+1$.
2. $k(G_{i-1},N_{i-1},A_i) \cap l(G_{j-1},N_{j-1},A_j) \neq \emptyset$.
3. $K(G_{i-1},N_{i-1},A_i) \cap u(G_{j-1},N_{j-1},A_j) \neq \emptyset$.
4. $q(G_{i-1},A_i) \cap r(G_{j-1},P_{j-1},A_j) \neq \emptyset$.
5. $q(G_{i-1},A_i) \cap v(G_{j-1},P_{j-1},A_j) \neq \emptyset$.

If the language permits cancellations not depending on the statements, the terms for cancellations in the conditions 2 and 4 must be restricted.
Thus we obtain chains

$$(A_i,R_i) \longrightarrow (A_j,R_j) \longrightarrow (A_k,R_k) \longrightarrow \quad \dots .$$

which define a net structure for the dialog and a subdivision of the dialog into connected components.

In a next step the structural model should be completely formalized. But this shall be done later.

6. Examples

a) A dialog system with ALGOL programs: operational, simple, primitive.

& & TRANSLATE/ 'begin'.........'end' & DATA/ .... & START EXECUTION	}	A_1
⟨printed result⟩		R_1

b) Another dialog system with ALGOL programs: operational, not simple (character condition).

& TRANSLATE progr1/ 'begin'...........'end'	}	A_1	
			$R_1 = \varepsilon$
& TRANSLATE progr2/ 'begin'...........'end'	}	A_2	
			$R_2 = \varepsilon$
& DATA alpha/	}	A_3	
			$R_3 = \varepsilon$
& EXECUTE progr1, alpha		A_4	
⟨printed result⟩			R_4

c) A dialog system with ALGOL statements: operational, not simple (name condition).

'integer' i, ...;	A_1	
		$R_1 = \varepsilon$
'real' x, y, ...;	A_2	
		$R_2 = \varepsilon$
i:=7;	A_3	
		$R_3 = \varepsilon$
print(......);	A_4	
⟨printed result⟩		R_4
'begin'........'end';	A_5	
⟨printed result related to A_5⟩		R_5

d) A JOSS-like system: operational and simple.

Set x=1.4142.	A_1	$R_1 = \varepsilon$
Set y=x/(2-x).	A_2	$R_2 = \varepsilon$
Type y.	A_3	
<printed result>		R_3
Let f(a,b)=(a*x - b*y)/(a - b).	A_4	$R_4 = \varepsilon$
1.1 a=i/10.	A_5	$R_5 = \varepsilon$
1.2 Type f(a,1).	A_6	$R_6 = \varepsilon$
Do part 1 for i=1(1)5.	A_7	
<printed result>		R_7

References

[1] Carracciolo di Forino, A., Programming Languages, in "Advances in Information Systems Science", Vol. 1, ed. by J. T. Tou, New York 1969

[2] Iverson, K. E., A Programming Language, Wiley & Sons, New York 1962

[3] Klerer, M., and Reinfelds, J., Interactive Systems for Experimental Applied Mathematics, New York and London 1968

[4] Sammet, J. E., Programming Languages, History and Foundations, chapter IV,6. Englewood Cliffs, N. J., 1969

THE STRUCTURE OF A FLEXIBLE AND EFFICIENT COMPILER FOR ALGORITHMIC CONVERSATIONAL LANGUAGES

by Hans Albrecht Schmid

1. Introduction

For the design of interactive systems it is necessary to consider some aspects in more detail which are not so highly significant for the design of batch systems.

Man and machine have to be regarded as a closed system its optimum efficiency to be attained only by fitting its interface to both man and machine, and not by independent optimization of its single components.
Because of the high degree of feedback between man and machine, the development of an algorithm in interaction with the computer allows the application of other methods and is therefore a process rather different from the process of the development of an algorithm in batch mode. Thus a system which is used to develop algorithms has to meet other requirements than a system to represent and carry out programs.

Fundamental investigations on psychological and statistic principles of interaction can not be done by the system designer, but system design has to take into account the results achieved in this area.

The second section of this paper deals with fundamental assertions and requirements of the conversational usage of a compiler.
In the third section two principles for the realisation of a data structure representing the users program in accordance with the established statements will be developed.
In the further sections a realisation of those principles in an interactive compiler will be shown based on a language of about the same complexity as ALGOL 60.

Greater emphasis is put on the description of logical structur than on detailed characteristics of implementation. This paper does not deal with problems concerning the special kind of the compiler's environment as are for instance scheduling and allocation of resources for terminal users, etc. The proposed compiler and generated program structur is sufficiently flexible to be adapted to special system and user profile requirements.

2. Interaction Fundamentals

2.1 User - Compiler Interface

Some of the principles established below are derived from the conventions of interactive compiler usage which have been proved practical and suitable in the past. On the other hand conventions not satisfying the user needs are the reason of establishing additional requirements.

The list of requirements discussed in this paper is as follows:

a) An increment is the unit of communication between user and compiler. After input of an increment a check of the local syntax is done.

b) Increments may be put in either in stored mode or in direct mode. In the stored mode they are entered into the program according to their increment number; in the direct mode they are executed immediatly. That may be used for desk-calculator purposes and for the setting, changing and testing of variables at program execution halts.

c) It is possible to put in or change increments independently from one another in any sequence.

d) Parts of programs may be executed; interleaving of program construction, program modification and execution is possible. At program halts caused either by execution errors or by user intervention the correct program environment is given, as regards for example the scope of identifiers.

e) There are two kinds of debugging: either static debugging aids. that are conditions imposed on variables or increments which may result in program interruption, or dynamic debugging by user intervention from the terminal.

f) Command and other statements do not work on different levels but are regarded to be equivalent in order to keep the user interface of the compiler as simple as possible. Hence there is only one "Terminal state" in which the user communicates with the compiler, and there are no different modes as for instance for program modifications in which only particular increments are permitted, with the exception of very particular commands which have only influence on the transmission line. The notion of "Terminal state" introduced by Parnas characterizes "all system conditions in which the set of interpreted messages and the set of interpretation (reaction of the system) is constant" [5].

2.2 User Behaviour and Psychological Needs

Research dealing with the response time [6], that is the time which passes until you get a response by the computer after an input has been given, had as a result that the response time has to be adequate to the kind of the input. For "human spontaneously organize their activities into clumps that are terminated by the completion of a subjective purpose or subpurpose". This subjective sense of completion is called a "closure". "More extended delays may be made in a conversation or transaction after a closure than in the process of obtaining a closure" [6].

The process represented by the input or modification of increments has then obtained a closure when the constructed part of the program is to be executed with the aim of testing its adequacy. Accordingly the response to the input of an increment should be given in a relative short time whereas it may take a longer time until you get the result of an execution.

There is another psychological need, that "is in the nature of response to an expectation" [6]. If you adress someone, you expect some kind of reaction.
This results in the fact, that the response to a demand can take a longer time when the user comprehends that and why it cannot be given in a shorter time by the computer.

There is still little known about the process of constructing an algorithm. But it is supposed that the variability concerning for example the program text or possible attributes or variables, is getting smaller in the course of completing the development of an algorithm [3]. Exact statements about this point would be quite important.

Statistic material about user behaviour and user program structures would be of interest, but are not yet available in a sufficient extent.

2.3 System Efficiency

A sequence of program construction (or program modification) and program execution is characteristic of interactive compiler usage. This means that neither the efficiency of solely compiling nor the efficiency of solely executing are of relevance, but only the efficiency of both compiling and executing together.

3. Flexibility versus Efficiency

Though it is required that the input of increments is independent of one another, there are cross references among the increments concerning program structure, program control transfer, and the data objects. In order to be able to execute an increment, these bindings have to be established, either temporary or fixed. The notion of "binding" being known for rather a long time, is used in the meaning of "the choosing of a particular . . . environment with which to implement a program construct" [7] (in our case an increment).

The problem is that when bindings are fixed, the change of the environment may cause an increment the bindings of which had been fixed, already, to become invalid, and that on the other hand temporarily established bindings adequated to every change of environment, demand to much expense for their execution when there is no change of the environment.

Two alternative models of interactive compilers are deduced from these points:

1. The Conversational Compiler.
The bindings are fixed in the generated code before the execution of incrments, mostly immediatly after their input, on the condition that information contained in increments already input is regarded as known. In this case, techniques used in one-pass compilers can be applied.
The generation of an increment code takes a considerable amount of time because of the establishing and fixing of global bindings, but the execution of an increment takes relatively a little amount of time (see L_I in diagram 1).
The modification of the program, however, causes a modification of the environment existing when the bindings were fixed at the generation of object code. Therefore, every modification of an increment has as its consequence a re-establishment of all the other bindings, that is the recompilation of the entire program. The flexibility at program modifications is rather small (see C_1 in diagram 2).

2. Interpretative Incremental Compiler.
The bindings are not fixed in the generated code; they are only established temporarily in an interpretive manner during the execution of an increment.
For this reason, the generation of an increment's code takes little amount of time, but the execution of an increment takes a considerable amount of time (see L_{II} in diagram 1).
The modification of an increment does not influence the code generated for the other increments. Consequently, the flexibility at program modification is very great (see C_2 in diagram 2).

It is obvious that neither of these two models of compilers does meet all of the established requirements. However, they are met by a new model based on the introduction of two principles, which are similar to ideas of Mitchell [3]:

1. Every function performed in the compiler has to be realized as late as possible, not before it is really needed. This means that the bindings are fixed and compiled code is generated at the moment when an increment is to be executed the first time.

In a program after a partial execution, there may exist non-compiled and compiled code together.

Execution of an increment demands somewhat more time than in the case of early compiled increments, as a test is necessary before every execution whether the increment is already compiled, and as a certain amount of time is indispensable during the run for providing the possibility of dynamic binding (see L_{III} in diagram 1).

Program modifications made before a compilation is carried out, take a little amount of time, whereas modifications after an execution necessitate one recompilation of the entire program (see C_3 in diagram 3).

Therefore it is necessary that
2. during the compilation additional information is generated indicating the environment in which the compiled code is valid. Then observation of the kind and position of a modification has the consequence that only those increments have to be recompiled which are actually affected by the modification.

This principle of the "localization of the effects of program modifications" can be applied to the conversational compiler model, too.

The localization of program modifications does not alter the compiler features shown in diagram 1 concerning the run effort.

In general the modification effort becomes smaller as shown in diagram 2(C_4 compared with C_1; C_5 with C_3); as its quantity, however, depends in a high degree on the program to be modified and on the kind of the modification, only qualitative statements can be made. Great discrepancies between idealized and actual values are possible.

Now the following classification of interactive compilers can be set up:

	bindings fixed early I	bindings fixed late III	bindings not fixed II
no localization of program modifications	Conversational Compiler 1	(Incremental Compiler) (3)	Interpretative Incremental 2
localization of program modifications	Conversational Compiler 4	Incremental Compiler 5	X

A comparison of the features of the different compiler models yields the result that an incremental compiler, which fixes the bindings late and localizes the effects of program modifications meets best the established requirements.
Incremental compilers, which do not localize modifications are not of great interest.

4. The Data Structure Representing the Source Program

The data structure generated during the input of increments serves for the representation of the source program and at the same time as the basis for further processing. For this reason it must have the following characteristics:
It has to be a reversible mapping of the source program under eventual loss of lay-out features.
As it serves as basis for further processing it should be compact.
Insertion or removal of increments should easily be possible.

These objectives can be realized by splitting up the information contained in an increment.
The program control dicitonary contains one entry for each increment, which consists of the line number, a pointer to the logical following increment, information on the type of the increment, and a pointer to the attached pseudo code. Additional information in a program control table entry will be explained later on.
The remaininginformation is contained in the pseudo code, which is given in infix- or postfix notation. The lexical scan is performed and the symbols are replaced by references to a symbol dictionary.

Thus the program control table represents the entire program structure containing all information necessary for the program control. The pseudo code contains the interrelations of data objects and is used only for the execution of an increment.

The representation of the source program by this linear data structure is superior to that by a tree structure as far as the following aspects are concerned.
In a linear structure, insertion or removal of increments are done more easily. In a tree structure, however, insertion of increments is contradictory to the demand of performing all functions as late as possible. The modification of an increment already fitted into a tree structure may require the modification of the entire tree.

5. Program Execution

The cross-references among the single increments are bound during the program execution. The binding takes place on two different levels, on the level of the program control table, concerning program structure and program control, and on the level of pseudo code, concerning the data objects.
For this purpose two stacks are set up and used during the execution, a symbol stack suggested by Griffith [1,2], and a control stack.

5.1 Program Structure and Control Interpretation

During the execution the control is passed from increment to increment in an interpretive manner.
The state of the control stack and the type of the increment, which is to be executed, determine, which functions are to be performed on the control and symbol stack, on the pseudo code and in the program control dictionary. A transition matrix may be used to select an appropriate routine.

Several levels of interpretation can be differentiated:

1. The interpretation of program and block structure implies, that parts of programs which are not to be executed, have to be parsed in a so-called "passive mode".

2. The global syntax of the sequence of increments is to be parsed. Either the static correctness of the entire program or the dynamic correctness of executed program parts can be proved.

3. The processing of the semantic program control information is done. If there are nested semantic structures adjoined to a sequence of increments this processing has to be performed in the control stack. This includes the processing of the nested structure of dynamically and statically chained blocks and of nested program executions.
For example in the case of the for-loop from the syntactical point of view there is only left recursion which is aquivalent to iteration. But for carrying out the program control transfer nesting of information in the control stack is necessary.

5.2 Data Objects

In the pseudo code the identifiers are replaced by references to a symbol table without consideration of the scope of variables.

Thus during the execution, these entrys in the symbol table are bound to the variables according to their scope in the symbol stack.

When entering a block one entry in the symbol stack is reserved for each variable by executing its declaration. This entry contains information about type and structure, the storage or a reference to the allocated storage and additional pointers, which are needed in order to chain variables having the same identifier. The corresponding pointer in the symbol table is set to the new symbol stack entry.

The allocation of storage to variables in the symbol stack is possible if the scope and the lifetime of the variables are identical. Otherwise the symbol stack is used as a dynamic identifier table only for processing the scope of variables.

If the storage is allocated in the symbol stack the variables can be accessed when machine code is generated, by indirect references in the symbol table. Then the pointers in the symbol table are to be adjusted to the correct symbol stack entry, when a block is entered or left. In the case of procedure call or parameter call by name when dynamic and static nesting of blocks do not correspond, this is rather complicated.

When the access to the symbol stack entries is done interpretively the pointers in the symbol table can contain at any moment the symbol stack entry, at which the chain for an identifier begins. Then the chain is searched in the stack until an entry with valid scope is found [2].

6. Compilation

The object program structure described in the last sections is very flexible with regard to program modifications. In order to make program execution more efficient, the bindings temporarily established in the control- and symbol stack have to be fixed, when they are established the first time during a program execution. On the one hand this is done on the level of the control dictionary, on the other hand on the level of code.

6.1 The Binding of Data Objects

During program execution the generation of machine code is done as late as possible, that is the first time, when an increment is to be executed. When the test if machine code exists already, has a negative result, compilation is done. Pseudo code and symbol stack comprise all information needed for generation of machine code. This compiled code is attached to the entry in the program control dictionary; a flag is set in it that the compiled code is valid, and the compiled code is executed.

There are two ways in order to localize the effects of data object modifications:
As mentioned in [3], an additional attribut can be attached to each variable. This consists of the set of those increments in which the variable is used.

A flag that the compiled code is not valid, is set in all those increments, when there are modifications of the attributes or the scope of a variable.

With regard to the generated object program structure another method is more suitable.
During the compilation of an increment additional information is generated, that indicates in which environment the compiled code is valid.

This information consists essentially of indicators of the attributes as are type, structure and eventually allocated storage of the variables which were compiled.

Program modifications causes now to set the flag that the compiled code is not valid, in an entire area of the program. Then before execution of each increment the test has to be done whether the code is still valid in the modificated environment.

6.2 The Binding of Program Structure and Program Control

The compilation of the program structure and the program control is done on the level of the program control dictionary, the first time when during program execution a structure is processed in the control stack.

This compilation may result in that pointers are added to the linear sequence of increments in the program control dictionary which enable jumps in the sequence of increments during program execution. The structure generated in the program control dictionary is then like the structure of machine code in the linear sequence of storage.

On the other hand a tree structure may be generated during compilation. It has in comparison to the linear structure the advantage that the effects of modifications can be localized exactly. Only the part of the tree has to be recompiled which is affected by the modifications. But the effort for the generation of a tree structure is much greater.

The extent to which the compilation is performed can differ according to the levels of interpretation, which were distinguished in section 5:

1. If block- and program structures are compiled it is not necessary to process these structures in the passive mode.

2. If the global syntax is compiled, the control transfer from one increment to another is done in correspondence to the types of the increments to be executed. The control stack has to be accessed only in order to fetch semantic information.

3. If the compilation of the program control is done completly, the control stack is used only for the processing of block structure and of nested executions.

An answer to the question which structure is to generate during compilation and to which extent compilation is to be done, can not be given in generality. This depends in a high degree on the characteristics of the language to be implemented.

In order to obtain a satisfying implementation two points have to be balanced:

On the one hand the effort for performing the compilation in comparison to the speed of program execution; on the other hand, the effort needed for the localization of program modifications in comparison to the exactness with which the effects of modifications are localized.

7. Summary

This paper had as objective to show

1. which requirements are in the nature of interaction

and

2. that by the application of the two principles presented in this paper, incremental compilers can be designed which meet these requirements, even if the used dialog-language is rather heavily structured.

8. References

[1] M. Peccoud, M. Griffiths and M. Peltier, Incremental Interactive Compilation, Proc. IFIPS 68, Amsterdam (69)

[2] M. Berthaud, M. Griffiths, Incremental Compilation and Conversational Interpretation, Grenoble

[3] James G. Mitchell, The Design and Construction of Flexible and Efficient Interactive Programming Systems, Carnegie-Mellon University (1970)

[5] David L. Parnas, On the Use of Transition Diagrams in the Design of a User Interface for an Interactive Computer System, Proc. 24th Nat. Conf. ACM (1969)

[6] Robert B. Miller, Response Time in Man-Computer Conversational Interaction, Proceedings AFIPS 68, New York (1968)

[7] F. J. Corbato and H. J. Saltzer, Some Considerations of Supervisor Program Design for Multiplexed Computer Systems, Proc. IFIPS 68, Amsterdam (69)

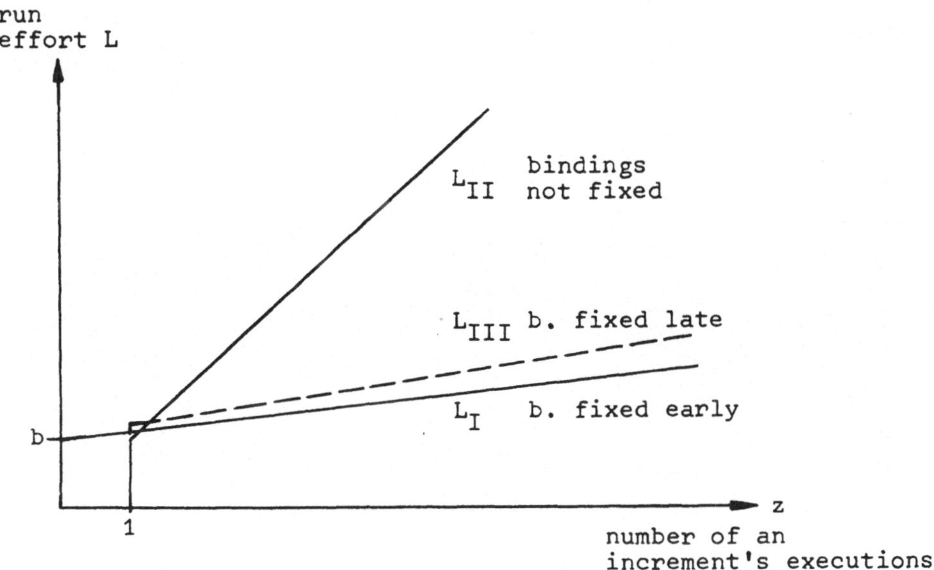

$L_I = c \cdot z + b$

$L_{II} = b \cdot z$

$L_{III} = (c+d) \cdot z + b$

The meaning of the parameters b, c, d is as follows:

b : mean effort for establishing the bindings of an increment and for compilation or for interpretive execution

c : mean effort for the execution of a compiled increment

d : mean effort for testing if an increment is already compiled and for providing the possibility of dynamic binding

For the representation of L_I, L_{II}, L_{III} the relations between the parameters b,c,d were chosen, as a result of practical experience, as follows:

$$b \gg c > d$$

Diagram 1 Run Effort

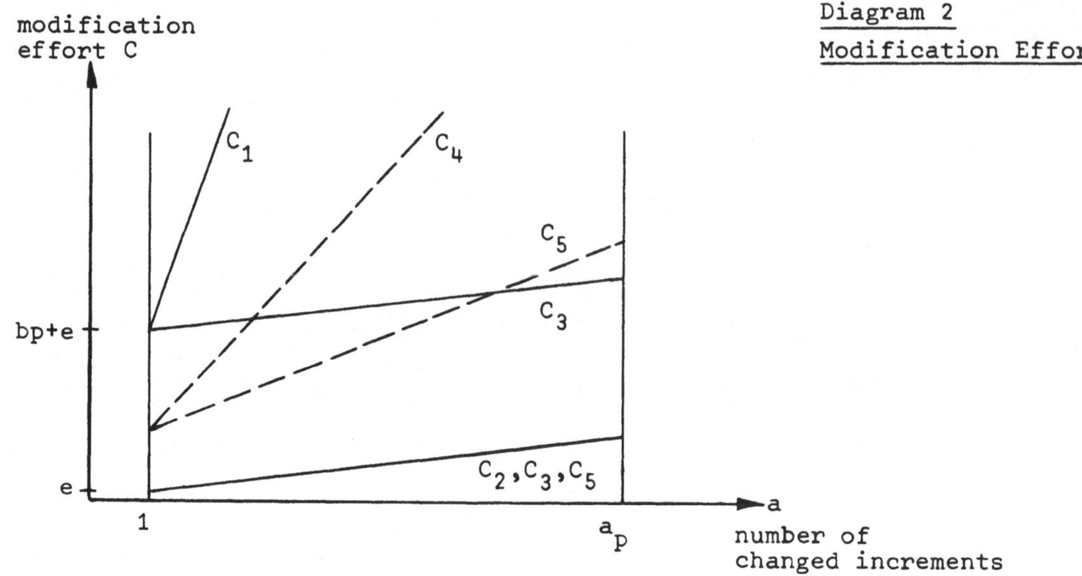

$C_1 = (bp+e)\cdot a$

$C_2 = e\cdot a$

$C_3 = \begin{cases} e\cdot a \\ e\cdot a + bp \end{cases}$ modifications are done before / after the first compilation is performed

$C_4 = e\cdot a + \sum_{i=1}^{a} (aa_i\cdot bp+la_i)$

$C_5 = \begin{cases} e\cdot a \\ e\cdot a + \sum_{i=1}^{a} (\Delta aa_i\cdot bp+la_i) \end{cases}$ "

The variable a denotes the number of the increments which are changed during the same period of program halt, before an execution is resumed or initiated.

The meaning of the parameters e, bp, aa_i, la_i, a_p is as follows:

e : mean effort for generation of an increment's pseudo code

bp : mean effort for compiling the entire program from pseudo code

aa_i : mean percentage of increments affected by the i-th modification

la_i : mean effort for localizing the effects of the i-th modification

a_p : number of all increments of the program

$\Delta aa_i = aa_i - (aa_o \vee \cdots \vee aa_{i-2} \vee aa_{i-1})$ where $aa_o = 0$.

The definition of Δaa_i represents that the sets of increments affected by a sequence of modifications may have a non empty conjunction.

PROGRAMMIERTER DIALOG ZUR ERZEUGUNG VON LEHRPROGRAMMEN

von Klaus-Dieter Graf

1. Zu einer an pädagogischen Problemen orientierten Programmiersprache

Lehrprogramme gehören in den Bereich der Pädagogik; es erscheint deshalb zunächst auffällig, wenn im Rahmen einer Fachtagung über Programmiersprachen über die Erzeugung von Lehrprogrammen gesprochen wird. Tatsächlich aber stellen diese nur eines der didaktischen Probleme dar, an denen man sich bereits seit längerem bei Überlegungen zur Entwicklung einer "pädagogischen" Programmiersprache orientiert hat.

Im Zusammenhang mit Ansätzen zum objektivierten Unterricht bzw. zur objektivierten Unterrichtsplanung sind nämlich Teilprozesse und -aufgaben aufgefunden bzw. herausgearbeitet worden, die einer Abwicklung oder Lösung mit Methoden der elektronischen Datenverarbeitung durchaus zugänglich sind. Nur exemplarisch sei dazu verwiesen auf die Steuerung von Lehrautomaten oder auf den automatischen Entwurf von Lehrprogrammen zu vorgegebenen Lehrstoffen und Lehrzielen nach informationstheoretischen Kriterien (vgl. Graf 1970). Ein von Uwe Lehnert herausgegebener Sammelband "Elektronische Datenverarbeitung in Schule und Ausbildung - Erfahrungen, Praxis, Planungen in Deutschland" macht deutlich, daß es bereits eine recht umfangreiche Praxis der Datenverarbeitung im schulischen Sektor gibt .(Lehnert 1970). Dennoch ist das Problem einer Spezialsprache für die dabei vorhandenen Probleme noch nicht entschieden angegriffen worden. Das liegt nicht zuletzt daran, daß man bei der Übertragung von Lehrertätigkeiten an Rechner natürlich zunächst einmal solche auswählte, die von verhältnismäßig rein numerischem Charakter sind. Dafür genügten i.a. Sprachen wie ALGOL oder FORTRAN. So wurden z.T. Probleme wie "Zensuren aus dem Computer", "automatische Auswertung programmierter Prüfungen", " Aufstellen von Stunden- und Raumplänen" oder "Rationalisierung in der Schulverwaltung" bewältigt.

Wie eingangs erwähnt bemüht man sich aber heute mehr und mehr um die Programmierung von Lehrertätigkeiten, die nicht mehr eindeutig numerischer Art sind. Lehnert faßt diese unter den Oberbegriffen "Planung und Vorbereitung von Unterricht" und "Vermitteln von Kenntnissen und Fertigkeiten" zusammen, wobei bislang jeweils vorwiegend die programmierte Unterweisung berücksichtigt wird. In diesem Problembereich wird nun sehr deutlich, daß man eine an didaktischen oder zumindest unterrichtstechnologischen Problemen orientierte Programmiersprache braucht, wenn man sich nicht in kaum noch übersehbarer Assemblerprogrammierung erschöpfen will. Die Entwicklung der Autorsprachen, die unter 3. noch näher erwähnt werden, wurde von diesem Aspekt mitbestimmt.

2. Lehrprogrammieren

Lehrprogramme sind eine besondere Form der Darstellung von Lehrstoffen, die einem Lernenden selbständige, kontrollierte Bearbeitung gestattet. Die Kontrolle wird durch Handlungsanweisungen im Lehrprogramm selbst und z.T. durch automatische Abläufe während der Lehrstoffdarbietung (bei Lehrautomaten) bewirkt.
Der Prozeß der Herstellung eines Lehrprogramms, kurz "Lehrprogrammieren", ist im Prinzip wie folgt organisiert: anfangs werden Lehrstoff und Lehrziel formuliert und Daten über die ins Auge gefaßten Adressaten des Lehrprogramms gesammelt, z.B. bezüglich der Vorkenntnisse und des Lernverhaltens. Davon ausgehend wird anhand eines didaktischen Konzepts das Lehrprogramm selbst aufgestellt, d.h. eine Folge von Lehrschritten, im einzelnen jeweils bestehend aus einem Urteil über eine vorhergehende Leistung des Adressaten, einem Lehrquant,(das einen kleinen Teil des Lehrstoffs darstellt) einem Verknüpfer,(das ist meist eine Frage zum Lehrstoff) und einem Aufruf zu einer Reaktion (i.a. eine Antwort auf die gestellte Frage). Die Reaktion bewirkt dann die Fortführung des Lehrprogrammes. Sind mehrere Reaktionen möglich, so kann die Lehrschrittfolge verzweigt fortgeführt werden, insbesondere sind Wiederholungen, Überspringungen, Zusatzbelehrungen u.ä. möglich.

3. Erfassungs- und organisatorische Hilfe durch Autorsprachen

Der Aufbau des Lehrprogramms ist natürlich bestimmt durch Überlegungen didaktischer Art; u.a. ist man bemüht, die wesentlichen Begriffe des Lehrstoffs logisch an bekannte anzuschließen bzw. auseinander zu entwickeln und die Zusammenhänge herzustellen. Hinsichtlich der Begriffsdichte und der Komplexheit der Aussagen ist dabei Rücksicht auf die genannten (psychostrukturellen) Daten des Adressaten zu nehmen.

Neben dieser Programmierung des Informationsflusses hinsichtlich des Lehrstoffs erfordert die Steuerung des Lernprozesses durch Darbietung von Lehrschritten und geeignete Verzweigungen die Beachtung besonderer Regeln. Dies gilt besonders dann, wenn es sich um Lehrprogramme handelt, die rechnergesteuert über Lehrautomaten dargeboten werden sollen. Zur Erleichterung der Lehrprogrammierung für solche Zwecke wurde der erste Ansatz zur Entwicklung einer Programmiersprache für pädagogische Zwecke unternommen, nämlich in Form der sogenannten "Autorsprachen". Diese umfassen im wesentlichen leicht verständliche Codewörter, die dem Autor bei Vorliegen des eigentlichen Lehrtextes eine Lehrprogrammierung direkt an dem Rechner gestatten, der das Lehrprogramm auch darbieten soll. Ein bekanntes Beispiel ist COURSEWRITER, eine Autorsprache, die insbesondere das Formulieren des Steuerteils eines Lehrprogramms gestattet (Text geben, Antwort entgegennehmen, externe Geräte wie Projektor oder Tonband steuern) sowie die Organisation des Lehrprogramms erleichtert (Anlegen von Verzweigungen, Numerierung, Löschen. Einfügen).

Die Autorsprachen sind nur ein sehr kleiner Schritt zur Bewältigung über numerische Aufgaben hinausgehender Tätigkeiten im Bereich von Unterricht. Nicht angesprochen wird dabei das Problem der Textverarbeitung für Unterrichtsprozesse und in Unterrichtsprozessen. Ein Aspekt von Unterricht ist z.B. ,daß Lehrstoffe und Schülerreaktionen in gewisser Weise didaktisch manipuliert werden müssen. Das bedeutet schon im Bereiche des CAI(Computer Assisted Instruction),

daß eigentlich nicht nur eine Sprache vorhanden sein muß, die dem Lehrer, bzw. Autor das Programmieren des Lehrautomaten erleichtert. Vielmehr braucht man auch eine Unterrichtsdialogsprache, die dem Schüler eine Konversation mit dem Lehrautomaten gestattet, die über das Drücken bestimmter Tasten oder das Markieren von Punkten auf einem Sichtgerät hinausgeht.
Ein erstes Ergebnis in dieser Richtung besteht z.B. darin, daß im Rahmen der Autorsprache LIDIA freiformulierte Schülerantworten beurteilt werden können. (Stahl 1969)

Das Hauptanliegen dieser Ausführungen geht nun dahin, die Möglichkeit der Anwendung des Verfahrens des programmierten Dialogs bei der Erzeugung von Lehrprogrammen zu erläutern.
Es geht also um den Einbezug elektronischer Datenverarbeitung in die Vorbereitung programmierten Unterrichts, nicht in dessen Durchführung.
Darüberhinaus soll umrissen werden, wie eine dafür geeignete Dialogsprache aussehen kann.

4. Lehrprogrammieren mit programmierter methodischer oder didaktischer Kontrolle

Vom Grundgedanken der Autorsprache ausgehend wird man zum eigentlichen Dialog zwischen Autor und Rechner durch die Erfahrung geführt, daß nicht nur die äußere Form eines Lehrprogramms verhältnismäßig streng formalisiert ist, also z.B. aus wenigen Bausteinen wie Lehrquanten, Fragen, Verzweigungen etc. in strenger Abfolge konstruiert ist. Vielmehr ist auch der semantische, bzw. der inhaltliche Anteil zumindest teilweise kalkülhaft gestaltet.
Das läßt sich an Strategien ablesen, die von verschiedenen Autoren für die Lehrprogrammestellung angegeben werden, wobei Lehrstoff und Lehrziel als bereits festgelegt vorausgesetzt werden. (Frank 1969, Lahn 1971)
D.h. konkret z.B. ,für die Konstruktion eines Lehrquants, einer Frage oder eines Urteils mit einem Verweis sind jeweils methodische und didaktische Regeln zu beachten,

die sich z.T. durch das Abzählen von Wörtern, das Führen von Strichlisten, die Berechnung von syntaktischen Informationswerten u.ä. formale Vorgänge prüfen lassen.
Solche Prüfungen lassen sich aber ohne großen Aufwand programmiert vornehmen, wenn an jede entsprechende Eingabe des Autors beim Lehrprogrammieren an einem protokollierenden Rechner eine entsprechende Anweisung angefügt wird. Durch zugehörige "Äußerungen" des Rechners entsteht dann ein echter programmierter Dialog, also nach einer Definition von Georg Nees ein " gesprächsartiger Informationsaustausch zwischen einem Menschen und einem Rechner" (Nees 1966). Auch die Bedingung, daß der Austausch in den " gewohnten zeitlichen Dimensionen eines Gesprächs" erfolgt, ist angesichts des Umfangs der Gesprächsobjekte, - Lehrquanten und Fragen erfüllt. Deren formale Kontrolle erfolgt nämlich - so jedenfalls die bisherigen Erfahrungen - vom Rechner her zeitlich unmittelbar. Besonders effektiv wird der Dialog, wenn die Überwachung nur bei "Regelverletzungen" zu einer Rechner-Äußerung führt; vergleichbar mit der Syntax - Überwachung bei der Dialog-Programmierung von Rechnen.

5. <u>Lehrprogrammieren mit programmierter didaktischer Konstruktionshilfe</u>

Der Dialog wird noch interessanter, wenn das vorgegebene didaktische Regelsystem nicht nur zur programmierten Kontrolle vom Menschen gelieferter Dialogbeiträge herangezogen wird, sondern auch zur Konstruktion von Vorschlägen zur Fortsetzung des Lehrprogramms, z.B. hinsichtlich des Begriffsaufbaua. Letzterer ist ja eine Funktion des vorgegebenen Lehrstoffs und des bereits entwickelten Lehrprogramms.Auch diese Rechnerfunktion kann automatisch am Anfang der Erstellung jedes neuen Lehrschritts stehen, ohne erst aufgerufen zu werden. Natürlich setzt das die Möglichkeit der Zurückweisung durch den menschlichen Partner voraus.(Näheres in Graf 1970a).

6. <u>Eine Sprache für den programmierten Lehrprogrammier-Dialog, bezogen auf die Struktur des Dialog-Verfahrens</u>

Die bisherigen Ausführungen deuteten nur ganz wenige Aspekte der Dialog- Möglichkeiten bei der Lehrprogrammierung an, verdeutlichten aber vielleicht schon, daß es sinnvoll ist, sich

der Rechnerunterstützung in diesem Zusammenhang zu bedienen.
Eine Programmier- und Dialogsprache für diese Zwecke hat sich an Begriffen wie Lehrquant, Begriffsfortschritt, Information (als Maß) usw. zu orientieren und muß Anweisungen bezüglich des Lernfortschrittes, des logischen Zusammenhanges, der Formatierung von Lehrschritten u.ä. ermöglichen.
Die Dialogsprache muß (und kann) bezüglich des Gesprächsgegenstandes "Lehrprogramm und seine Bestandteile" sowohl syntaktische als auch semantische und pragmatische Funktion haben.

Darüberhinaus ist eigentlich eine eigene Programmiersprache erforderlich, in der a) das den Dialog steuernde Programm und b) die zusätzlichen Aktionen des Rechners, die nicht zum Gespräch gehören, erfaßt werden. Solche Aktionen sind z.B. eben die Überprüfung von Kriterien, die selbständige Konstruktion von Fortsetzungsvorschlägen oder das Protokollieren bzw. Abspeichern der fertigen Teile des Dialog-Objekts, also des Lehrprogramms.

Wir sind nun weit davon entfernt, einen geschlossenen Ansatz vorstellen zu können, hoffen aber, vom Stand der allgemeinen Theorie der Programmiersprachen in dieser Hinsicht bald profitieren zu können.
Es wurde bisher für den Versuch einer Realisierung eines Lehrprogrammier-Dialogs lediglich ein Programmsystem entwickelt, dessen Leistungen u.a. als die eines "Übersetzers" interpretiert werden können. Der Übersetzer hat zwei Funktionen: einmal werden didaktische Anweisungen des Lehrprogrammierers entgegengenommen und bearbeitet, zum anderen werden Mitteilungen oder Anfragen bezüglich des Lehrprogrammierprozesses vom Rechner generiert und ausgegeben. Zusätzlich übernimmt das Programmsystem die Dialog-Leitung, indem es bestimmt, welche Leistungen zur Fortsetzung des Lehrprogramms von wem zu erbringen sind. Der menschliche Dialogpartner kann durch geeignete Aufrufe oder Entscheidungen in dieses Verfahren eingreifen.
Die Dialog-Leitung durch den Rechner ist deshalb vorteilhaft, weil einerseits die Konstruktion der Lehrprogramm-

Makrostruktur ebenfalls nach formalisierten Regeln zu erfolgen hat und andererseits die Zahl der Alternativen für die Lehrprogramm-Fortsetzung hinsichtlich der Begriffsentwicklung i.a. verhältnismäßig klein ist. Diese können also dem Lehrprogrammierer jeweils vorgeschlagen werden, wodurch er von der Beachtung der Makrostruktur z.T. entlastet wird.

Das bereits realisierte Dialog-Verfahren DIALOG-ALZUDI kann anhand der Abbildung 1 kurz erläutert werden. Zunächst sei wiederholt,daß beim Lehrprogrammieren im wesentlichen vier Faktoren von Belang sind:

1. der Lehrstoff; er wird in einem sog. Basaltext erfaßt,
2. das Lehrziel,
3. ein Modell vom Adressaten des Lehrprogramms,
4. der Autor.

Alle Strategien der Lehrprogrammierung, auch die rein personal durchgeführten, gehen im Grunde so vor, daß der Autor - nachdem er Lehrstoff und Lehrziel festgelegt hat - in jedem Arbeitstakt den tatsächlichen Zustand seines Modells vom Adressaten prüft und dann unter didaktischen Gesichtspunkten einen Lehrschritt entwirft, der dieses Modell in Richtung auf den "Sollzustand", bestimmt durch das Lehrziel, hin ändert. Geeignete Lehrschritte werden protokolliert - und so entsteht das Lehrprogramm. In der Abbildung ist dieser Takt als Regeltakt eines Regelkreises interpretiert.

In den Regelprozeß wird nun der Rechner auf mehrfache Weise einbezogen:

1. als formaler Prüfer für die geplanten Lehreinwirkungen des Autors,
2. als selbständiger Generator für solche Lehreinwirkungen, die vom Autor erst hinsichtlich ihrer Eignung für das Adressatenmodell geprüft werden,
3. als Simulator für den Adressaten. D.h. wir interpretieren den Lehrprogrammierprozeß einfach so, als solle das Adressatenmodell durch den Autor belehrt werden, also aus einem Anfangszustand über zahlreiche Zwischenzustände in einen Zielzustand überführt werden.
4. als Protokollant für das Dialog-Objekt, also das nach und nach entstehende Lehrprogramm.

In der Notation des Beitrags von Kupka in diesem Band: "Ein Strukturmodell für Dialogsprachen" haben wir also 'results' $R_i = f(Z_{i-1}, A_i)$ bei Zuständen Z_{i-1} des Adressaten-Modells und 'statements' A_i des Autors, und $Z_i = g(Z_{i-1}, A_i)$. Es erscheint entgegen der Voraussetzung dieses Strukturmodells auch angebracht, die Funktionen $A_i = h(Z_{i-1}, R_i, M_i)$ einzuführen, wobei M_i für gewisse innere Motivationszustände steht, die das Agieren des Autors auf ein Dialog-Ziel hin beeinflussen.

Mit diesem System ist bereits ein Dialog möglich, der die besondere Kapazität des Rechners zur Abwicklung formaler Generier- und Prüfaufgaben ausnützt. Für den Autor wird ein solcher Dialog allerdings dann mühselig, wenn sich bestimmte Aufrufe für bestimmte Rechnerleistungen in jedem Takt nahezu zyklisch wiederholen müssen. Denn für jeden Lehrschritt sind im wesentlichen formal dieselben Abläufe erforderlich.
Hier liegt es nun nahe, deren Abwicklung selbst wieder zum Gegenstand einer Rechnersteuerung werden zu lassen. Dies geschieht tatsächlich durch die Einführung des sog. "Moderators", eines Programmes, das Einfluß auf den Dialog-Ablauf nimmt. Es richtet sich nicht auf die Interpretation von Autor-Anweisungen und deren Ausführung, sondern regelt lediglich, wann welche Maßnahmen überhaupt erforderlich sind und welcher der System-Partner dafür heranzuziehen ist. Insbesondere erteilt der Moderator also stellvertretend für den Autor selbständig Aufträge für den Rechner (Als Prüfer oder Generator).

Damit findet kein völlig freier Dialog mehr statt, der nur vom Autor gesteuert wird. Vielmehr werden die Sachzwänge des Dialoggegenstandes, hier z.B. die feste Makro- und Mikrostruktur von Lehrprogrammen, programmiert berücksichtigt.
Es läßt sich vielleicht einwenden, daß dies nicht mehr dem Wesen eines Dialogs entspricht und hier lediglich Stapel-Verarbeitung unter Einbeziehung manueller Eingaben des Autors abläuft. Eine solche Einschränkung der Autorleistung durch den Formalismus des Generators oder des Moderators läßt sich aber unterbinden, wenn man ein Übergehen von

Moderator-Anweisungen durch den Autor vorsieht und u.U. auch die Protokollierung vom Rechner abgelehnter Eingaben erzwingen läßt. Wesentlich ist ja nur, daß der Autor jeweils auf die formalen lerntheoretisch oder informationstheoretisch bedingten Anforderungen der Lehrprogrammierung hingewiesen wird.

7. Zulässige 'statements' der verwendeten Sprache

Die von uns verwendete Dialogsprache ist sehr einfach aufgebaut: sie reichte aber bisher aus, um einige Modelldialoge zu führen. Sie dient neben der Lehrprogrammprotokollierung vornehmlich dem Dialog über die Erreichung des Lehrziels und den Begriffsfortschritt. Außerdem ist der Rechner in der Lage, selbst Formulierungsvorschläge für Lehrquanten, Fragen und Antworten zu machen, indem er sich auf den anfangs eingegebenen Lehrstoff stützt. Der Dialog findet unter der Voraussetzung statt, daß die tragenden Begriffe des Lehrstoffs in einer numerierten Liste erfaßt sind, es wird nur auf diese Nummern Bezug genommen.

a) statements des Autors:

```
(lehrquant)::= "text in bezug zum lehrstoff"
(frage)     ::= "text in bezug zum lehrstoff"
(antwort)   ::= "text in bezug zum lehrstoff"
(begriffsnummer)::= 0/1/2/3/.../100/ende zyklus
(urteil)    ::= +/-
((aufruf)   ::= gib lehrquant/gib frage/gib antwort/
                gib begriffsnummer/gib urteil/gib bemerkung/
                gib aufruf/gib anfrage)
```

b) statements des Rechners:

```
(lehrquant)::= "text in bezug zum lehrstoff"
(frage)     ::= "text in bezug zum lehrstoff"
(antwort)   ::= "text in bezug zum lehrstoff"
(begriffsnummer)::= 1/2/3/.../100
(urteil)    ::= Ø/#/zu gross
(bemerkung)::= letzte erwähnung/nur begriff (begriffs
                nummer) verwenden/ soll für (begriffs
                nummer) erreicht
```

(aufruf) ::= gib lehrquant/gib frage/gib antwort/
gib begriffsnummer/gib urteil

(anfrage) ::= lehrschritt erwünscht/lehrschritt später/
zyklus/enden/neueinführung (begriffsnummer)/
überhaupt etwas neues/lehrquant mit (begriffs
nummer)/frage mit (begriffsnummer)/selbst/
schon fertig - dennoch

Objektsprache und Metasprache sind hier vereinigt: zur Objektsprache gehören jeweils "lehrquant", "frage", "antwort" und "begriffsnummer".

Die statements gehen jeweils von den Generatoren aus, vom Rechnergenerator kommen auch auf Veranlassung des Moderators die Anfragen. Zu den statements der Prüfer gehören die Urteile und die Bemerkungen.
Vom Moderator werden einerseits, wie bemerkt, über den Rechnergenerator Anfragen an den Autor veranlaßt, andererseits gehen direkte Aufrufe an den Autor.

Im Interesse eines flüssigen Dialogs entfallen die Aufrufe des Menschen, stattdessen erfolgen an den Stellen im Dialog, an denen solche überhaupt möglich wären, Anfragen des Rechners, z.T. mit konstruktiven Vorschlägen, was gemäß den didaktischen Regeln z.Zt. zur Fortsetzung des Lehrprogramms erforderlich bzw. möglich ist.
Die Abbildung 2 gibt in Form eines "Sprachablaufplans" einen Überblick über die Dialog-Möglichkeiten im Verlaufe der Erzeugung eines Lehrschritts.
Die Operationskästchen in diesem Plan enthalten jeweils zulässige Sprachelemente, solche des Menschen sind durch doppelte untere Begrenzung und durch Kleinschreibung gekennzeichnet. Bei den Entscheidungskästchen sind zwei Arten zu unterscheiden. Einmal handelt es sich um Anfragen des Rechners, die zu einer Verzweigung je nach dem Urteil des Menschen (+/-) führen. Die nur mit Zahlen (1-12) beschrifteten Entscheidungskästchen dagegen stellen didaktische Entscheidungen des Rechners dar, auf die der Autor keinen unmittelbaren Einfluß hat.
Zur vollständigen Erklärung des Dialog-Verfahrens und insbesondere der Sprachregelung sei auf Graf 1969 und 1970a verwiesen.

8. Implementierung

Das Rechner-Programmsystem (DIALOG-ALZUDI) ist in der Assemblersprache PROSA unter Einbeziehung der Zeichenarithmetik (durch Simulation) abgefaßt und wird an einer DVA Siemens 303 P abgewickelt. Es belegt 10 000 Festwörter im Kernspeicher, der Dialog findet über den Bedienungsblattschreiber statt. Die Versorgung des Programms mit den Eingangsdaten erfolgt über Lochstreifenleser, das protokollierte Lehrprogramm wird unmittelbar über Lochstreifenstanzer ausgegeben.

9. Abschluß

Unser Problem war zunächst einmal eine elementare eigentliche Dialogsprache, die dem Autor gestattet, mit einem Rechner über seinen Gegenstand "Lehrprogramm" in geeigneten Termini zu kommunizieren.
Eine ebenso wichtige, allerdings noch viel schwierigere Aufgabe ist eine Spezialsprache zur Programmierung des Generators, des Prüfers und des Moderators selbst. Diese stellt sich u.a. auch deswegen, weil seitens der Autoren der Wunsch vorliegt, jeweils ihre eigene, spezielle Didaktik zugrunde zu legen. Dessen Erfüllung scheitert, solange er von einer Programmierung in Assemblersprache abhängig ist.

10. Literatur

Frank, H.: Kybernetische Grundlagen der Pädagogik, 2 Bde. (1969)

Graf, K.-D.: Eine Sprache für den Lehrprogrammierdialog. In: Grundlagenstudien aus Kybernetik und Geisteswissenschaft, 10/4 (1969)

- . - : Zur Entwicklung einer an didaktischen Problemen orientierten Programmiersprache. In: Sprache im Technischen Zeitalter, 33 (1970)

- . - : Programmierter Dialog zur Erzeugung von Lehrprogrammen. In: Zeitschrift für erziehungswissenschaftliche Forschung, 4 (1970a)

Lahn, W.: Ein Beitrag zum didaktischen Programmieren: Das Entwickeln der Programmstruktur aus einer Analyse des Lehrgegenstandes durch ein Satzgerüst in Folgesätzen.

In: Programmiertes Lernen. Unterrichtstechnologie und Unterrichtsforschung, Heft 2/1971.

Lehnert, U.: Elektronische Datenverarbeitung in Schule und Ausbildung, 1970.

Nees, G.: Programmierter Dialog. In: H.Frank (Hsg.): Lehrmaschinen in kybernetischer und pädagogischer Sicht 4, (1966)

Stahl, V.: Ein algorithmierbares Verfahren zur Beurteilung frei formulierter Adressatenantworten. In: Grundlagenstudien aus Kybernetik und Geisteswissenschaft, 10/2 (1969)

Anschrift des Verfassers:
Pädagogische Hochschule Rheinland, Abt. Neuß
404 Neuß, Humboldtstr. 2.

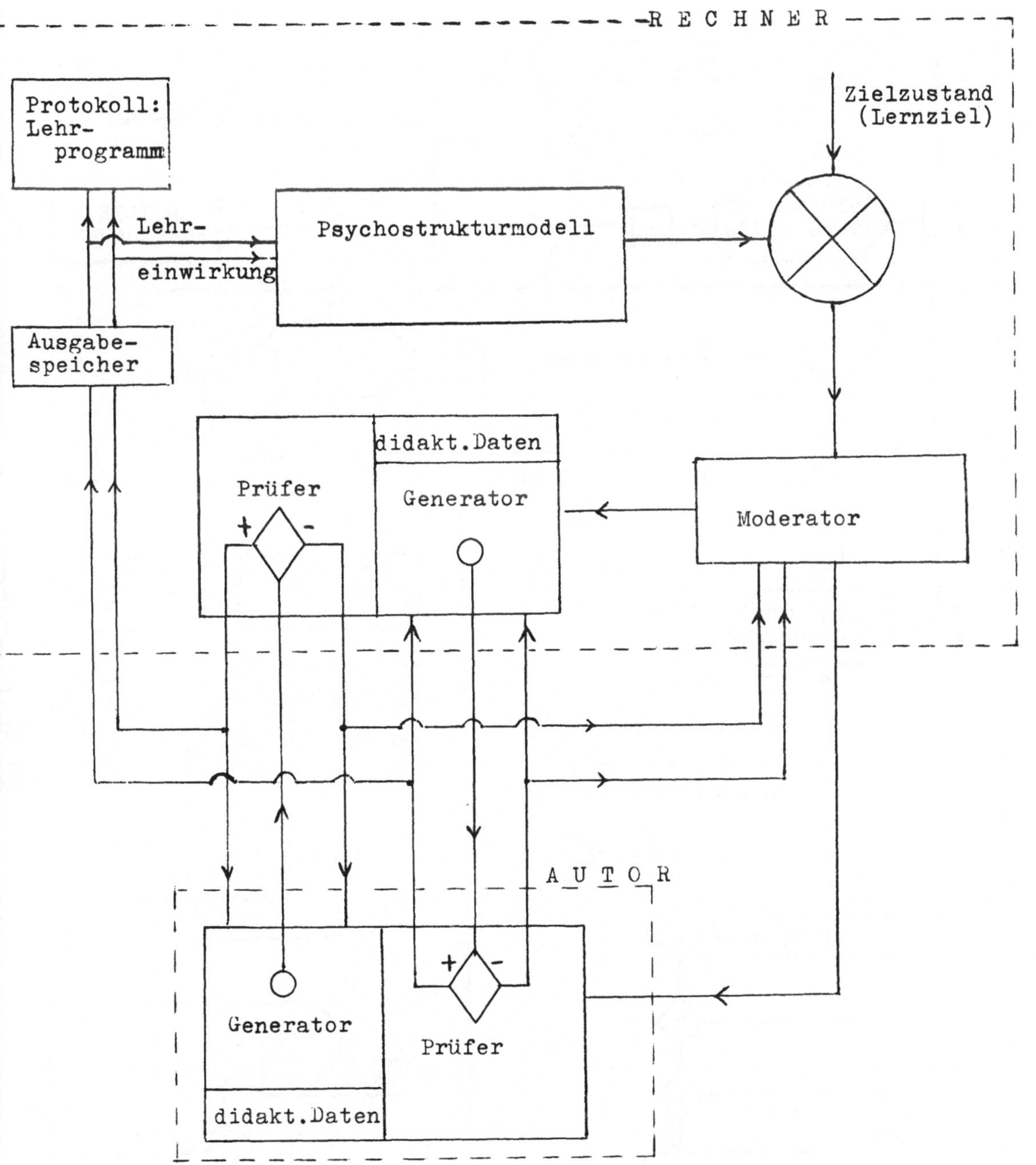
R E C H N E R
Protokoll: Lehr- programm
Zielzustand (Lernziel)
Lehr-
einwirkung
Psychostrukturmodell
Ausgabe- speicher
didakt.Daten
Prüfer
+
-
Generator
Moderator
A U T O R
+
-
Generator
Prüfer
didakt.Daten

Abb. 1

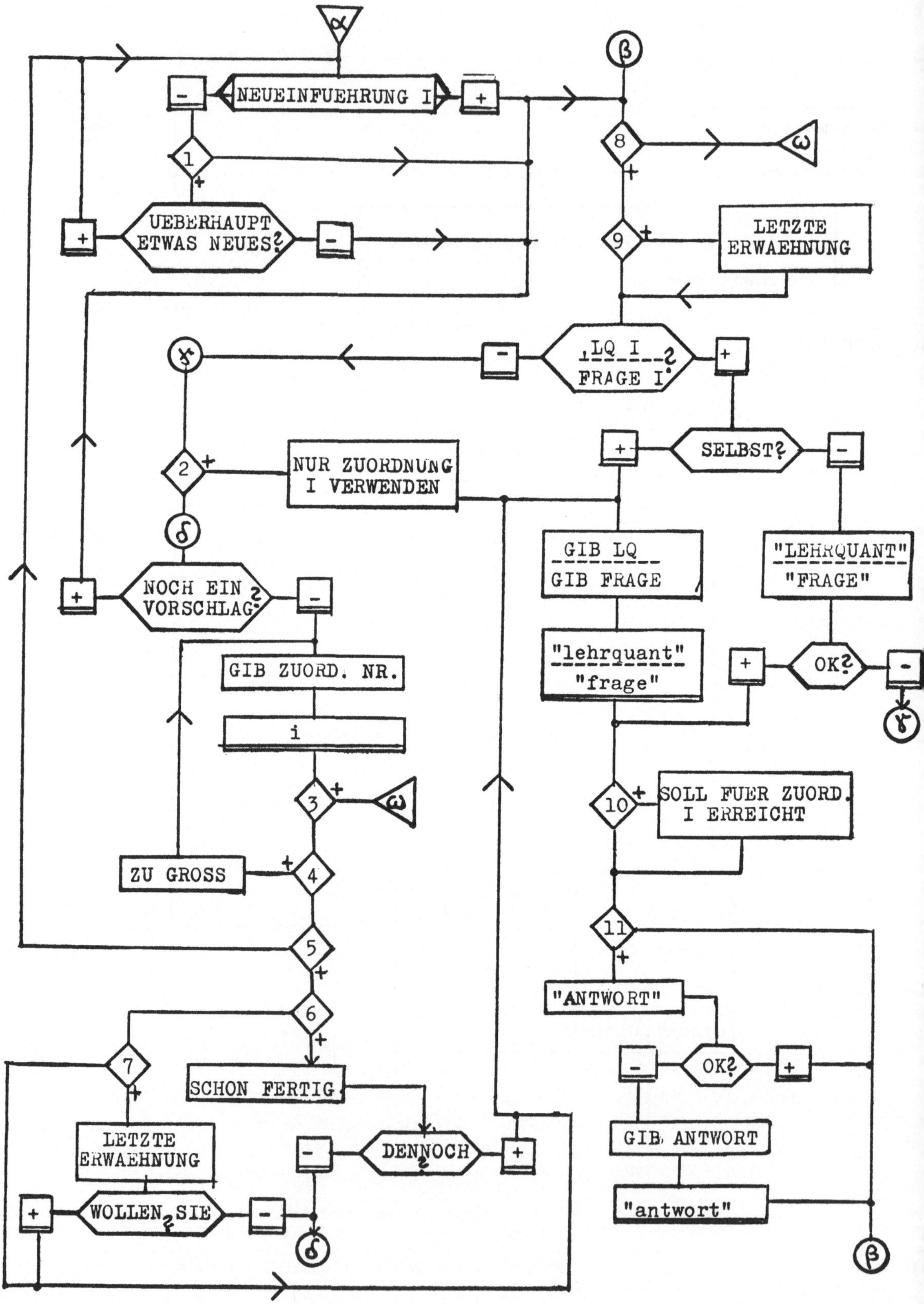

α

NEUEINFUEHRUNG I

\-

\+

β

1

8

ω

UEBERHAUPT ETWAS NEUES?

\+

\-

9

LETZTE ERWAEHNUNG

LQ I
FRAGE I?

\-

\+

γ

2

NUR ZUORDNUNG I VERWENDEN

SELBST?

\+

\-

δ

GIB LQ
GIB FRAGE

"LEHRQUANT"
"FRAGE"

NOCH EIN VORSCHLAG?

\+

\-

GIB ZUORD. NR.

"lehrquant"
"frage"

OK?

\+

\-

γ

i

3

ω

10

SOLL FUER ZUORD. I ERREICHT

ZU GROSS

4

5

11

6

"ANTWORT"

7

SCHON FERTIG

OK?

\-

\+

LETZTE ERWAEHNUNG

DENNOCH?

\-

\+

GIB ANTWORT

WOLLEN SIE?

\+

\-

δ

"antwort"

β

Abb.2

ÜBER DEN EINSATZ VON MAKROPROZESSOREN IM GENERATORTEIL EINES ÜBERSETZERSYSTEMS

von G. Heldmann und H.T. Krüger

1. Einleitung

Das Makrokonzept diente bisher im wesentlichen dazu, existierende Programmiersprachen (in der Regel Assembler-Sprachen) durch die Einführung neuer Sprachelemente zu erweitern. Makros wurden hauptsächlich als spezielle Sprachmittel angesehen, die es dem Programmierer gestatteten, sich mit einer einzelnen Instruktion auf eine Gruppe von Anweisungen der Grundsprache zu beziehen.

Die meisten Makroprozessoren sind auch heute noch fest mit einer Programmiersprache verknüpft; der Prozessor bildet mit dem Übersetzer der Programmiersprache ein festes Übersetzersystem, welches dann z.B. Makro-Assembler genannt wird.

In den letzten Jahren sind nun mehrere Makroprozessoren, z.B. LIMP, ML/I ... entwickelt und publiziert worden, die unabhängig von einer bestimmten Grundsprache sind. Diese universellen Prozessoren haben im Bereich der Systemprogrammierung immer mehr an Bedeutung gewonnen.

In diesem Bericht wird über Erfahrungen mit einem universellen Makroprozessor, genannt GPSP, berichtet, der über eine Reihe von Eigenschaften verfügt, die unter anderem den Einsatz des Prozessors in einem Übersetzersystem ermöglichen.

Als konkretes Einsatzgebiet für GPSP ist z.Zt. der SIEMENS PL/I-Compiler vorgesehen; hier wird der Makroprozessor die Aufgabe der Befehlsauflösung, d.h. der Code-Erzeugung übernehmen.

Das folgende Bild gibt die Grobstruktur des PL/I-Übersetzers wieder:

Bild 1:

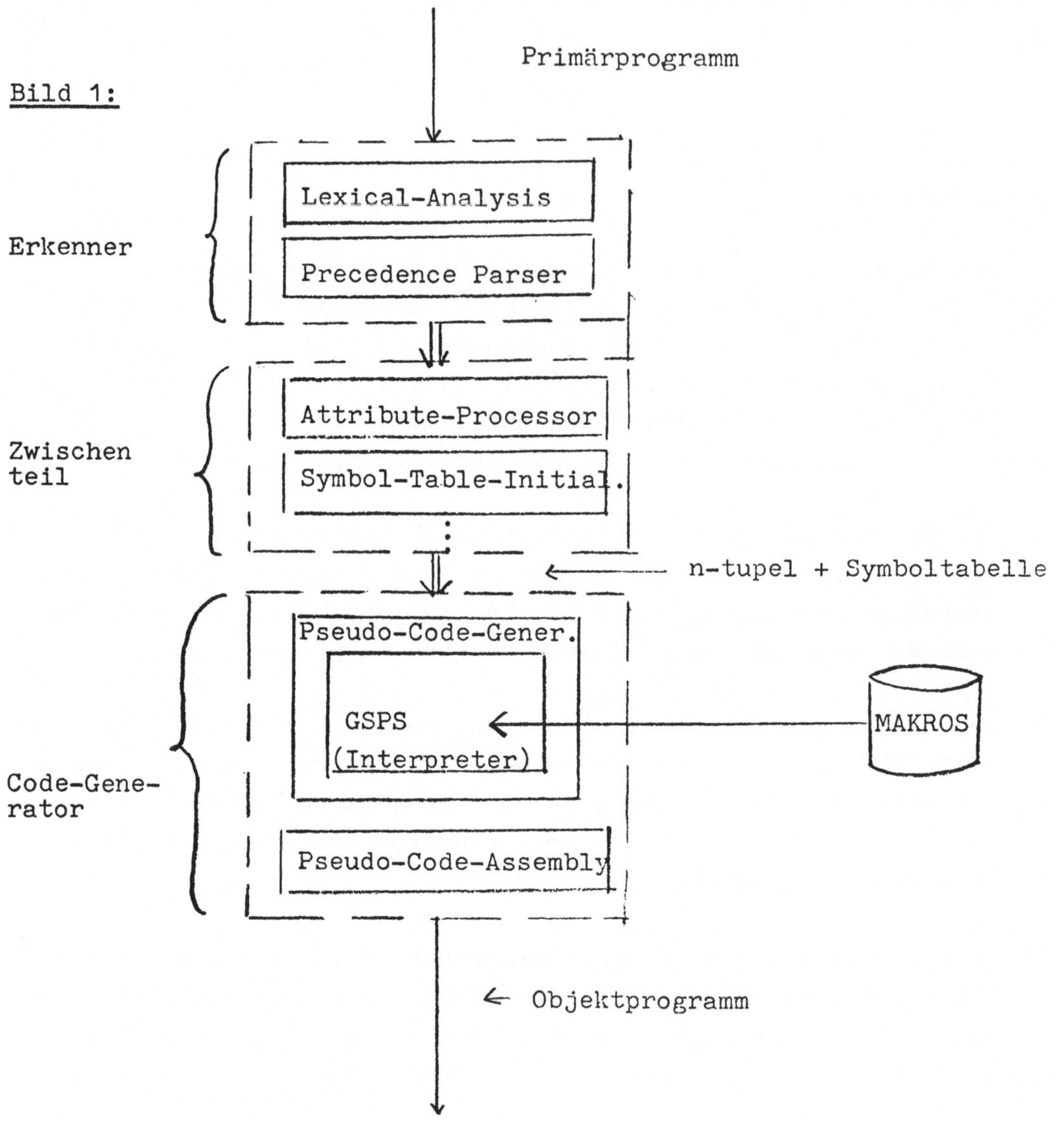

Der Übersetzer zerfällt in mehrere logische Phasen. Das vordere Ende (Erkenner) und das Mittelstück des Compilers erzeugen die Phrasen-Struktur der Quellensprache in der internen Form von n-tupeln ("multi-address-code with named results").

Beispiel: Aus der PL/I-Anweisung

A = X * (Y+Z);

wird

```
+ stref (Y), stref (Z), T1
* stref (X), T1, T2
= T2, stref (A)
```

erzeugt.

Hier steht "stref" für symbol-table-reference; "stref (X)" ist Zeiger auf den Symboltabelleneintrag der Variablen X und TN bezeichnet ein Zwischenergebnis. Die erste Phase des Code-Generators arbeitet den oben beschriebenen Zwischentext, sequentiell ab. Die einzelnen n-tupel werden in eine Sequenz von Pseudo-Instruktionen aufgelöst. Die Pseudo-Instruktionen stellen eine 1:1 symbolische Darstellung der Maschinensprache dar. Mit anderen Worten, eine Pseudo-Instruktion entspricht genau einer Maschinen-Instruktion. Die Pseudo-Instruktionen haben als mögliche Operanden Zeiger auf Symboltabelleneinträge und/oder symbolische bzw. physikalische Register.

Die Überführung der n-tupel in Pseudo-Code wird durch eine Reihe von Durchläufen erzielt; jeder Durchlauf ersetzt eine bestimmte Menge von n-tupeln durch Pseudo-Instruktionen.

Die einzelnen n-tupel werden als Makro-Aufrufe interpretiert. Die Ersetzungsroutinen sind die zugehörigen Makro-Definitionen, die vom Makroprozessor GPSP interpretativ abgearbeitet werden.

Die zweite Phase des Code-Generators, die "Pseudo-Code-Assembly" ersetzt im wesentlichen die Symboltabellen-Referenzen durch Basisregister und Distanzadressen, adressiert den Code und führt die physikalische Registerzuordnung durch. Dieser Assemblierungs-Lauf erzeugt auch die für den "Linkage Editor" notwendigen Steuerinformationen.

Für diesen Aufgabekomplex der Befehlsauflösung muß ein Makroprozessor die folgenden Forderungen erfüllen:

1. Hohe Verarbeitungsgeschwindigkeit
2. adäquate höhere Makro-Sprache, um die Abbildungsfunktion n-tupel $\rightarrow$ Pseudo-Code formulieren zu können,
3. adäquate Syntax für Makro-Aufrufe (Verarbeitung der "intermediate language"),
4. der Makroprozessor kann als Unterprogramm aufgerufen werden.

Inwieweit nun GPSP diesen Forderungen gerecht wird, soll in Kapitel 2 gezeigt werden; dort werden die wesentlichen Eigenschaften von GPSP näher beschrieben. In Kapitel 3 wird anhand von Beispielen demonstriert, wie man mit GPSP ein "high-level-language-code-generation-system" aufbauen kann. Das Kapitel 4 faßt die wesentlichen Erkenntnisse, die beim Einsatz von GPSP gewonnen wurden, zusammen.

2. Der Makroprozessor GPSP

2.∅. Vorbemerkung

Die Hauptmerkmale des Makroprozessors GPSP lassen sich wie folgt zusammenfassen

- GPSP ist "umwelt-unabhängig"
- GPSP verfügt über eine mächtige Makro-Sprache
- GPSP ist schnell

2.1. Die Struktur von GPSP

Die Umweltunabhängigkeit von GPSP wird durch folgende Struktur erreicht:

Bild 2:

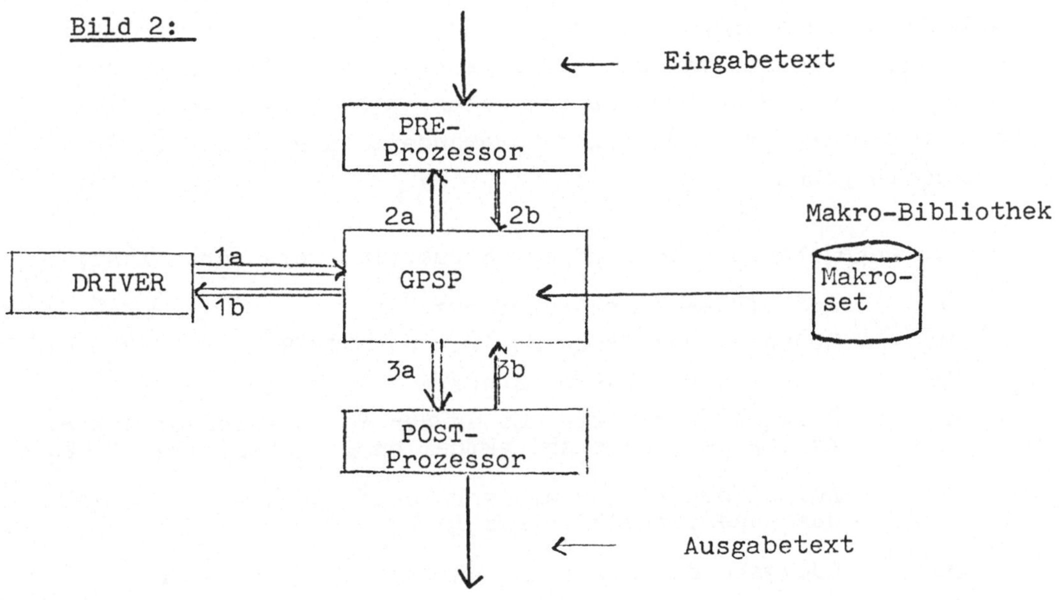

Der Makroprozessor fungiert als Unterprogramm, das von einem Steuerprogramm - hier DRIVER genannt - aufgerufen wird. Das Steuerprogramm übergibt in einer Parameterliste die folgenden Informationen:

- Adresse des PRE-Prozessors
- Adresse des POST-Prozessors
- Name der Makro-Set
- Informationen, die die Speicherorganisation von GPSP festlegen und den Anschluß von Code-Prozeduren ermöglichen (vgl. hierzu die CALL-Anweisung der Makro-Sprache)

Die Ein-/Ausgabeoperationen, d.h. das Lesen des Eingabetextes und die weitere Verarbeitung der vom Makroprozessor generierten Stringterme, werden von den Prozessoren PRE und POST ausgeführt. Diese Prozessoren sind vom Makroprozessor unabhängige Routinen. Der PRE-Prozessor stellt in einem Puffer P_E dem Makroprozessor einen Stringterm des Eingabetextes zur Verfügung. Stellt dieser Stringterm einen Makro-Aufruf dar, so wird die zugehörige Makro-Definition abgearbeitet und evtl. generierte Strings in einem Puffer P_A dem POST-Prozessor übergeben. Alle Stringterme die keine Makroaufrufe sind werden unverändert in P_A dem POST-Prozessor übergeben.

Im oben angegebenen Bild wird der Steuerfluß veranschaulicht:

1a	Aufruf des Makroprozessors
1b	Rückgabe der Steuerung an den DRIVER
2a	Aufruf des PRE-Prozessors
2b	Rückgabe der Steuerung an den Makroprozessor unter Angabe der Länge des aktuellen Eingabestrings in P_E
3a	Aufruf des POST-Prozessors unter Angabe der Länge des generierten Strings in P_A
3b	Rückgabe der Steuerung an den Makroprozessor

Mit dem Aufruf 1a wird die Initialisierungsphase des Makroprozessors eingeleitet. Der Makroprozessor liest die vom DRIVER spezifizierte Menge der Makro-Definitionen (Makro-Set) die die Verarbeitung des Eingabetextes steuern sollen in den vom DRIVER festgelegten Speicherbereich. In dieser Initialisierungsphase wird auch die Makro-Namenstabelle und die Tabelle der globalen Makro-Variablen aufgebaut. Im Anschluß daran geht der Makroprozessor in die Verarbeitungsphase über, es erfolgt der Aufruf 2a.

2.2. Makro-Sprache

Die GPSP-Sprache ist eine Variante der Makro-Sprache des IBM/360 Makro-Assemblers.

In GPSP gibt es drei Datentypen:

arithmethisch (A), Bitstring (B) und Charakterstring (C). Die Arithmetik ist auf integer Arithmetik beschränkt. Den Datentypen entsprechend gibt es A-, B- und C-Variable. Der Gültigkeitsbereich (Nature) der Variablen kann lokal (LCL) oder global (GBL) sein. Neben einfachen Variablen können auch eindimensionale Felder vereinbart werden. Die Erklärung der Variablen erfolgt mit den deklarativen Anweisungen LCLA, LCLB, LCLC, GBLA, GBLB und GBLC.

Neben expliziten Erklärungen ist für einfache Variable auch eine implizite Erklärung durch den Namen der Variablen möglich. Ist z.B. die Variable &BG1Ø nicht explizit erklärt, so wird für die Variable Typ B und Gültigkeitsbereich global angenommen.

Den Variablen werden mit der SET-Anweisung Werte zugewiesen.

Als arithmetische Operatoren fungieren +, -, * und /. Als Stringoperator gibt es den Concatenationoperator und den Substring-Operator. Beide Operatoren können auf Bit und Characterstring angewandt werden. Als Bitstring der Länge 1 werden auch Vergleichsausdrücke gezählt. Vergleichsoperatoren sind EQ, NE, LE, GT,... Ist der Vergleich wahr, dann ist der Wert des Vergleichsausdrucks der Bitstring B'1', ist der Vergleich falsch, dann ist der Wert des Vergleichsausdrucks der Bitstring B'Ø'.

Beispiele:

```
&X      SET     (&X+1)*2
&CLØ    SET     '&CLØ'(1,1).'XXX'
&BLØ    SET     (&X EQ Ø)
```

(In der zweiten SET-Anweisung wird des erste Zeichen von &CLØ mit dem String 'XXX' gekettet und der Variablen &CLØ zugewiesen).

Zur Steuerung des Konstrollflusses gibt es in GPSP als unbedingte Sprunganweisungen die AGO-Anweisungen, als bedingte Sprunganweisungen die AIF-Anweisungen und die "Computed GOTO-Anweisungen".

Beispiel:

```
AGO   .NOTIN
AIF   (&I LE 1Ø).LOOP
GOTO  .L1,.L2,.L3,&ALØ
```

(Ist der Wert von &ALØ 1, 2, bzw. 3 dann wird zu den Marken .L1, .L2, bzw. .L3 verzweigt, ansonsten geht der Kontrollfluß zu der statisch folgenden Anweisung über).

Mit Hilfe der SPLIT-Anweisung kann ein SNOBOL-ähnlicher "pattern-matching"-Prozeß formuliert werden.

Beispiel:

```
SPLIT    &S1=&HEAD,&OP='A',&TAIL
```

Diese SPLIT-Anweisung bedeutet: "Suche in dem String &S1 das erste Auftreten des Zeichens 'A'. Ist der Suchprozeß erfolgreich, d.h. wird 'A' im String &S1 gefunden, dann wird der erste Teil des String S1 der Variablen &HEAD zugewiesen, der Rest des Strings &S1 der Variablen &TAIL und &OP wird der Wert 'A' zugewiesen.

Ist der Suchprozeß nicht erfolgreich, dann wird &HEAD der Wert des Strings &S1, &TAIL der Nullstring und &OP das Zeichen Zwischenraum '␣' zugewiesen.

Die INDEX-Anweisung impliziert wie die SPLIT-Anweisung einen Suchprozeß. Während jedoch bei der SPLIT-Anweisung ein String durchsucht wird, wird bei der INDEX-Anweisung ein Feld durchsucht.

Beispiel:

```
&I          INDEX    &A = 'OMA'
```

&A ist der Name eines Feldes. Der Suchprozeß beginnt beim ersten Element des Feldes. Ist der Wert des Elements &A(m) der String 'OMA' dann wird &I auf m gesetzt und der Suchprozeß ist beendet. Ist der Suchprozeß nicht erfolgreich, dann erhält &I den Wert Ø.

Mit der RETR-Anweisung kann man einen durch absolute Adresse und Länge beschriebenen Kernspeicherinhalt einer GPSP-Variablen zuweisen und mit der STOW-Anweisung kann der Wert einer GPSP-Variablen in angegebene Kernspeicheradressen geschrieben werden.

Beispiel:

```
&CLØ    RETR    &ALØ(2,3)
&CLØ    SET     &CLØ.'1'
&CLØ    STOW    &AL1(Ø,4)
```

Der Wert von &ALØ wird als absolute Speicheradresse interpretiert. In dieser Speicheradresse wird die Distanz 2 addiert. Die an dieser Adresse stehenden 3 Bytes werden der Variablen &CLØ zugewiesen. An diesem String wird durch die folgende SET-Anweisung das Zeichen '1' gekettet. Dieser String wird dann an die durch den Wert von &ALØ gegebenen Kernspeicheradressen geschrieben.

Für Ein-/Ausgabeoperation gibt es in GPSP die <u>FEED-Anweisung</u> und die <u>DELVR-Anweisung</u>.

<u>Beispiel:</u>

```
FEED    &CG1Ø
DELVR   &STRING1
```

Das FEED-Statement fordert vom PRE-Prozessor einen Bytestring an und ordnet diesen der Variablen &CL1Ø zu. Das DELVR-Statement übergibt den String &STRING1 dem POST-Prozessor.

Die <u>CALL-Anweisung</u> dient zum Ansprung von Unterprogrammen die sich im DRIVER befinden.

<u>Beispiel:</u>

```
CALL   &SUBR1Ø (&ALØ,&CG1Ø)
```

&SUBR muß eine A-Variable sein. Der Wert dieser A-Variablen wird als Relativadresse zur Basis CALLBASE verstanden (CALLBASE ist eine Adresse, die GPSP als Parameter vom DRIVER erhält). Unter dieser Adresse ist die Adresse der anzuspringenden Routine gespeichert. Parameter werden "per reference" übergeben,

2.3. Über die Vorübersetzung von Makro-Definitionen

Die hohe Verarbeitungsgeschwindigkeit von GPSP wird durch eine Vorübersetzung der Makro-Set erzielt. GPSP verarbeitet nicht Makro-Definitionen auf der Ebene der Quellensprache (=Makro-Sprache) sondern in einer sogenannten Skeleton-Darstellung. Diese Skeleton-Darstellung gleicht weitgehend dem Befehlsrepertoire einer 1-Adress-Maschine. So wird z.B. der bedingte Sprungbefehl

```
AIF   (&AG1 EQ 1).X
```

in folgende Skeleton-Befehle aufgelöst:

LA &AG1	Lade arithmetisches Register RA mit &AG1
EQ RA,='1'	Vergleiche RA mit 'immediate operand 1' und setzte logisches Register RB auf 'TRUE' bei Gleichheit, sonst auf 'FALSE'
AIF .X	Springe nach X, wenn RB den Wert 'TRUE' hat.

Das interne Format eines Skeleton-Befehls hat folgende Struktur.

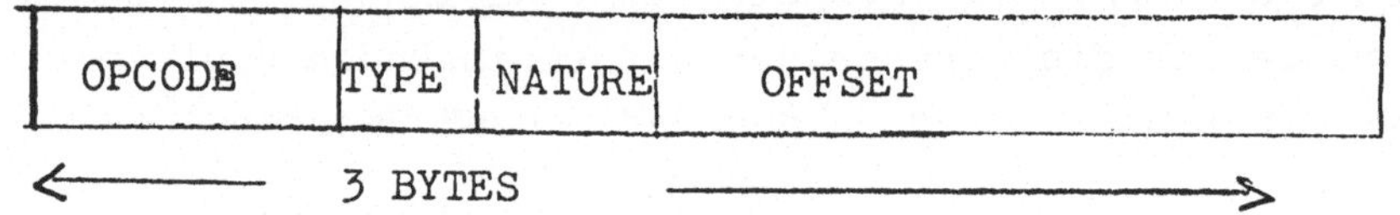

wobei OPCODE der Operations-Code des Befehls
TYPE der Typ (arithmetisch, bit character) des Operanden
NATURE der Gültigkeitsbereich (global, lokal) des Operanden ist und
OFFSET die Relativ-Adresse des Operanden bezogen auf einen durch TYPE und NATURE bestimmten Pegel ist.

Die Übersetzung der Makros in Skeletons wird von einem Übersetzungsprogramm, im folgenden EDITOR genannt, ausgeführt. Die erzeugten Skeletons werden vom EDITOR in der Makrobibliothek hinterlegt.

Eine für den Benutzer sehr wesentliche Funktion des Übersetzers ist der sogenannte "update-mode". Damit ist es möglich einzelne Makro-Definitionen zu ändern, neue Definitionen hinzuzufügen und/ oder alte Definitionen zu eliminieren ohne die gesamte Makro-Set neu zu übersetzen.

Das folgende Bild veranschaulicht das gesamte System GPSP

Bild 3:

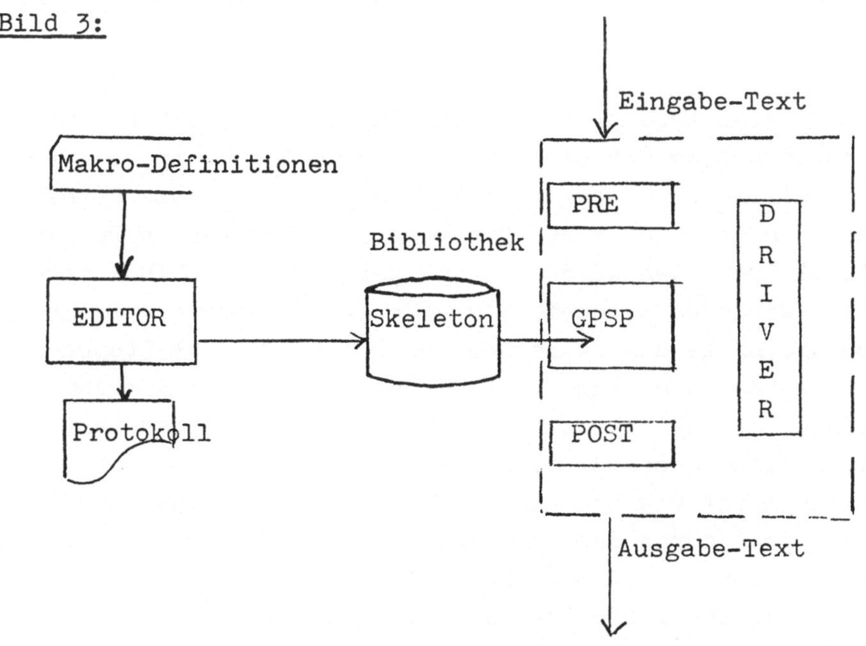

3. Der GPSP-Code-Generator

3.1. Der Eingabe-Text

Die Texteinheit des Eingabestrings ist ein n-tupel

Operator operand1 operand2 ..... operand n

Vom GPSP Code-Generator wird das n-tupel als Makroaufruf interpretiert. Der Operator ist der Name des Makros und die Operanden sind die Argumente des jeweiligen Makroaufrufs. Der PRE-Prozessor hat die Aufabe die Texteinheit "n-tupel" im Eingabe-string zu erkennen, den Operator (=Makronamen) zu lokalisieren und den Makroprozessor GPSP den Stringterm "n-tupel" (=Makroaufruf) zu übergeben.

Die Syntax der n-tupel ist jedoch nicht die klassische Syntax der Makroaufrufe, wo die Liste der Argumente durch ein oder mehrere Zeichen "Zwischenraum" begrenzt ist, und die Argumente selbst durch Kommata getrennt sind. Die n-tupel haben festes Format. Alle n-tupel Operanden werden durch zwei Zeichen (BYTES) dargestellt. Für jedes n-tupel, d.h. für jeden Operator, liegt wiederum die Länge der Operanden fest. Irgendwelche Steuerzeichen wie "Zwischenraum" und/oder Komma sind daher nicht notwendig, um die syntaktischen Einheiten Operator, erster Operand, zweiter Operand,... zu kennzeichnen. Das Format eines n-tupels ist wie bei einem IBM 360 oder Siemens 4004 Maschinenbefehl durch den Operationsteil eindeutig festgelegt. Der Makroprozessor GPSP muß also über ein Sprachelement verfügen das eine Lokalisierung der Argumente des Makroaufrufs über deren Längen ermöglicht. In GPSP ist dieses Sprachelement durch den sog. Substring-Parameter realisiert worden.

Beispiel:

&LENGTH(6,2)

Diese Parameteroperation bedeutet, daß der formale Parameter &LENGTH das 6-te und 7-te Zeichen in einem Makroaufruf repräsentiert.

3.2. Die Code-Generator-Sprache (CGL)

Nachdem der PRE-Prozessor dem Makroprozessor GPSP ein n-tupel als Makroaufruf übergeben hat wird die entsprechende im Skeletonformat vorliegende Makro-Definition abgearbeitet.

Die Makro-Definitionen können als Semantik von PL/I angesehen werden; sie beschreiben die Abbildung der Phrasen-Struktur des PL/I-Programms auf Pseudo-Code. Zur Formulierung der Makro-Definitionen steht die im vorigen Abschnitt besprochene Makro-Sprache zur Verfügung. Die Makro-Sprache GPSP ist jedoch eine "general purpose"-Sprache und enthält keine auf besondere Anforderungen des Code-Generators zugeschnittenen Formulierungsmöglichkeiten.

Eine spezielle Code-Generator-Sprache (CGL) kann aber aus der Makro-Sprache GPSPentwickelt werden, wenn zur GPSP-Sprache neue Sprachelemente "per definition" hinzugefügt werden. Schreibt man die Definitionen der neuen Sprachelemente in der Form von GPSP-Makros so kann man den Makroprozessor GPSP zur Übersetzung von CGL in GPSP verwenden.

Dieses Übersetzungssystem wird bei uns PRE-EDITOR genannt und besteht aus dem Makroprozessor GPSP und der PRE-EDITOR Makro-Set, die Syntax und Semantik der zu GPSP hinzugefügten Sprachelemente in GPSP beschreibt.

Die Semantik der PL/I Phrasen wird in CGL formuliert. Der PRE-EDITOR übesetzt die CGL-Programme in GPSP-Makro-Definitionen und diese werden schließlich mit Hilfe des EDITOR's in Skeletons übersetzt.

Das folgende Bild soll diesen Zusammenhang veranschaulichen:

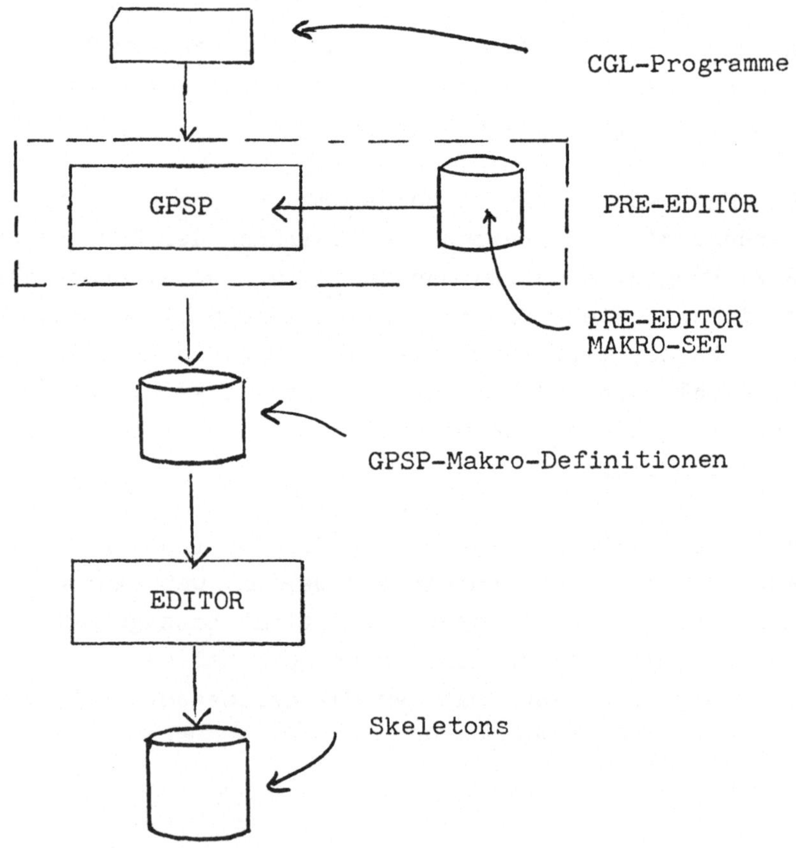

Die in Skeletònformat übersetzten Makro-Definitionen bilden mit dem Makroprozessor GPSP und einem speziellen DRIVER, PRE- und POST-Prozessor den PL/I Code-Generator.

Es soll nun etwas näher auf CGL eingegangen werden. Eine vollständige Syntax kann zum augenblicklichen Zeitpunkt noch nicht angegeben werden, da immer noch neue Sprachelemente hinzukommen, die es dem Programmierer ermöglichen, die Befehlsauflösung noch einfacher und klarer zu formulieren. Es wäre auch nicht sinnvoll, hier zu versuchen, ein möglichst vollständiges Bild des gerade aktuellen Sprachumfangs von CGL zu vermitteln, da sehr viele Sprachelemente nur bei Kenntnis des Innenlebens des Compilers und des "object layouts" verstanden werden können. Anhand eines konkreten Beispiels sollen jedoch einige typische Elemente von CGL erläutert werden.

Die Problemstellung lautet: Es ist eine Pseudo-Instruktion zu erzeugen die einen 4-BYTE langen Eintrag der Symboltabelle in ein symbolisches Register lädt. Der Eintrag hat die Distanzadresse 16 zu einer Symboltabellenreferenz welche durch den formalen Parameter &P1 repräsentiert wird.

In CGL kann dieser Sachverhalt wie folgt formuliert werden:

```
SYMREG   &REG1Ø (FIXED)
CODE     L  &REG1Ø,&P1+16
```

Symbolische Register werden in CGL mit Hilfe der SYMREG-Anweisung erklärt. Der Typ des symbolischen Registers kann FIXED oder FLOAT sein. Es können Registerpaare definiert werden und auch symbolische Register fest mit physikalischen Registern verknüpft werden.

```
E.g.            SYMREG  &REG1  (FIXED, PAIR (&REG2,EO))
                SYMREG  &REG14 (FIXED,ABS (14))
```

Durch diese Anweisung werden ®1 und ®2 als gerade-ungerades symbolisches Registerpaare und ®14 als Name des physikalischen Registers 14 erklärt.

Der PRE-EDITOR übersetzt die SYMREG-Anweisung in eine GPSP CALL-Anweisung. Mit der CALL-Anweisung wird eine DRIVER-Routine angesprungen, die für die Verwaltung der symbolischen Register zuständig ist. Der in CGL zum symbolischen Register erklärten GPSP Variablen (Typ: C, Nature:LCL) wird durch diese Routine der folgende Wert zugewiesen:

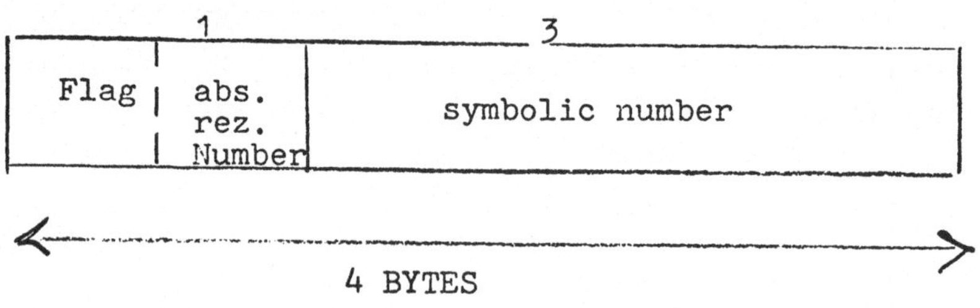

Flag zeigt an ob das Register zu einem Registerpaar gehört, ob das Register das erste Register eines Registerpaares ist, ob ein Register ein physikalisches Register ist. Ist das Register ein physikalisches Register so enthalten Bit 5-8 die Nummer des physikalischen Registers. Die Nummer des symbolischen Registers ist für zwei Register eines Registerpaares die gleiche und ist für ein gerade - ungerades Registerpaar immer gerade.

Zur Erzeugung von Pseudo-Code steht in CGL die CODE-Anweisung zur Verfügung. Diese Pseudo-Instruktion wird in der CODE-Anweisung in einem Assembler-ähnlichen Format angegeben. Die folgende Grammatik beschreibt die Syntax einer Klasse von Pseudo-Instruktionen der auch die oben angegebenen Pseudo-Instruktion L angehört.

<RX1-format> ::= <opname> <blanks>
{ <register>, <stref>[+<offset>] [(<index>)]
| <register>, <offset>([<index>,] <base>)
| <register>, <symb. address> }

mit

<index> , <base> , <register>::= <symb.reg.> | <A-const>

<stref> ::= <formal parameter> | <C-Variable>

<offset> ::= <A-Variable> | <A-Const>

<symb.addr.> ::= LAST/NEXT/TODBAS1/TOENTRY/ADF2/...

Als Register können symbolische Register angegeben werden, d.h. Variable die in einer CGL SYMREG-Anweisung als symbolische Register erklärt worden sind oder eine dezimale Konstante die direkt ein physikalisches Register bezeichnet.

Die Symboltabellenreferenz (stref) wird im allgemeinen ein formaler Parameter sein der einen n-tupel Operand des Eingabestrings repräsentiert. Es kann aber auch eine C-Variable eine Symbo tabellenreferenz enthalten. Symboltabellenreferenzen sind wie symbolische Register 4 BYTES lang und bestehen aus einer Blocknummer und einem Index.

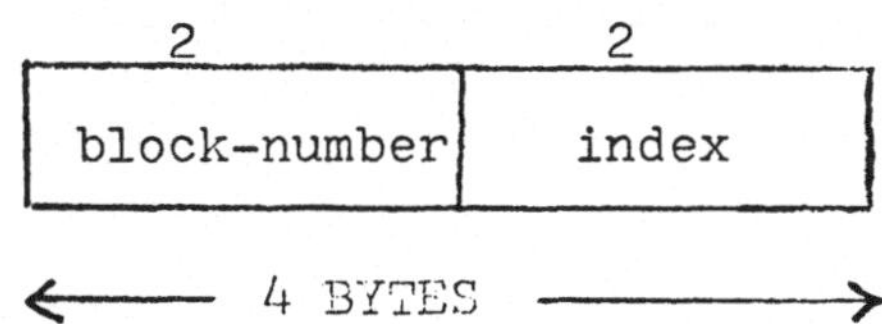

Symbolische Adressen repräsentieren Konstante deren Wert i.a. das Format

<offset> (<base>)

hat. So stellt etwa ADF2 eine mnemotechnische Bezeichnung für 88(13) dar.

Der PRE-EDITOR hat nun die Aufgabe, den Operanden einer CODE-Anweisung entsprechend der Syntax der Pseudo-Instruktionen zu analysieren, einen Concatenations-Ausdruck aufzubauen dessen Auswertung das interne Format der Pseudo-Instruktion ergibt und eine Ausgabe-Anweisung zu erzeugen, welche dann diesen Bytestring dem POST-Prozessor des Code-Generators übergibt, d.h. der GPSP-EDITOR bildet die CGL CODE-Anweisung auf eine GPSP-SET-Anweisung und eine DELVR-Anweisung ab.

Das interne Format der hier beschriebenen RX1-Pseudo-Instruktion (L, ST,....) sieht wie folgt aus:

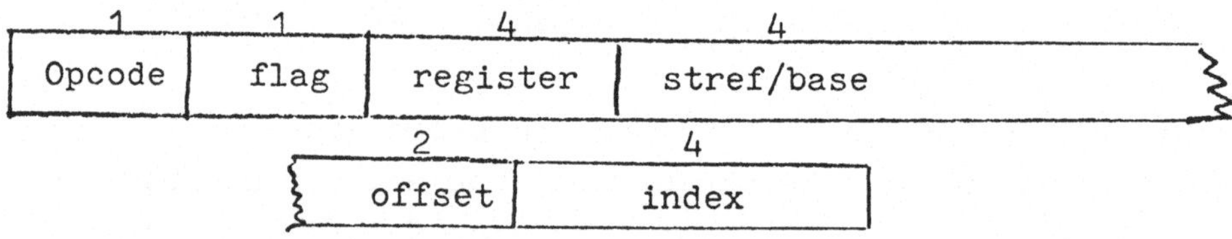

Flag zeigt an ob der zweite Operand eine Symboltabellenreferenz oder ein Basisregister ist, ob offset angegeben ist, ob ein Indexregister angegeben ist. Die Länge dieser Pseudo-Instruktion ist also 16 Bytes, wenn sowohl offset und Index angegeben ist und entsprechend kürzer, wenn offset und/oder Index nicht spezifiziert sind.

4. Zusammenfassung

Es wurde ein universeller Makroprozessor vorgestellt, der über eine Reihe von Eigenschaften verfügt, die ihn zu einem mächtigen Werkzeug für den Übersetzerbau machen. Anhand von Beispielen wurde demonstriert, wie man mit GPSP eine höhere Code-Erzeugungssprache definieren kann.

Die praktische Anwendbarkeit der oben ausgeführten Code-Erzeugungs-Technik basiert im wesentlichen auf der Verarbeitungsgeschwindigkeit des Interpreters. Durch die Vorübersetzung (EDITOR) der Makros konnte eine Verarbeitungsgeschwindigkeit des Interpreters erreicht werden, die ungefähr das 20-fache des Makroprozessors des 4004-Assemblers beträgt.

Die wesentlichen Vorteile der mit GPSP realisierten Code-Erzeugungstechnik lassen sich wie folgt zusammenfassen:

a) Erweiterbarkeit

Der Code-Generator ist gegenüber Sprachmodifikationen oder Erweiterungen der Quellensprache weitgehend unabhängig; neue Anweisungen bzw. Sprachelemente oder Änderungen der Semantik bestehender syntaktischer Kategorie können durch Hinzufügen neuer Makros und/oder Änderungen an vorhandenen Makros abgefangen werden. Eingriffe in den Übersetzer selbst sind nicht notwendig!

b) Austestbarkeit

Die Erfahrung zeigt, daß das Austesten des Genratorteils eines Übersetzers mit einem großen Aufwand verbunden ist. Mit der oben eingeführten Technik gewinnt der Compiler-Schreiber zwei entscheidende Vorteile. Die Befehlsauflösungs-

Routinen, d.h. die Abbildungsfunktionen von n-tupel auf Pseudo-Code können in einer höheren Programmiersprache problemorientiert formuliert werden, und der zu erzeugende Code läßt sich in einer symbolischen Form notieren. Damit wird sowohl der Übersetzer als auch das generierte Objekt (Objektprogramm) relativ leicht austestbar.

RTS - EINE SPRACHE ZUR BESCHREIBUNG VON REGISTERNETZEN

von H. Hoehne

1. Einleitung

Das Problem, einen Automaten zu konstruieren, der in der Lage ist, sich oder seinesgleichen zu reproduzieren, hat auf dem Gebiet der automatischen Konstruktion von Computern durch Computer schon heute reale technisch-wissenschaftliche Bedeutung. Allerdings handelt es sich hierbei um Teillösungen des obigen Problems, da man im rechnergestützten Entwurfsprozeß von Rechnern noch keineswegs ohne menschliche Intervention auskommt, ja sogar wesentliche Entwurfsaufgaben nach wie vor von der Person des Konstrukteurs gelöst werden müssen. Verständigungsmittel zwischen Konstrukteur und entwerfendem Computer sind auf allen Stufen des Entwurfsprozesses formale Sprachen. Sie dienen zur Dokumentation der jeweiligen Entwurfsstufe einerseits und zur Steuerung der automatisierten Entwurfsvorgänge andererseits.

1.1. Einsatz von Registertransfersprachen zur Entwurfsdokumentation

Es erscheint sinnvoll, die verschiedenen Entwurfsstufen von Computern nach ihrem Detailierungsgrad der Hardwarebeschreibung voneinander zu unterscheiden (Bild 1.1). Eine dieser Stufen ist die der Registernetze, deren Dokumentationssprachen als Registertransfersprachen bezeichnet werden. Charakteristisch für diese Entwurfsstufe ist, daß in ihr sämtliche Informationsspeicher (Register) und Informationswege (Verknüpfungsnetze) festgelegt werden - nicht jedoch deren innerer Aufbau.

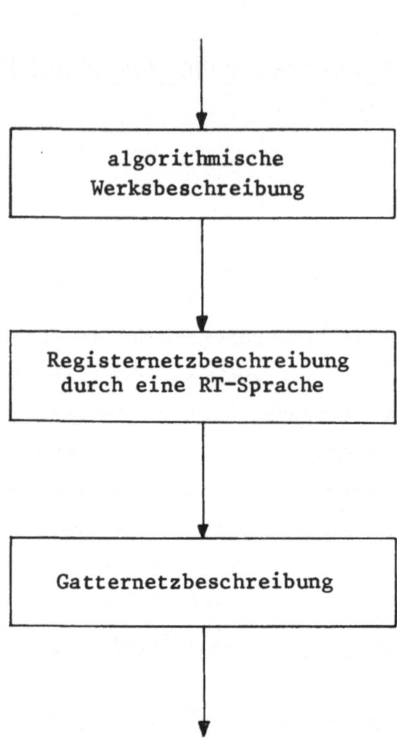

Bild 1.1: Entwurfsstufen eines Computers

Die typische Grundoperation des Informationstransportes von mehreren Quellregistern aus über ein Boole'sches Verknüpfungsnetz in ein Zielregister und dies in Abhängigkeit von einer Bedingung wird als Registertransfer bezeichnet (Bild 1.2). (Der Registertransfer entspricht der Ergibtanweisung in herkömmlichen, algorithmischen Programmiersprachen.)

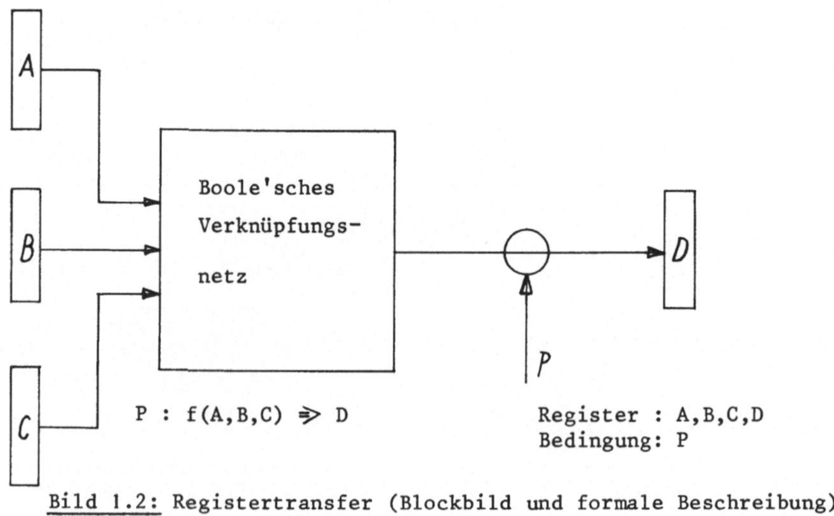

Bild 1.2: Registertransfer (Blockbild und formale Beschreibung)

Abgrenzen läßt sich eine Registernetzbeschreibung nach "oben" von einer rein algorithmischen Beschreibung ganzer Werke eines Computers und nach "unten" von der Gatternetzbeschreibung, in der jeder im Schaltwerk vorhandene, logische Baustein mit seien Verbindungen zu anderen Bausteinen explizit ausgewiesen wird.

1.2. Registernetzsimulationen

Neben der reinen Dokumentation einer Entwurfsstufe besteht das Bedürfnis, die formalen Beschreibungen eines Schaltwerks auf jeder Entwurfsstufe automatischen Kontrollen zu unterwerfen. Es lassen sich derartige Kontrollverfahren in statische und in dynamische Verfahren unterteilen, wobei unter dynamischen solche Verfahren zu verstehen sind, die das Durchspielen des Entwurfs mit speziellen Testwerten erfordern.

Die Simulation einer Entwurfsstufe ist folglich notwendig zur Durchführung dynamischer Kontrollen eines Schaltwerkes. Als Ausgangspunkt für eine derartige Simulation ist eine formale Beschreibung des Entwurfs auf dieser Stufe zwar notwendig, jedoch nicht hinreichend. Zur Simulation wird über die formale Darstellung des Simulationsobjekts hinaus noch eine Simulationssteuersprache für folgende Aufgaben benötigt:

1.) Ablaufsteuerung der Simulation

2.) Verkehr des Schaltwerkes mit der Umwelt

3.) Steuerung der Simulationsergebnisausgabe

4.) automatischer Vergleich der Simulationsergebnisse mit den Ergebnissen einer algorithmischen Beschreibung des Schaltwerks.

1.3. Statische Kontrollverfahren von Registernetzen

Wie unter 1.2 bereits erwähnt, kann die formale Beschreibung eines Registernetzes auch Objekt statischer Kontrollverfahren sein, d.h. Objekt von Kontrollverfahren, die Aussagen über die Korrektheit des Entwurfs allgemein, also ohne Rücksicht auf spezielle Testwerte ermöglichen.

Derartige Verfahren beginnen bei den einfachen, kontextfreien Syntaxkontrollen der RT-Beschreibung und lassen sich ausdehnen über die Anwendung kontextsensitiver Regeln bis hin zu automatisierten Beweisverfahren.

Soweit möglich ist grundsätzlich den statischen Kontrollverfahren der Vorzug vor dynamischen Verfahren zu geben, da sich nur mit ihnen allgemeine Korrektheitsaussagen machen lassen. Da es bislang jedoch auf der Registernetzebene noch nicht gelungen ist, statische Kontrollverfahren zu entwickeln, die alle Fehlermöglichkeiten überdecken, wird man in praxi immer eine Kombination beider Verfahren wählen müssen.

1.4. Äquivalenztransformationen

Mittels einer RT-Sprache sind im allgemeinen verschiedene Beschreibungsformen desselben Registernetzes möglich, die sich durch den Grad der Isomorphie zur Hardware voneinander unterscheiden. Soweit sich kanonische Transformationsregeln für den Übergang von einer Beschreibungsform zu einer anderen angeben lassen, steht einer Automatisierung derartiger Äquivalenztransformationen nichts im Wege. Die automatisierte Anwendung von Äquivalenztransformationen läßt sich auch auf Beschreibungsformen ausdehnen, die sich außerhalb der Registernetzstufe befinden. So sind z.B. aus Registertransferanweisungen automatisch die entsprechenden Flipflopansteurungsgleichungen für das Transferziel abgeleitet worden.

1.5. Einsatz von RT-Sprachen in der Lehre

Als formales Beschreibungsmittel in Lehrveranstaltungen über Rechnerstrukturen ist die Verwendung einer Registertransfersprache nahezu unumgänglich. Aus diesem Bedürfnis heraus ist auch die überwiegende Zahl der existenten RT-Sprachen an Hochschulen entstanden.

Die Motivation für die Entwicklung spezieller Registertransfersprachen dürfte ausreichend deutlich geworden sein. Im folgenden werden der Stand der Technik, der Werdegang, die Sprachphilosophie und die wesentlichen Aspekte einer Registertransfersprache vorgestellt.

2. Stand der Technik

Um den prinzipiellen Unterschied zwischen Gatternetzsprachen und Registertranssprachen noch deutlicher hervorzuheben, soll hier zunächst kurz auf die Gatternetzsprachen eingegangen werden.

2.1. Gatternetzsprachen

Wesentliches Merkmal derartiger Sprachen ist, daß sie Hardware-Bauelement-orientiert sind [1 bis 9]. Ihren Namen haben sie daher, daß das am häufigsten verwendete Bauelement das logische Gatter ist. Ein Schaltwerk stellt sich als Netz aus derartigen Bauelementen (Bild 2.1) dar bzw. mathematisch als gerichteter Graph (Bild 2.2), dessen Knoten die Bauelemente und dessen Kanten die Leitungszüge zwischen den Bauelementen sind, bzw. softwaremäßig als Plex, (Bild 2.3), d.h. als verallgemeinerte Listenstruktur mit vielfach verzweigenden Listenelementen.

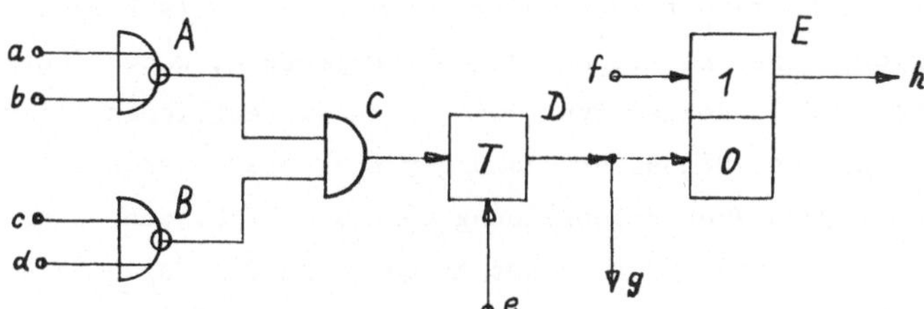

Bild 2.1: Beispiel eines Ausschnittes aus einem Gatternetz

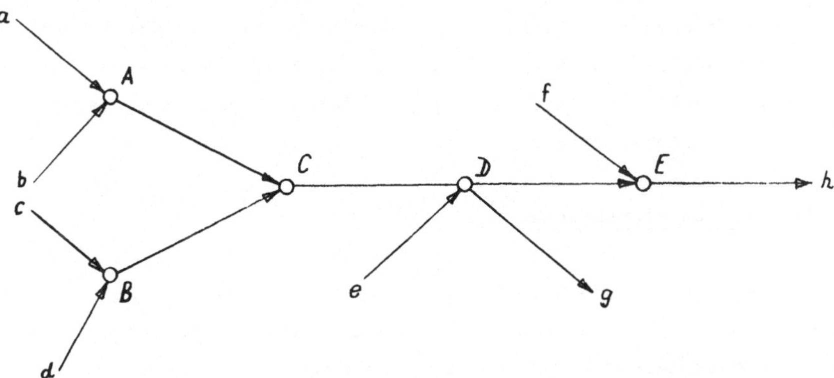

Bild 2.2: Darstellung eines Gatternetzes als gerichteter Graph

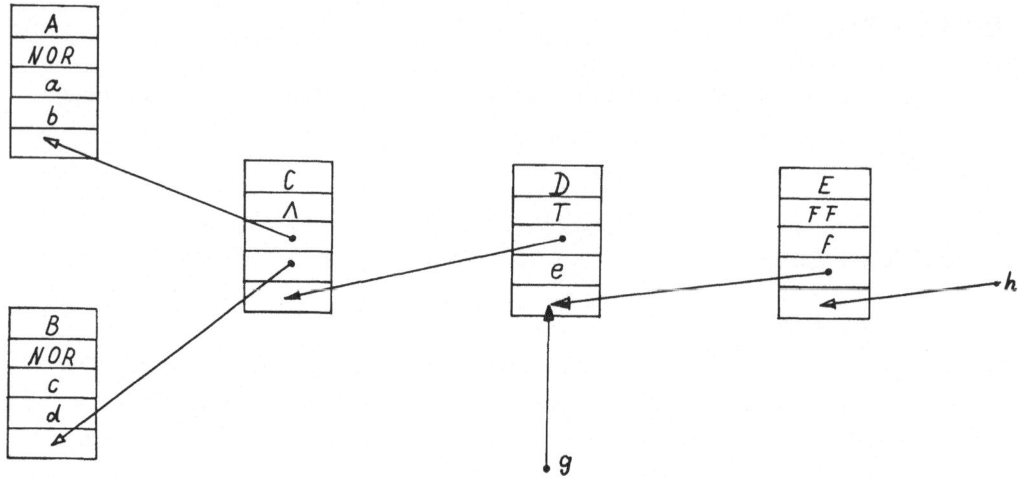

Bild 2.3: Darstellung eines Gatternetzes als Plex

Es liegt nun nahe - und dieser Weg wird auch bei den meisten Gatternetzsprachen beschrittten - , derartige Gatternetze knotenorientiert, d.h. als Plex zu beschreiben. Dies entspricht einer Auflistung aller Bauelemente, wobei jedes mit einem Namen versehen und in seinem Typ sowie seinen wesentlichen Eigenschaften wie Zahl der Eingänge, Signalverzögerungen etc. charakterisiert wird. Weiterhin werden in jeder Bauelementbeschreibung noch die Verbindungen entweder seiner Eingänge zu Ausgängen oder seiner Ausgänge zu Eingängen anderer Bauelemente oder sogar beide aufgeführt, wobei die letzte Möglichkeit redundant ist und zu Kontrollzwecken dient.

Der Vorteil einer solchen Plexbeschreibung liegt einerseits in der Isomorphie zur Hardware und andererseits in der einfachen Umsetzbarkeit in eine simulier- und prüfbare Datenstruktur im Entwurfscomputer. Der Umsetzalgorithmus ist nämlich im Prinzip ein Assemblierprozeß.

2.2. Erste Registertransfersprachen

Wohl die erste Registertransfersprache wurde von I.S. Reed entwickelt [1o bis 12], von dem auch die Grundidee stammt, alle Vorgänge in (taktgesteuerten) Schaltwerken als Informationstransporte von Quellregistern aus in Zielregister, eben als Registertransfers zu beschreiben. In der Reed'schen RT-Sprache werden noch Vorgänge im Kontrollteil und im Operationsteil eines Schaltwerks einheitlich, d.h. mit denselben sprachlichen Mittel beschrieben.

Doch schon die von Y. Chu entwickelte Sprache CDL [13] kennt den Unterschied zwischen Transfers im Operationsteil und solchen im Kontrollteil, die als Sprünge und Tue-Anweisungen auftreten. Auch ist bereits im CDL eine Unterteilung des Schaltwerkes in Sequenzen möglich .

(Mit der Iverson-Language sind zwar ebenfalls umfangreiche Registernetze beschrieben worden [14-17] ; doch ist die Zahl der in dieser Sprache verwendeten Operationen ohne klar definierbares Hardware-Äquivalent so groß, daß man die Iverson-Language nicht mehr zu den Registertransfersprachen zählen kann, sondern sie zu den algorithmischen Beschreibungssprachen rechnen muß.)

2.3. LOTIS und DDL

Als zwei Vertreter von Registertransfersprachen mit besonders umfangreichen sprachlichen Möglichkeiten seien hier LOTIS [18] und DDL [19] hervorgehoben. Beide sehen die prinzipielle Trennung von Operations- und Kontrollteil eines Schaltwerks vor, indem sie spezielle Ablaufsteuerungsbefehle zur Verfügung stellen. Weiterhin ist es mit ihnen möglich, ein Schaltwerk nicht nur in Sequenzen, d.h. in Teilgraphen eines zusammenhängenden Zustandsgraphen, sondern auch in voneinander unabhängige Werke, d.h. in selbständige Unterautomaten, aufzuteilen. Diese Zerlegung führt bei parallel und asynchron zueinander arbeitenden Unterautomaten zu einer erheblichen Reduzierung der Zustandszahl und verringert durch die gewonnene Modularität die Fehlerhäufigkeit im Entwurfsprozeß großer Registernetze. In beiden RT-Sprachen ist ferner die Möglichkeit vorgesehen, einzelne Werke eines Rechnerentwurfs aus der strukturellen RT-Beschreibung herauszunehmen, und entweder nur durch einen Kommentar zu charakterisieren oder durch eine rein funktionelle Beschreibung u.U. mittels einer algorithmischen Programmiersprache festzulegen. Beide Sprachen gestatten es auch, asynchrone Schaltwerke, die allerdings Flipflopregister im Rückkoppelungszweig enthalten müssen, darzustellen.

Im Gegensatz zu Software-Programmen, bei denen es in der Zeitdimension im allgemeinen nur auf die Topologie ankommt, kann man beim Entwurf von Schaltwerken nicht auf zeitliche Metrik verzichten.

Diesem Bedürfnis wird besonders in LOTIS dadurch Rechnung getragen, daß die Syntax Möglichkeiten vorsieht, einzelnen Operationen oder auch Operationsgruppen Signallaufzeiten zuzuordnen. In DDL hingegen können nur Takte vereinbart, und es kann ein spezielles Verzögerungselement benutzt werden, das etwa den Charakter eines monostabilen Kippschalters hat.

2.4. Entwicklung von RTS

Ende 1967 wurde am Institut für Nachrichtenverabeitung der Technischen Hochschule Darmstadt RTS I für den Einsatz in der von Prof. Piloty und seinen Assistenten durchgeführten Lehrveranstaltung "Schaltwerktheorie" konzipiert und bis Mitte 1969 zu seiner endgültigen Form weiterentwickelt [2o]. Pate gestanden haben bei dieser Entwicklung Reeds Registertransfersprache und Chus CDL.

Die Syntax von RTS I wurde bewußt einfach gehalten, damit sie von den Studenten in etwa einem Viertelsemester im Rahmen der Lehrveranstaltung "Schaltwerktheorie" erlernbar ist. (Dieses Ziel ist leider noch nicht befriedigend erreicht worden - nicht zuletzt, weil nicht bei allen Teilnehmern Programmierkenntnisse vorausgesetzt werden können.)

Als einzige ausführbare Anweisung ist in RTS I der Transfer vorgesehen, so daß keine syntaktische Trennung von Kontroll- und Operationsteil im Schaltwerk möglich ist. Außerdem wurde im RTS I auf eine Blockstruktur verzichtet; d.h. ein RTS I - Programm besteht aus nur einem Deklarations- und einem Ausführungsteil.

Um für eine noch aufzustellende Lehrveranstaltung "Rechnerstrukturen" ein geeignetes, formales Ausdrucksmittel zur Verfügung zu haben und im Hinblick auf den möglichen industriellen Einsatz in der Rechnerentwicklung wurde im Rahmen einer Studienarbeit die erste Version der RT-Sprache, RTS II , festgelegt [21-23] , die etwa die Ausdrucksmöglichkeit von LOTIS und DDL bietet und darüberhinaus eine bessere Erfassung der Zeitverhältnisse in einem Registernetz ermöglicht. RTS II ist außerdem im wesentlichen aufwärtskompatibel zu RTS I.

3. Beschreibung von synchronen Einphasentaktsystemen in RTS

Unter synchronen Einphasentaktsystemen sollen Registernetze verstanden werden, in denen Übertragungsoperationen nur zu bestimmten, periodisch wiederkehrenden Zeitpunkten stattfinden können, die durch ein entsprechendes Signal, den Takt, festgelegt werden. Da in derartigen Systemen die Einhaltung der Zeitbedingungen leicht überprüft werden kann, wird auf die Einführung einer zeitlichen Metrik in der Beschreibung der Einphasentaktsysteme zunächst verzichtet.

3.1. Sprachphiliosophie von RTS für Einphasentaktsysteme

Wie bereits unter 2.2. anegedeutet ist es beim Entwurf einer RT-Sprache sehr wesentlich, auf eine klare Trennung zwischen Operationen und Objekten, denen ein wohldefiniertes Hardwareäquivalent entspricht, sogenannten "harten" Sprachelementen, und solchen, bei denen dies nicht der Fall ist, sogenannten "weichen" Sprachelementen zu unterscheiden. Mit der Einführung "weicher" Sprachelemente in eine RT-Sprache sollte sparsam umgegangen werden, damit diese nicht den Charakter einer Strukturbeschreibungssprache verliert. Bei den "harten" Sprachelementen besteht hingegen die Gefahr, daß man sich durch zu starke Spezialisierung und einseitige Auswahl auf eine bestimmte Technologie festgelegt und damit den Anwendungsbereich der Sprache einschränkt.

Im Gegensatz zu algorithmischen Programmiersprachen, in denen - bis auf ALGOL 68 - von der Sequentailität der Anweisungen ausgegangen wird und die Parallelität von Anweisungen - wenn überhaupt - nur durch besondere Maßnahmen des Programmierers erreicht werden kann, ist in RTS das Grundkonzept die potentielle Parallelität aller Operationen, die - soweit unerwünscht - durch zusätzliche Bedingungen und Marken eingeschränkt werden muß. Wie in Programmiersprachen das Verhalten von Computern im Maschinencode so spiegelt sich in RT-Sprachen die innere Parallelarbeit von Schaltwerken wieder. Sieht man von dem Strukturbeschreibungsaspekt jeder RT-Sprache ab, so kann man RTS auch als "ereignisorientiert" im Gegensatz zu "ablauforientiert" bezeichnen, wobei das Zutreffen einer einschränkenden Bedingung als "Ereignis" gesehen wird.

3.2. Verknüpfungsnetze in RTS

Da die eigentliche Informationsverarbeitung von Schaltwerken in den Verknüpfungsnetzen stattfindet, die Register hingegen nur zur Informationsspeicherung dienen, sollen hier zuerst die verschiedenen Darstellungsformen von Verknüpfungsnetzen in RTS behandelt werden.

Unter der Annahme, daß die Überprüfung der Signallaufzeiten in Verknüpfungsnetzen bei Einphasentaktsystemen nicht auf der Registernetzebene stattfindet, ist eine gatterisomorphe Beschreibung von Verknüpfungsnetzen im allgemeinen zu aufwendig und reicht eine funktionelle Beschreibung derselben aus. Dies drückt sich nicht nur im Fehlen jeglicher Vereinbarungsmöglichkeiten für bestimmte Gattertypen, sondern auch in der Zulässigkeit von Verknüpfungsoperationen mit beliebiger Operandenzahl und von Makroverknüpfungsoperationen in RTS aus. Benutzt wird in RTS als Beschreibungsmittel für Verknüpfungsnetze eine vektorielle Boole'sche Algebra, in der jedes "Coercing", d.h. automatische Anpassung von Operanden verschiedener Binärstellenzahl aneinander, verboten ist. Neben den 3 Grundverknüpfungen des Boole'schen Verbandes, $\wedge$ (UND) , $\vee$ (ODER) und ' (NEGATION), stehen als syntaktischer Komfort noch weitere Verknüpfungen zur Verfügung (z.B. $\oplus$(EXOR), $\subset$ (Implikation) und NAND).

(Im Rahmen dieser Arbeit wird zwar auf das Eingehen auf syntaktische Details weitergehend verzichtet; eine Besonderheit von RTS sei hier jedoch erwähnt: Es wurde auf die Einführung jeglicher Operatorprioritäten verzichtet und dabei ein etwas erhöhter Klammerungsbedarf bewußt in Kauf genommen). Dyadische Operatoren, für die das Assoziativgesetz Gültigkeit hat, dürfen in RTS auch polyadisch

z.B. $A \wedge B \wedge C \wedge D$

und monadisch verwendet werden; sie haben im 2. Fall eine Dimensionsreduktion des Ergebnisses gegenüber dem Operanden zur Folge:

z.B. $(vA) = A_1 vA_2 vA_3 \ldots\ldots vA_n$

Zu diesen Boole'schen Verknüpfungsoperatoren treten noch die oben erwähnten Makroverknüpfungsoperationen hinzu, von denen einige für in praxi auftretende Verknüpfungsnetze, wie Addier- und Vergleichnetze, in RTS bereits vordefiniert wurden:

z.B. ADD(A,B)

Da sie syntaktisch in derselben Weise wie in algorithmischen Programmiersprachen die Funktionsprozeduren aufgerufen werden, haben sie die Bezeichnung "RTS-Funktionen" erhalten.

Über diese "harten" Beschreibungsmittel für V-Netze hinaus werden in RTS noch einige "weiche " Mittel wie die Konkatenation von mehreren Operanden:

z.B. $\{A,B,C,D\} = A \circ B \circ C \circ D$

die Verkürzung eines Operanden (bei selektiver Stellenauswahl):

z.B. $A[1, 3:5] = \{A_1, A_3, A_4, A_5\}$

und die Dimensionserhöhung (Potenzierung) "quer" zur Wortrichtung eines Operanden:

z.B. FAE(A,3) = $\{A,A,A\}$

Auch die Vereinbarungmöglichkeit von neuen Makroverknüpfungsoperationen ist zu den "weichen" Beschreibungsmitteln zu zählen, da mit einer Makrovereinbarung noch nicht die Existenz eines bestimmten Verknüpfungsnetzes ausgedrückt wird. Es ist im Gegenteil mittels einer Vereinbarung sogar möglich, eine ganze Klasse von Verknüpfungsnetzen unter einem Namen zusammenzufassen (z.B. wenn Operanden veriábler Stellenzahl in der Vereinbarung zugelassen werden). Erst der bereits oben erwähnte Aufruf einer Makrooperation bedeutet die Spezifikation eines ganz bestimmten Verknüpfungsnetzes.

3.3. Register, Boole'sche Konstante, Anschlüsse und Indizes

Die unter 3.2 mehrfach angesprochenen Operanden von Boole'schen Verknüpfungsoperationen sind neben geklammerten Boole'schen Ausdrücken in erster Linie Register und Boole'sche Konstante:

z.B. $7B5 = \{o,o,1,1,1\}$

(7 = Wert der B-Konstante, 5 = Binärstellenzahl)

Darüberhinaus besteht in RTS die Möglichkeit, sogenannte Anschlußvariablen zu vereinbaren, deren Hardwareäquivalent ein Anschlußpunkt ohne Speichereigenschaft ist. Mit Werten versorgt werden Anschlußvariable entweder ständig von einem bestimmten Verknüpfungsnetz (ständige Durchschaltung auf einen Anschluß) oder temporär (Durchschaltung auf einen Anschluß) - gegebenenfalls zu verschiedenen Zeitpunkten auch von verschiedenen Verknüpfungsnetzen. Eine besondere Sorte von Anschlüssen wird aus der Schaltwerksumgebung versorgt (Eingangsanschlüsse).

Als "weiche" Operanden stehen in RTS Indizes zur Verfügung. Sie werden als Konstante in der Verkürzungsoperation (Teilregister und -anschluß in RTS):

z.B. $X[0,2:4,7] = \{X_o,X_2,X_3,X_4,X_7\}$

und in einigen Makrooperationen zur genaueren Auswahl einer Operation aus einer ganzen Klasse von Operationen:

z.B. $MINT(X,5)=X'_1 \wedge X'_2 \wedge X'_3 \wedge \dots \wedge X'_{n-3} \wedge X_{n-2} \wedge X'_{n-1} \wedge X_n$

sowie als Variable bei der Definition einer räumlichen Iteration, z.B. in der Deklaration von Makrooperationen, benötigt.

3.4. Übertragungsanweisungen

Prinzipiell wäre es möglich - in RTS I geschieht dies auch so -, Registernetze ausschließlich mit Transferanweisungen als einziger Übertragungsanweisung und einigen ständig durchgeschalteten Anschlüssen, um die gemeinsame Benutzung von Verknüpfungsnetzen ausdrücken zu können, zu beschreiben. In einer derartigen RT-Sprache werden auch Informationsverarbeitungen innerhalb eines Registers, wie z.B. Zählen oder zyklisches Shiften, als Informationstransporte beschrieben:

z.B. ZAUF(Z) ⇛Z (entspricht : Z:=Z+1)
oder RVZ (A) ⇛A (entspricht: $\{A_n, A_1, A_2, \ldots\ldots, A_{n-1}\} \Rightarrow A$)

Mit Hilfe der (temporären) Durchschaltung jedoch lassen sich einige häufig in Registernetzen auftretende Konstellationen wesentlich eleganter formulieren - insbesondere z.B. das "bus-Sharing", d.h. die gemeinsame Benutzung eines Übertragungsweges durch verschiedene Transfers.

Auch die Beschreibung von registerinternen Informationsverarbeitungen mittels Transferanweisungen erscheint etwas gewaltsam, und außerdem wird dadurch als unerwünschter Nebeneffekt die Möglichkeit eröffnet, die eigentlich nur zu einem ganz bestimmten Zweck definierten Makrooperationen, ZAUF, RVZ usw. in einem nicht vorgesehenen Kontext zu verwenden:

z.B. ZAUF(Z)$\vee$B ⇛C

Aus diesem Grunde wurden in RTS II zur Darstellung registerinterner Informationsverarbeitungen die Registeroperationen eingeführt:

z.B. <u>zauf</u>(Z).

3.5. Schritte und bedingte Anweisungen, Verbundanweisungen

Übertragungsanweisungen, die beim Zutreffen einer gemeinsamen Bedingung parallel, d.h. gleichzeitig auszuführen sind, können in RTS zu einem Schritt (Phase) zusammengefaßt werden:

z.B. SB:T1;T2;D1;D2.

(SB = Schrittbedingung; T1,T2 = Transferanweisungen; D1, D2 = Durchschaltungen).

In diesem Zusammenhang muß noch auf einen Unterschied in der Semantik von Transfers und Durchschaltungen hingewiesen werden: Bei Transfers wird die über den Informationsübertragungsweg (Transferquelle = "linke Seite" des Transfers) bereitgestellte Information durch das eintreffende Taktsignal einmalig in das Zielregister (Transferziel = "rechte Seite" des Transfers) übernommen. Bei der Durchschaltung hingegen hat das Durchschaltungsziel (Anschluß) solange den Wert der Durchschaltungsquelle, wie die Schrittbedingung zutrifft, d.h. den Wert 1 hat. Da der Anschluß keine Speichereigenschaft hat, besitzt er den Wert undefiniert, wenn keine Durchschaltung, die diesen Anschluß als Ziel hat, wirksam ist.

Prinzipiell reicht das Verfahren der einstufigen Bedingung zur Steuerung von Übertragungsanweisungen aus. Aus praktischen Gründen ist es jedoch von Vorteil, eine Bedingungshierarchie vorzusehen, so daß Übertragungsanweisungen mit ähnlichen Steuerbedingungen unter einer Gruppenbedingung in einem Schritt zusammengefaßt werden können. Man bedient sich dabei in RTS der bedingten Anweisung, die anstelle von Übertragungsanweisungen in Schritten stehen kann:

z.B. <u>if</u> TB <u>then</u> T1 <u>else</u> T2;

(TB = Transferbedingung; T1,T2 = Transferanweisungen).

Weiterhin wurde aus denselben Gründen wie in ALGOL 60 die Verbundanweisungen eingeführt:

z.B. <u>begin</u> T1;T2;D1 <u>end</u>;

Dadurch ist es nicht nur möglich, mehrere Anweisungen unter eine gemeinsame Transferbedingung zu stellen, sondern auch Schachtelungen von bedingten Anweisungen (hinter <u>then</u>) zu erzeugen.

3.6. Parallel- und Serienarbeit in Registernetzen

Wie bereits erwähnt wird in RTS von der prinzipiellen Parallelarbeit aller Anweisungen ausgegangen. Aus diesem Grunde ist es gleichgültig, in welcher Reihenfolge die einzelnen Schritte eines RTS-Programmes aufgeführt werden.

Der zeitliche Ablauf verschiedener Schritte - gleichzeitig oder hintereinander - wird durch entsprechende Schrittbedingungen die im RTS-Programm explizit gesetzt werden, gesteuert.

Um die in Schaltwerken aus Aufwandsgründen häufig auftretende, rein sequentielle Schrittfolge durch zusätzliche Sprachmittel zu begünstigen, wurden in RTS Sprunganweisungen und Schrittmarken eingeführt:

z.B. L1-SB1:....; <u>goto</u> L2
L2-SB2:....; <u>goto</u> L3

usw.

(L1 bis L3 sind Schrittmarken, SB1 und SB2 Schrittbedingungen)

Ausgegangen wird dabei von der Existenz eines im allg. nicht näher spezifizierten Ablaufsteuerungsregisters (Kontrollregister). Jede Schrittmarke entspricht dann der Speicherung eines bestimmten Wertes im Ablaufsteuerungsregister, der durch eine Sprunganweisung auf diese Marke in das Register hineintransferiert wird. Diese Deutung von Schrittmarken und Sprungsanweisungen läßt zwar im Prinzip noch die Zahl der vorhandenen Ablaufsteuerungsregister offen, z.B. wäre es denkbar, durch 2 Sprunganweisungen innerhalb eines Schrittes 2 verschiedene Nachfolgerschritte parallel anzustoßen.In RTS II wurde jedoch die Zahl der Ablaufsteuerungsregister auf eines eingeschränkt und dadurch (innerhalb eines Werkes) nur die rein sequentielle Berabeitung von Schritten mit Marken zugelassen. Dies hat zur Konsequenz, daß in jedem markierten Schritt zur eindeutigen Kennzeichnung des Nachfolgerschrittes genau eine Sprunganweisung ausgeführt werden muß.

Hat ein markierter Schritt außerdem eine Schrittbedingung wie im obigen Beispiel, so gilt die logische Konjunktion von Aktivierung der Marke und Zutreffen der Schrittbedingung. Wird also ein markierter Schritt durch eine Sprunganweisung auf seine Marke aktiviert, und trifft seine Schrittbedingung nicht zu, so wartet das Schaltwerk an dieser Stelle mit der Ausführung des Schrittes, bis die Bedingung zutrifft.

Die Kombination von Schrittmarken und Sprunganweisungen läßt auch eine automatentheoretische Deutung zu. Die Schritte entsprechen hierbei den symbolisch gekennzeichneten Zuständen und die Sprunganweisungen den Zustandsübergängen eines Automaten.

Die Zustände dieses Automaten werden also nicht durch die Werte in allen Elementen des Automaten mit Speichereigenschaft sondern nur durch die Werte im Ablaufsteuerungsregister bestimmt. Allgemeiner kann in derartigen Automaten zwischen "zustandsträchtigen" Registern und Datenregistern unterschieden werden; es wird durch diese Unterscheidung eine erhebliche Verminderung der Zustandszahl und damit eine Überschaubarkeit der Funktionsweise des Automaten erzielt.

3.7. Hierarchie der zusammengesetzten Anweisungen

Gebilde, die über eine eigene Ablaufsteuerung verfügen, die also eine abgeschlossenes Zustandsdiagramm haben, werden in RTS gemäß obiger Definition "Automat" genannt. Dies hat zur Folge, daß weder Sprünge von außen in einen Automaten hinein noch aus ihm heraus führen dürfen. Jedoch dürfen sich verschiedene Automaten gegenseitig beeinflussen. Da sich die Definition des RTS-Automaten in etwa mit dem Hardwarebegriff des Werkes deckt, ist für jeden Automaten in RTS ein eigener Vereinbarungsteil vorgesehen. RTS-Programme, die RTS-Automaten beschreiben, sind also programmtechnisch autark. Dies wird insbesondere durch das Prinzip des vollständigen Vereinbarungs- und Spezifikationszwanges aller in einem Automaten auftretenden Variablen erreicht. Der RTS-Automat ist also eine statisch und - bei geeigneter Versorgung durch die Umwelt - auch dynamisch prüfbare Einheit.

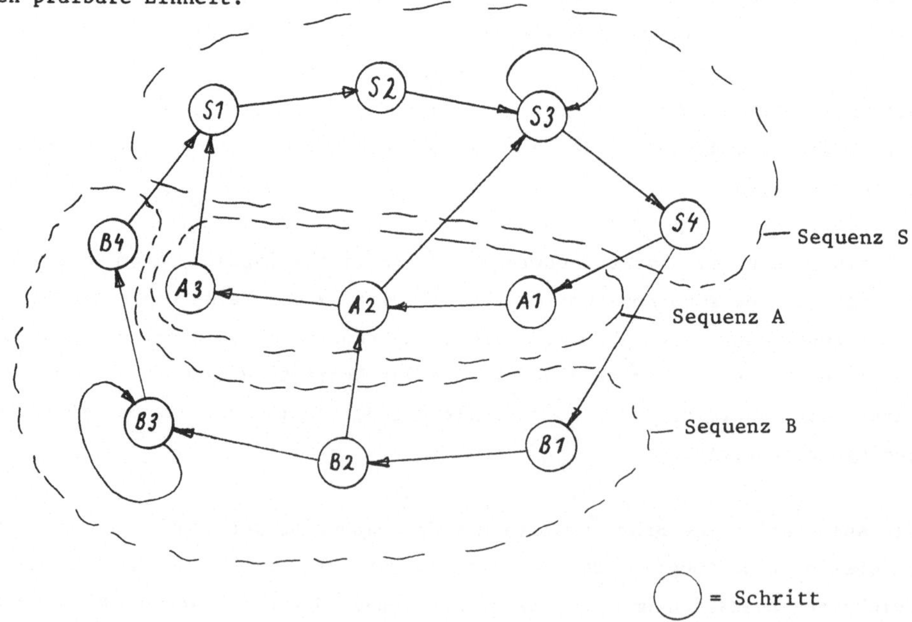

Bild 3.1: Beispiel der Unterteilung eines Automatenzustandsdiagrammes in Sequenzen

Geht man weiterhin von der Ablaufsteuerung durch Marke und Sprünge aus, so erschien es sinnvoll als Zwischenstufe zwischen dem Automaten und dem Schritt die (Schritt-) Sequenz einzuführen; sie entspricht einem Teilgraphen des Automatenzustandsdiagrammes (Bild 3.1), wobei die zweckmäßige Zerschneidung des Zustandsdiagrammes naturgemäß dem Benutzer der RTS-Sprache überlassen bleibt. Da es sich bei der Sequenz nicht um ein autarkes Gebilde handelt, wurde in RTS darauf verzichtet, ihr einen Vereinbarungsteil zuzuordnen. Wohl ist es aber möglich, eine globale Sequenzbedingung vorzusehen.

```
        automat  BEISPIEL

BEISPIEL: begin
                 } Deklarationen des Automaten  BEISPIEL

        SEQUS: begin

                S1:.........goto  S 2.
                S2:.........goto  S 3.
                S3:....if...then goto S 4 else goto  S 3.
                S4:....if...then goto SEQUA(A1) else goto  SEQUB(B1).
                end of Sequence SEQUS;

        SEQUA: begin

                A1:.........goto A 2.
                A2:.....if...then goto A3 else goto SEQUS(S3).
                A3:.........goto SEQUS(S1).
                end of Sequence SEQUA;

        SEQUB: begin

                B1:.........goto B 2.
                B2:....if....then goto SEQUA(A2) else goto B3.
                B3:....if....then goto B3 else goto B4.
                B4:.........goto SEQUS(S1)
                end of Sequence SEQUB

                end of Automaton BEISPIEL;
```

Sequenzen können in RTS auch geschachtelt werden; d.h. Sequenzen dürfen Sequenzen enthalten. Andererseits kann auch auf die Unterteilung eines Automaten in Sequenzen ganz verzichtet und die Schritte dieses Automaten direkt in seinem Ausführungsteil angeordnet werden.

Als dem Automaten übergeordnete Einheit wurde in RTS noch das System eingeführt. Es dient dazu, mehrere Automaten zu einer größeren Einheit zusammenzufassen und dieser gewisse, gemeinsam benutzte Einrichtungen, wie z.B. Register und Anschlüsse, zur Verfügung zu stellen. Folgerichtig bestehen Systeme nur aus einem Vereinbarungsteil und den Automatenausführungsteilen. Die Schachtelung von Systemen ist in RTS zulässig. Umfaßt werden alle Systeme von einem RTS-Programm:

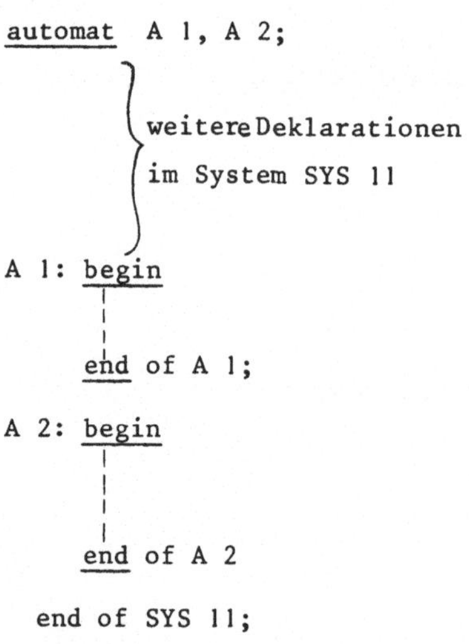

```
begin
  system SYS 1, SYS 2;
SYS 1: begin
  system SYS 11, SYS 12;
SYS 11: begin
        automat  A 1, A 2;
                  ⎫
                  ⎬ weitere Deklarationen
                  ⎪ im System SYS 11
                  ⎭
        A 1: begin
             |
             |
             end of A 1;
        A 2: begin
             |
             |
             end of A 2
          end of SYS 11;
SYS 12: begin
        |
        |
        end of SYS 12
    end of SYS 1;
```

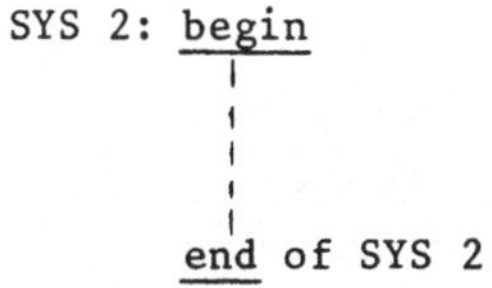

end of RTS-Program;

Zur Verdeutlichung der Hierarchie der zusammengesetzten Anweisung mag noch der folgende Graph dienen:

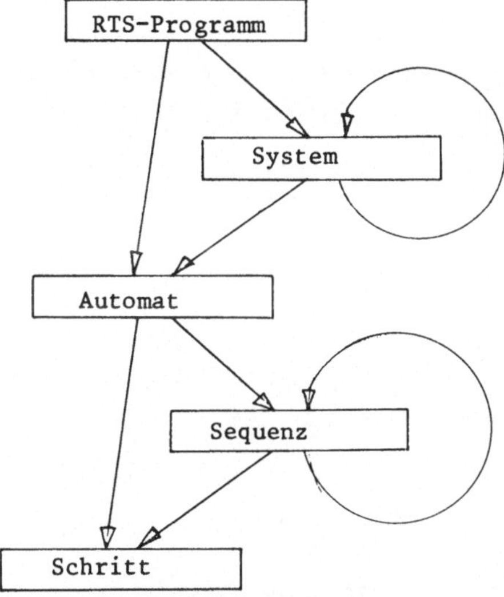

(der Pfeil bedeutet in Pfeilrichtung gelesen: "enthält")

Da die Simulation der vollständigen Strukturbeschreibung eines größeren Registernetzes zu aufwendig bezüglich Rechenzeit und Kernspeicherbedarf würde, können in RTS Automaten und Systeme durch funktionelle Beschreibungen dieser Blöcke ("black-box"-Werke) ersetzt werden. Eine derartige "black-box"-Beschreibung umfaßt einen RTS-Vereinbarungsteil aller nach außen wirksamen Größen dieses Werkes und einen Funktionsbeschreibungsteil, der z.B. in einer algorithmischen Programmiersprache abgefaßt sein kann.

4. Erweiterung des Konzepts von RTS

Dehnt man den Anwendungsbereich von RTS auf die in Verbindung mit ungepufferten Flipflops vielfach gebräuchlichen, mehrphasigen Takte und auf asynchron betriebene Registernetze aus, so wird die Einführung einer zeitlichen Metrik, die Erfaßbarkeit von Signallaufzeiten und die Vereinbarungsmöglichkeit von Takten unumgänglich.

4.1. Mehrphasentaktsysteme

Zunächst soll an einem Beispiel kurz erläutert werden, was hier unter einem Mehrphasentaktsystem verstanden wird (Bild 4.1).

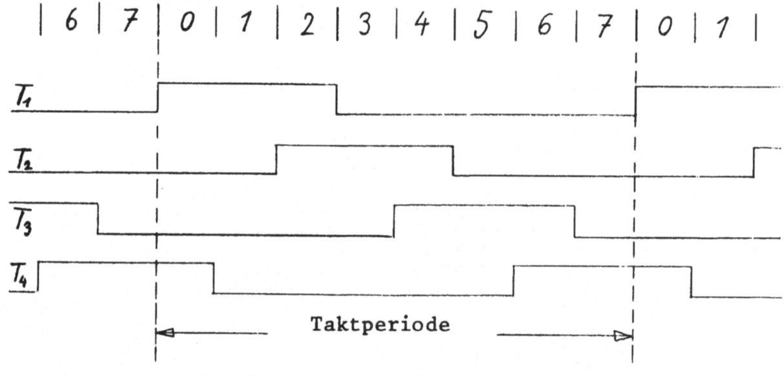

Bild 4.1: Mehrphasiges Taktsystem

Bei geeigneter Wahl des Tastverhältnisses der einzelnen Taktphase (im Beispiel 3:5) und der Phasenlage der Taktphasen zueinander lassen sich durch einfache Verknüpfungsfunktionen aus den Taktphasen Steuersignale ableiten, deren Einsatzpunkte und deren Dauer sich relativ fein abstufen lassen (Bild 4.2). In RTS werden derartige Steuersignale als Pulse bezeichnet und können fest vereinbart werden.

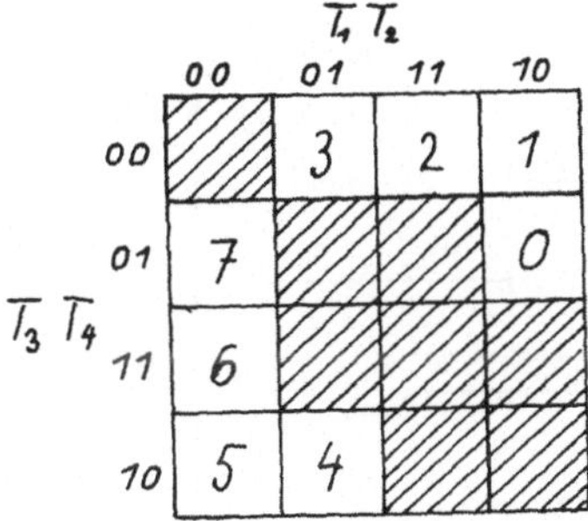

Bild 4.2: Karnaugh-Diagramm der abgeleiteten Einheitssignale

Der Vorteil eines Mehrphasentaktsystems liegt darin, daß man sich mittels der abgeleiteten Steuersignale wesentlich besser an die unterschiedlichen Zeitbedürfnisse der auszuführenden Übertragungsanweisungen (Transfers und Durchschaltungen) anpassen kann und dadurch insgesamt eine Beschleunigung des Rechners gegenüber einem Einphasentaktsystem erreicht. Diese Feinabstufung der Steuersignale ist besonders bei der Verwendung ungepufferte Flipflopregister erforderlich, da sich die Zahl der auszuführenden Transfers in derartigen Systemen erhöht gegenüber Systemen mit gepufferten Flipflopregistern und insbesondere reine "Register zu Register" - Transfers (ohne Verknüpfungsnetz zwischen Quelle und Ziel) mit sehr kurzen Signallaufzeiten häufiger auftreten.

Prinzipiell wäre es für die Erfassung von Taktsystemen in einer RT-Sprache ausreichend , lediglich die Vereinbarungsmöglichkeit des Taktsystems vorzusehen und außerdem zu fordern, daß Taktvariable bzw. davon abgeleitete Größen grundsätzlich mit in die Schrittbedingungen aufgenommen werden. In RTS wurde jedoch unter Inkaufnahme einer gewissen Spezialisierung der Sprache davon ausgegangen, daß Zustandswechsel der Ablaufsteuerung nur von Taktperiode zu Taktperiode auftreten. Wie unter 3.6. bereits ausgeführt entspricht einem Zustand der Ablaufsteuerung in RTS genau ein Schritt (mit Schrittmarke). Diese Definition des Schrittes wurde auch für Mehrphasentaktsysteme aufrechterhalten, so daß hier zwangsläufig eine Unterteilungsmöglichkeit des Schrittes in Einheiten, die von jeweils einem Steuersignal abhängen, vorgesehen werden muß. Diese Einheiten werden in RTS II als Phasen bezeichnet. Gekennzeichnet werden diese Phasen durch Beginn und Dauer des sie steuernden Pulses. (Bei der Rückkehr zum Einphasentakt fällt diese Definition der Phase mit der des Schrittes zusammen.)

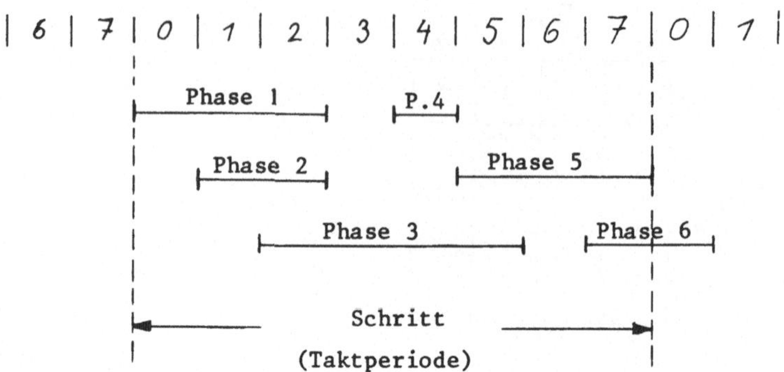

Bild 4.3: Beispiel für Phasen innerhalb eines Schrittes

Da die einzelnen Phasen eines Schrittes zeitlich beliebig zueinander liegen können (z.B. Bild 4.3), wird der Begriff "Parallelphasen" derart modifiziert, daß Phasen, die sich zeitlich überlappen, als zueinander parallel bezeichnet werden. (Im Bild z.B. Phase 1 mit den Phasen 2 und 3 oder Phase 3 mit den Phasen 1,2,4 und 5, jedoch Phase 1 nicht mit Phase 4). Dieser Parallelphasen-Begriff ist wichtig bei der Definition von zeitlichen Konsistenzbedingungen. Weiterhin ist es in RTS zulässig, Phasen zu definieren, deren Aktivierungsraum über eine Schrittgrenze hinaus geht; sie werden in dem Schritt definiert, in dem sie beginnen (Im Bild z.B. Phase 6).

Um den besonderen Charakter der Pulse als auslösende Steuersignale stärker hervorzuheben, dürfen sie nicht in Phasenbedingungen mit hineingezogen werden; sondern sie stehen an spezieller, syntaktischer Position innerhalb der zu steuernden Phase. Außerdem gehorcht die Bezeichnung von Pulsen eigenen Syntaxregeln.

4.2. Erfassung der Signallaufzeiten in synchronen Registernetzen

Das zeitliche Zusammenspiel von Übertragungsanweisungen wird in Mehrphasentaktsystemen schwer überschaubar. Aus diesem Grunde sind Fragen wie:

> " Haben die Eingangsgrößen eines Registers beim Eintreffen des Steuersignals (zur Auslösung des Transfervorganges) bereits ihren gewünschten Wert erreicht und bleibt dieser Wert konstant, während das Steuersignal anliegt?"

schlecht manuell zu beantworten. Erste Voraussetzung für die automatische Beantwortung derartiger Fragen ist die formale Spezifikationsmöglichkeit von Signallaufzeiten.

Solange synchrone Registernetze beschrieben und kontrolliert werden sollen, genügt die Erfassung der maximalen Signallaufzeiten im Übertragungsweg einer Übertragungsanweisung und braucht die zeitliche Interaktion verschiedener Signalübergänge in Verknüpfungsnetzen nicht betrachtet zu werden. Weiterhin wird davon ausgegangen, daß Verknüpfungsnetze im allgemeinen auf der Registernetzebene nur funktionell beschrieben werden. Aus diesem Grunde ist es sinnvoll, die formale Laufzeitspezifikation von den logischen Verknüpfungsoperationen zu trennen. In RTS wird all diesem durch die Einführung einer speziellen Verzögerungsfunktion Rechnung getragen.

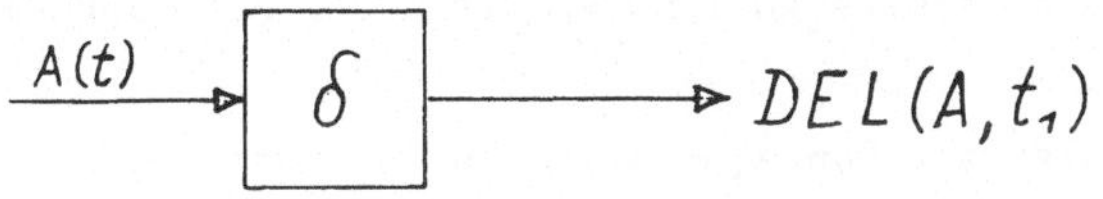

$A(t)$ → δ → $DEL(A,t_1)$

(Das Signal A wird um t_1 Zeiteinheiten verzögert am Ausgang wieder abgegeben.)

Syntaktisch spielt die Verzögerungsfunktion die Rolle einer RTS-Funktion, kann aber darüberhinaus auch auf der Zielseite einer Übertragungsanweisung und in Verbindung mit Registeroperationen und Sprunganweisungen verwendet werden, um Schaltzeiten in Registerzellen (Flipflops) mit erfassen zu können.

(Im Hinblick auf die einfachere Simulierbarkeit wird in RTS die Zeit in quantisierter Form eingeführt. Dies geschieht durch die Vereinbarung eines Zeitrasters, auf das sich alle weiteren Zeitangaben bei der Vereinbarung von Takten und bei der Spezifikation von Signallaufzeiten beziehen.)

Erwähnt werden soll in diesem Zusammenhang noch, da es bei zeitlichen Konsistenzkontrollen nicht unwesentlich ist, daß in RTS die Möglichkeit vorgesehen ist, bei der Vereinbarung von Registern zwischen gepufferten und ungepufferten Flipflops sowie zwischen Flanken- und Niveauansteuerung der Flipflops zu unterscheiden.

4.3. Asynchrone Automaten in RTS

Asynchron gesteuerte Registernetze können in RTS auch beschrieben werden, nicht jedoch allgemeine asynchrone Schaltwerke, unter die auch direkt rückgekoppelte Gatternetze fallen.

Der wesentliche Unterschied zwischen synchronen und asynchronen Registernetzen ist der, daß in asynchronen Netzen die von der Ablaufsteuerung kommenden Signale Transfers nicht nur möglich machen, d.h. die entsprechenden Tore im Informationspfad öffnen, sondern auch auslösen, d.h. gleichzeitig die Rolle der Taktsignale in synchronen Netzen mit übernehmen. Dies stellt an das zeitliche Zusammenspiel zwischen Übertragungsanweisungen und Steuersignalen relativ große Anforderungen.

Für eine RT-Sprache hat dies zur Konsequenz, daß nicht nur maximale, sondern auch minimale Signallaufzeit erfaßbar sein müssen und daß weiterhin der transiente Teil eines Signals zeitlich eingrenzbar sein muß. Man kann sogar noch einen Schritt weitergehen und Aussagen über monotonen bzw. nichtmonotonen Signalverlauf im transienten Teil von Signalen (Hazards) machen.

In RTS wurde zu diesem Zweck die Verzögerungsfunktion stärker eingegrenzt zur "verschleifenden Verzögerungsfunktion":

$$\mathrm{DEL}(A,t_1) = \begin{cases} A(t-t_1) & \text{für } t \geq t^* + t_1 \\ \text{don't care} & \text{für } t^* \leq t < t^* + t_1 \end{cases}$$

(t^* ist der Zeitpunktdes letzten Wechsels des Signals A;
t ist der augenblickliche Zeitpunkt und t_1 ist die Verschleifungszeit.)

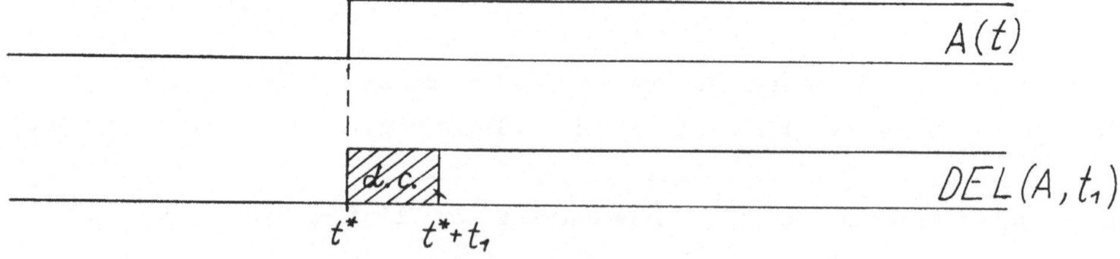

Außerdem wurde die "träge Verzögerungsfunktion" neu eingeführt; sie hat für Signalwechsel, die in größerem zeitlichen Abstand als die Verzögerungszeit auftreten, die Wirkung einer idealen Verzögerung. Im anderen Fall liefert sie den Wert don't care:

$$TAU(A,t_1) = \left\{ \begin{array}{ll} A(t-t_1) & \text{für } t^{(i+1)} - t^{(i)} \geq t_1 \\ \text{don't care} & \text{für } t^{(i+1)} - t^{(i)} < t_1 \end{array} \right\} \quad \text{für } t^{(i)} + t_1 < t < t^{(i+1)} + t_1$$

($t^{(i)}$ ist der Zeitpunkt des i-ten Wechsels des Signals A, $t^{(i+1)}$ der des (i+1)-ten Wechsels.)

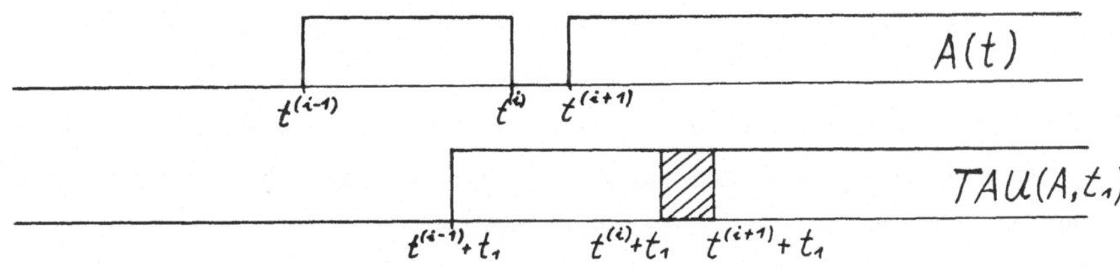

Durch Zusammensetzung dieser beiden Verzögerungsfunktionen lassen sich alle in Verknüpfungsnetzen auftretenden, zeitlichen Signalverschiebungen ausreichende genau nachbilden. Auf die Nachbildung des Hazardverhaltens von Verknüpfungsnetzen wird in RTS verzichtet.

5. Bemerkungen zur Implementierung von RTS

Implementierung bedeutet hier "Benutzung der formalen Beschreibung eines Registernetzes zu seiner Simulation".

Zwei Verfahren standen für die Implementierung zur Auswahl:

1.) Vollkompilation von RTS-Programmen in den Maschinencode einer Wirtsmaschine.

2.) Teilkompilation in eine interne Datenstruktur (IDS) und Interpretation dieser IDS durch einen Simulationsinterpreter.

Die Entscheidung fiel zugunsten des 2. Verfahrens aus; es wurde dabei ein gewisser Effiziensverlust in Kauf genommen. Der Vorteil des 2. Verfahrens liegt neben der Maschinenunabhängigkeit und der Einfachheit des Kompilers in der Modularität der IDS und des Simulationsinterpreters. Da die IDS alle Informationen des Quellprogrammes enthält, ist sie außerdem prinzipiell dekompilierbar, und es können Fehlerausschriften quellsprachenorientiert ausgegeben werden.

Für die erste Version, RTS I, liegt am Institut für Nachrichtenverarbeitung eine Implementierung auf der IBM 7o4o teils in ALGOL 6o und teils in FORTRAN IV vor. Eine reine FORTRAN-Implementierung für RTS I ist in Arbeit. Für die erweiterte RTS-Version, RTS II, ist die Planung der IDS und des Simulationsinterpreter in der Endphase.

Zu erwähnen ist noch, daß in der Syntaxprüfphase des RTS-Kompilers auch alle sonstigen statischen Kontrollen des Registernetzes durchgeführt werden und daß der Simulationsinterpreter die IDS während der Simulation auf ihre Konsistenz überprüft.

6. Schlußzusammenfassung

Im ersten Teil dieses Vortrages wurden die wesentlichen Motive für die Entwicklung spezieller Registertransfersprachen und ihre Abgrenzung gegenüber anderen Schaltwerksbeschreibungssprachtypen geschildert. Es wurden dann im zweiten Teil die Sprachphilosophie und die wesentlichen Eigenschaften von RTS vorgestellt, insbesondere wurde auf die Einführung einer zeitlichen Metrik in RTS eingegangen. Der Vortrag schließt mit Erwähnung des Implementierungsprinzip von RTS.

7. Literaturhinweise

[1] P.W. Case, H.H. Graff, L.E. Griffith, A.R. LeClercq.,W.B. Murley, T.M. Spence, Solid Logic Design Automation, IBM J. Res.&Dev. 8(Apr. 64), pp. 127-14o.

[2] H. Clausert, I. Kahlert-Warmboldt, Untersuchung digitaler Schaltungen mit dem Programmsystem DICAP, El. DV. 11,9 (Sept. 69), S. 443-451 und El. DV. 12,2 (Feb. 7o), S. 75-82.

[3] G.G. Hays, Computer-Aided Design: Simulation of Digital Design Logic, IEEE-Trans.Comp. C-18,1 (Jan 69), pp. 1-1o.

[4] J.S. Jephson, R.P. McQuarrie, R.E. Vogelsberg, A Three-Value Computer Design Verification System, IBM Syst. J. 8,3 (1969), pp. 178-188.

[5] W. Jost, TIPSI-Ein Time-Sharing-Programm zur Simulation von Digitalschaltungen, EL.DV. 12,12 (Dez. 7o), S. 583-586.

[6] M. Lehmann, R. Eshed, Z. Netter, The Checking of Computer Logic by Simulation on a Computer, Comp. J. 6,2 (July 63), pp. 154-162.

[7] L. Shalla, Automatic Analysis of Electronic Digital Circuits Using List-Processing, Com. ACM 9,5 (May 66), pp. 372-38o.

[8] E.G. Ulrich, Time-Sequenced Logical Simulation Based on Circuit Delay and Selective Tracing of Active Network Paths, Proc. ACM 2oth Nat. Conf. , 1965 , pp. 437-448.

[9] E.G. Ulrich, Exclusive Simulation of Activity in Digital Networks, Com. ACM 12,2 (Feb. 69), pp. 1o2-11o.

[1o] I.S. Reed, Symbolic Systhesis of Digital Computers, Proc. ACM (Sept. 52), pp. 9o-94.

[11] Y. Chu, Digital Computer Design Fundamentals, New York: McGraw-Hill, 1962.

[12] H. Schorr, Computer Aided Digital Systems Design and Analysis Using a Register Transfer Language, IEEE-Trans. El. Comp. EC-13, 12(Dez. 64), pp.73o-737

[13] Y. Chu, An ALGOL-like Computer Design Language, Com. ACM 8,1o (okt. 65), pp. 6o7-615.

[14] K.E. Iverson, A Programming Language, New York: Wiley, 1962.

[15] K.E. Iverson, A Common Language for Hardware, Software, and Applications, AFIPS Proc. 22 (Fall 62), pp.121-129.

[16] K.E. Iverson, A Programming Notation in System Design, IBM Syst. J.2(June 63), pp. 117-128.

[17] A.D. Falkoff, K.E. Iverson, E.H. Sussenguth, A Formal Description of System /36o, IBM Syst. J. 3,3 (1964), pp. 198-262.

[18] H.P. Schlaeppi, A Formal Language for Describing Machine Logic, Timing, and Sequencing (LOTIS), IEEE-Trans. El. Comp. EC-13,4 (Aug. 64), pp. 439-448.

[19] J.R. Duley, D.L. Dietmeyer, A Digital System Design Language (DDL), IEEE-Trans. Comp. C-17,9 (Sept. 68), pp. 85o-861.

[2o] R. Piloty, RTS I (Registertransfersprache), 3. Auflage, Institut für Nachrichtenverarbeitung, T.H. Darmstadt, 1969.

[21] H. Hoehne, Entwicklung und Implementierung einer Sprache zur Darstellung und Simulation komplexer Schaltwerke, Institutsbericht des Institutes für Nachrichtenverarbeitung, T.H. Darmstadt, 1969.

[22] H. Hoehne, Einführung der Zeitdimension in RTS, Institutsbericht des Institutes für Nachrichtenverarbeitung, T.H. Darmstadt, 1969.

[23] U. Blumenschein, W. Langner, Entwicklung und Definititon der Registertransfersprache RTS II, Studienarbeit Nr. NVST 83 des Institutes für Nachrichtenverarbeitung, T.H. Darmstadt, 197o.

STRUCTURAL SIMILARITY OF PROGRAMS AND SOME CONCEPTS OF ALGORITHMIC METHOD

by Karel Čulík

A concept of a programming language scheme (as a programming theory) and of its programming language (as its programming model) for a particular computer are introduced and in this way "machine dependency and independency of programming languages" are clarified. Certain elementary changes are described, by which some structural similarities among the program schemes are defined. In each programming language a functional equivalency of programs is introduced by a requirement that by both programs the same function is computed. Briefly the definitions of flow-diagrams and algorithmic diagrams of a program are introduced. Three concepts of algorithmic method are discussed but always a class of functionally equivalent programs is in the base of them.

1. Programming language scheme

An unclear concept of a programming language which is "machine independent" or which is an "universal computer language" [1] may be clarified by the following introduction of a programming language scheme (PLS).

The alphabet of a PLS is the union of five sets of symbols (each two of them are disjoint) Opr, Pred, Var, Mar, Sep the elements of which are called names of operations, names of relations, variables (or identifiers), markers (or labels) and separators respectively where the following decompositions are prescribed: $\mathrm{Opr}=\bigcup_{i=1}^{\infty}\mathrm{Opr}^{(i)}$ and $\mathrm{Pred}=\bigcup_{i=1}^{\infty}\mathrm{Pred}^{(i)}$ (i.e. $\mathrm{Opr}^{(i)}\cap\mathrm{Opr}^{(j)}=\emptyset=\mathrm{Pred}^{(i)}\cap\mathrm{Pred}^{(j)}$ if $i\neq j$ and $i,j=1,2,\ldots$), and $\mathrm{Sep}=\{,()[\,]\langle\rangle;\ =:\ \underline{\mathrm{Stop}}\}$. Further $\mathrm{Cond}^{(i)}=\{g[m_1,m_2];\ g\in\mathrm{Pred}^{(i)}\text{ and }m_1,m_2\in\mathrm{Mar}\}$ and the elements from the set $\mathrm{Cond}=\bigcup_{i=1}^{\infty}\mathrm{Cond}^{(i)}$ are called names of conditions (it is clear that $|\mathrm{Cond}^{(i)}|=|\mathrm{Pred}^{(i)}|\cdot|\mathrm{Mar}|^2$ for each $i=1,2,\ldots$).

The operational or conditional type of a PLS is the following sequence of non-negative integers (or cardinalities) $(|\mathrm{Opr}^{(1)}|,\ |\mathrm{Opr}^{(2)}|,\ldots)$ or $(|\mathrm{Pred}^{(1)}|,\ |\mathrm{Pred}^{(2)}|,\ldots)$ respectively and storage type of the PLS consists in its variable type $|Var|$ together with its marker type $|Mar|$ respectively (the storage type may be generalized - if different sorts of memory cells, e.g. registers, or storage units are distinguished - by a proper decomposition of Var). Two PLSs having the same operational, conditional, variable and marker types need not be distinguished.

Let Com be the set of all commands (or better command schemes) of the PLS, i.e. of all strings over its alphabet having one of the following forms:

(operational command): $f(x_1,x_2,\ldots,x_n)=: x_o$ where $f \in Opr^{(n)}$ and $x_i \in Var$ for $i=0,1,\ldots,n$;

(conditional jumping command): $g[m_1,m_2](y_1,y_2,\ldots,y_n)$ where $g[m_1,m_2] \in Cond^{(n)}$ and $y_i \in Var$ for $i=1,2,\ldots,n$;

(stopping command): Stop;

(for the purpose of this paper all other kinds of commands, e.g.

(output command): print (x) where $x \in Var$;

(unconditional jumping command): k where $k \in Mar$;

(restoring command): x =: y where $x,y \in Var$;

etc., may be omitted).

Further let $MarxCom=\{\langle k,C\rangle ; k \in Mar \text{ and } C \in Com\}$ be the set of all marked commands $\langle k,C\rangle$ and $Prog=\{(K^{(1)};K^{(2)};\ldots$ $\ldots;K^{(n)});\ K^{(i)} \in Com \cup (MarxCom) \text{ for } i=1,2,\ldots,n\}$ be the set of all programs (or better program schemes) of the PLS (certain reasonable restrictions should be accepted here, e.g. if $K^{(i)}=\langle k^{(i)},C^{(i)}\rangle$ and $K^{(j)}=\langle k^{(j)},C^{(j)}\rangle$ where $i\neq j$ then $k^{(i)}\neq k^{(j)}$, etc.).

A <u>flow-tree</u> FT_P of a program (scheme) $P=(K^{(1)},K^{(2)},\ldots$ $\ldots,K^{(n)})$ is an oriented rooted tree $\langle V,\varrho\rangle$ with a labelling η of its vertices from V (the binary relation $\varrho\subset V^2$ is the set of its oriented edges) which is defined inductively as follows:

(i) first of all let us take a vertex v_1 as the root for ever and let us put $V_1=\{v_1\}$, $\varrho_1=\emptyset$ and $\eta_1(v_1)=K^{(1)}$;

(ii) let us assume that $1\leqslant i$ and that V_i, ϱ_i and η_i have already been determined and let us investigate all leafs in $\langle V_i,\varrho_i\rangle$, i.e. all vertices $v\in V_i$ such that there does not exist a vertex $w\in V_i$ such that $(v,w)\in\varrho_i$; if $v\in V_i$ is a leaf then $\eta_i(v)=K^{(j)}$ where $1\leqslant j\leqslant n$ and $K^{(j)}$ contains a command $C^{(j)}\in$ Com and therefore the following possibilities may occur: 1) $C^{(j)}$ is an operational command; in this case either $j<n$ and then we take a new vertex $w\notin V_i$ and we define $V_{i+1}=V_i\cup\{w\}$, $\varrho_{i+1}=\varrho_i\cup\{(v,w)\}$ and $\eta_{i+1}=\eta_i\cup\{(w,K^{(j+1)})\}$, or j=n and then the vertex v is called <u>blind</u> and no new vertex is taken; 2) $C^{(j)}$ is a conditional jumping command, i.e. $C^{(j)}=g[m_1,m_2](y_1,y_2,\ldots,y_k)$; in this case either there exist two integers p and q such that, $1\leqslant p$, $q\leqslant n$ and $m_1=k^{(p)}$, $m_2=k^{(q)}$ where $k^{(s)}$ is a marker contained in $K^{(s)}$, and then we take two new vertices $w,t \notin V_i$ (obviously if $m_1=m_2$ then w=t also) and we define $V_{i+1}=V_i \cup \{w,t\}$, $\rho_{i+1}=\rho_i \cup \{(v,w),(v,t)\}$ and $\eta_{i+1}=\eta_i \cup \cup \{(w,K^{(p)}),(t,K^{(q)})\}$, or there exists just one of those integers and then the corresponding one vertex is added or there does not exist any of them and then v is called blind; 3) $C^{(j)}$ is a stopping command; in this case v is called <u>stopped</u> and no further vertex is taken;

(iii) thus either there exist a leaf in $\langle V_i, \rho_i \rangle$ being neither blind nor stopped and then according to (ii) $\langle V_{i+1}, \rho_{i+1} \rangle$ is defined in such a way that $V_i \subset V_{i+1}$, $\rho_i \subset \rho_{i+1}$ and $\eta_i \subset \eta_{i+1}$, or all leafs of $\langle V_i, \rho_i \rangle$ are either blind or stopped; in this last case one puts $V=V_i$, $\rho=\rho_i$ and $\eta=\eta_i$ and otherwise one puts $V=\bigcup_{i=1}^{\infty} V_i$, $\rho=\bigcup_{i=1}^{\infty} \rho_i$ and $\eta=\bigcup_{i=1}^{\infty} \eta_i$.

A path in FT_P starting in its root and terminating in a stopped leaf is called a <u>stopped branch</u> of FT_P. If $(v_1,v_2,\dots,v_m)$ is a stopped branch, then $(\eta(v_1);\eta(v_2);\dots;\eta(v_m))$ is a program of the PLS also which is called a <u>branch program</u> of P. The set B_P of all branch programs of P may be empty, finite or infinite, and it is an important characteristics of P itself (some restrictions concerning

B_P are useful, e.g. only those branch programs are admitted which contain at least one operational command and in fact all markers and conditional commands may be omitted as superflous, etc.).

Each program $P \in Prog$ is a string over an alphabet and therefore it can be assumed that all occurrences of a variable x in P are clearly distinguished by their numbering from the left to the right, i.e. the h-th occurrence of x is considered as replaced by a new symbol h_{x_P} where h is an integer such that $1 \leqslant h \leqslant sc_P(x)$ and $sc_P(x)$ is the total number of all occurrences of the variable x in the program P (if VarP denotes the set of all variables occurring in P than $x \in VarP$ implies $sc_P(x) \geqslant 1$).

An occurence of a variable in a program is always an occurrence of this variable in a command. If this occurence is on the right of the separator =: it is called a <u>defining occurrence</u> and in all other cases it is called an <u>applied occurrence</u>.

An occurrence ${}^{i}x$ in a $B \in B_P$ where $1 \leqslant i \leqslant sc_B(x)$ is called an <u>input occurrence of</u> x (and the variable x is called an <u>input variable of</u> B) if all occurrences ${}^{j}x$ in B are applied for j=1,2,...,i. It is convenient to admit the zero-th occurrence ${}^{o}x$ if x is an input bariable. The (non-empty) set of all input occurrences of a variable x is called an <u>input scope of x</u> and denoted $Sc_B({}^{o}x)$.

The <u>scope</u> of a defining occurrence ${}^{i}x$ in B is the following set of occurrences $Sc_B({}^{i}x)=\{{}^{i+1}x, {}^{i+2}x, \ldots, {}^{i+k}x\}$ where $k \geqslant 0$ is the maximal integer such that ${}^{i+j}x$ is an applied occurrence of x for each $j=1,2,\ldots,k$.

An occurrence ${}^{i}x$ in B is called an <u>output occurrence</u> of x (and the variable x is called an <u>output variable of</u> B) if ${}^{i}x$ is a defining occurrence and if each ${}^{j}x$ is an applied occurrence belonging to a conditional jumping command for each $j=i+1,i+2,\ldots,sc_B(x)$ (there are other possibilities how to determine the output variables, e.g. by using the output commands, etc., but the difference is not essential). If ${}^{i}x$ is a defining or zero occurrence and $Sc_B({}^{i}x)= =\{{}^{i+1}x,\ldots,{}^{i+k}x\}$ then the <u>command scope of ${}^{i}x$ in</u> B is the following set of commands $CoSc_B({}^{i}x)=\{K_j,K_{j+1},\ldots,K_{j+h}\}$ where ${}^{i}x$ belongs to (j-1)-st and ${}^{i+k}x$ to (j+h)-th command in B.

Let I_B or O_B be the set of all input or output addresses of B B_P and let us define the set of <u>input variables</u> and <u>output variables of</u> P as follows: $I_P= \bigcup_{B \in P_B} I_B$ and

$$O_P= \bigcup_{B \in P_B} O_B.$$

In order to define the scopes and command scopes of the defining or zero occurrences in P it is necessary to describe some auxiliary constructions.

Let P^* arise from P by replacing of the i-th occurrence of x by a new symbol x^i (differing from ${}^i x_P$) for each $x \in VarP$ and each $i=1,2,\dots,sc_P(x)$ and let B^* be determined by P^* and FT_{P^*} in the same way as $B \in B_P$ by P and FT_P does (in fact in P^* , FT_{P^*} and B^* only some distinguishing integers are added). Then there is an one-to-one correspondence cod_B among all occurrences ${}^k x_B$ on the one hand and all the occurrences ${}^i(x^j)_B$ on the other hand because obviously

$$sc_B(x) = \sum_{i=1}^{sc_P(x)} sc_{B^*}(x^i) \text{ for each } x \in VarB \text{ and each } B \in B_P,$$

i.e. one may write $cod_B({}^k x_B) = {}^i(x^j)_{B^*}$ for suitable i and j, if $1 \leqslant k \leqslant sc_B(x)$ where $x \in VarB$ and $x^j \in VarB^*$ where $1 \leqslant j \leqslant sc_P(x)$ and $1 \leqslant i \leqslant sc_{B^*}(x^j)$.

Now if ${}^h x_P$ is a defining or zero occurrence of x in P then its scope is again a set of applied occurrences of x in P defined as follows:

$$Sc_P({}^h x_P) = \Big\{ {}^j x_P;\ \text{there exists } B \in P_B \text{ such that } x^j \in VarB^* \text{ and there exists i such that } 1 \leqslant i \leqslant sc_{B^*}(x^j) \text{ and it holds } {}^i(x^j)_{B^*} \in cod_B\big[Sc_B(cod_B^{-1}({}^1(x^h)_{B^*}))\big] \Big\},$$

which, in fact, again corresponds to a union of certain scopes in the branches $B \in B_P$.

If x^i is a defining or zero occurrence of the variable x in P and if $Sc_B({}^1(x^i)) = \{{}^a x, {}^{a+1}x, \dots, {}^{a+k}x\}$ then let K_{b_j} be that command which contains the occurrence ${}^{a+j_x}$ in B. Further there are integers j_h such that $0=j_0<1\leqslant j_1<j_2<\dots$ $\dots<j_m\leqslant k$ and K_{b_h} is a conditional command if and only if $h=j_1,j_2,\dots,j_m$. Therefore the ordered set of commands $\{K_{b_0},K_{b_1},\dots,K_{b_k}\}$ is divided into m (if $j_m=k$) or into m+1 (if $j_m<k$) parts $R_1=\{K_{b_0},K_{b_0+1},\dots,K_{b_{j_1}}\}$, $R_2=\{K_{b_{j_1}+1},K_{b_{j_1}+2},\dots$ $\dots,K_{b_{j_2}}\},\dots,R_m=\{K_{b_{j_{m-1}}},K_{b_{j_{m-1}}+1},\dots,K_{b_{j_m}}\}$,$R_{m+1}=\{K_{b_{j_m}+1},\dots$ $\dots,K_{b_k}\}$. If $K^{(p)}$ or $K^{(q)}$ is the first or the last command of any of this ordered sets respectively, e.g. $K^{(p)}=K_{b_{j_{h-1}}+1}$ and $K^{(q)}=K_{b_{j_{h+1}}}$ then $p<q$ (because of the construction of the flow-tree of P) and therefore the set of commands $\bar{R}_h=\{K^{(p)},K^{(p+1)},\dots,K^{(q)}\}$ is determined uniquely and it is possible to define

$$\mathrm{CoSe}_P({}^1(x^i))=\bigcup_{h=1}^{m+1}\bar{R}_h.$$

The set of all scopes in P of all defining or zero occurrences of a variable x is the set of vertices of an unoriented graph in which two vertices=scopes are joined by an edge iff their set-theoretical intersection is not empty. The set of all scopes belonging to a connected component of this graph is called a <u>family of scopes of ${}^i x$</u> and denoted by

$FaSc_P({}^i x)$ and then a <u>family of command scopes of ${}^i x$</u> is defined as follows $CoFaSc_P({}^i x) = \bigcup_{Sc_P({}^j x) \in FaSc_P({}^i x)} CoSc_P({}^j x)$.

2. Flow-diagrams and algorithmic diagrams

A <u>flow-diagram</u> FD_P of a program (scheme) $P=(K^{(1)},K^{(2)},\ldots$ $\ldots,K^{(n)})$ is a finite oriented graph $\langle W,\varphi\rangle$ with one distinguished vertex and with a labelling ψ of vertices defined as follows: $W=\{w_1,w_2,\ldots,w_n\}$ and $\psi(w_i)=K^{(i)}$ for $i=1,2,\ldots,n$; the distinguished vertex is that one labelled by $K^{(1)}$, i.e. here w_1; if the command $C^{(i)}$ contained in $K^{(i)}$ is operational and if $i<n$ then $(w_i,w_{i+1})\in\varphi$, otherwise if $i=n$ there is no edge starting in v_i; if the command $C^{(i)}$ is conditional, e.g. $C^{(i)}=g[m_1,m_2](y_1,y_2,\ldots,y_m)$, and if there are commands $K^{(p)}$ and $K^{(q)}$ such that the markers $k^{(p)}$ and $k^{(q)}$ contained in them satisfy $k^{(p)}=m_1$ and $k^{(q)}=m_2$, then $(v_i,v_p)\in\varphi$ and $(v_i,v_q)\in\varphi$, otherwise only one or no of these edges is starting in v_i; finally if $C^{(i)}$ is a stopping command then no edge is starting in v_i.

An <u>algorithmic diagram</u> AD_P of a program (scheme) $P=$ $=(K^{(1)},K^{(2)},\ldots,K^{(n)})$ is a multi-graph $\langle W^*,\psi^*,E,\iota,\lambda_E\rangle$ being an extension of $\langle W,\varphi,w_1,\psi\rangle$ i.e. $W\subset W^*$ and $\psi\subset\psi^*$, defined as follows:

1) $W^*=W\cup W_I\cup W_O$, $W\cap W_I=W_I\cap W_O=W\cap W_O=\emptyset$, and $|W_I|=|I_P|$, $|W_O|=|O_P|$;

2) $\psi^*=\psi\cup\psi_I\cup\psi_O$, where ψ_I or ψ_O is a one-to-one

mapping of W_I onto I_P or of W onto O_P respectively;

3) the set E of oriented edges of the second type (which must be distinguished from the edges of the first type in φ) with the incidence ι , which mapps E into $W^* x W^*$, are defined as follows: if $w \in W_I$ then $\psi'_I(w)=x \in I_P$ and by each input occurrence $^i x_P \in Sc(x)$ a vertex $v \in W^*$ is determined such that $^i x_P$ is an occurrence in $\psi^*(v)$ and simultaneously an integer a is determined showing that $^i x_P$ is the a-th variable from the left to the right appearing in the command $\psi^*(v)$ and therefore one requires the existence of an edge $e \in E$ such that $\iota(e)=[w,v]$ and $\lambda_E(e)=a$; if $w \in W$ then $\psi'(v)=K^{(b)}$ and the command $C^{(b)}$ contained in $K^{(b)}$ is either operational and then the single defining occurrence of a variable in this $C^{(b)}$ is an occurrence $^h x_P$ and therefore by each applied occurrence $^j x_P \in Sc(^h x_P)$ a vertex $v \in W$ is determined such that $^j x_P$ is an occurrence in $\psi(v)$ and simultaneously an integer a is determined showing that $^j x_P$ is the a-th variable in $\psi(v)$ and therefore the existence of an edge $e \in E$ is required such that $\iota(e)=[w,v]$ and $\lambda_E(e)=a$, or the command $C^{(b)}$ is conditional or stopping and then no edge of the second type is starting in w; if $w \in W_O$ then $\psi'_O(w)=y \in O_P$ and there is unique output occurrence $^h y_P$ determined which appears in a command $\psi(v)$ for some $v \in W$ and therefore one requires the existence of an edge $e \in E$ such that $\iota(e)=[w,v]$ and λ_E is not defined for e; thus the AD_P is completely determined.

Finally it is easy to see that it is possible to omit all the occurrences of all variables anywhere in AD_P, because they are in some sense unessential and redundant (they can be refound again). In this way arises an <u>variableless</u> (or <u>addressless</u>) <u>algorithmic diagram</u> of P, which is completely independent on any variable (of course its vertices are labelled by the names of operations or of conditions only).

<u>Example 1</u> If $P=(K^{(1)}=\langle m_1, x+y=:z\rangle;\ K^{(2)}=\langle m_3, x/y=:y\rangle;\ K^{(3)}=z<_{[m_1,m_2]} y;\ K^{(4)}=\langle m_2, x<_{[m_3,m_4]} z\rangle;\ K^{(5)}=\langle m_4, \mathrm{Stop}\rangle)$ then in Fig. 1 is represented schematically a part of its flow-tree FT_P and in Fig. 2 or Fig. 3 there is represented its flow-diagram FD_P or its algorithmic diagram AD_P respectively (where the occurrences of variables are already distinguished).

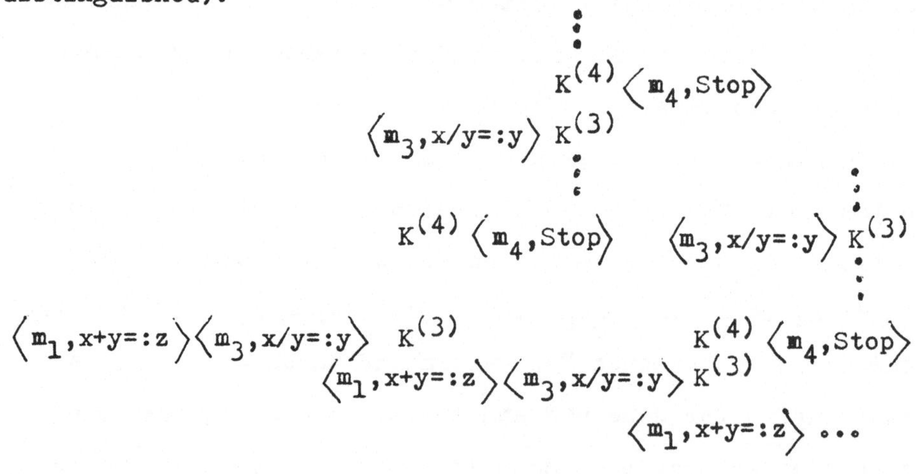

$$
\begin{array}{l}
\qquad\qquad\qquad\qquad\qquad\qquad \vdots \\
\qquad\qquad\qquad\qquad\qquad\qquad K^{(4)}\ \langle m_4, \mathrm{Stop}\rangle \\
\qquad\qquad\qquad\qquad \langle m_3, x/y=:y\rangle\ K^{(3)} \\
\qquad\qquad\qquad\qquad\qquad\qquad \vdots \qquad\qquad\qquad\qquad \vdots \\
\qquad\qquad\qquad K^{(4)}\ \langle m_4, \mathrm{Stop}\rangle \qquad \langle m_3, x/y=:y\rangle\ K^{(3)} \\
\qquad\qquad\qquad\qquad\qquad\qquad\qquad\qquad\qquad\qquad \vdots \\
\langle m_1, x+y=:z\rangle\langle m_3, x/y=:y\rangle\ K^{(3)} \qquad\qquad\qquad K^{(4)}\ \langle m_4, \mathrm{Stop}\rangle \\
\qquad\qquad\qquad \langle m_1, x+y=:z\rangle\langle m_3, x/y=:y\rangle\ K^{(3)} \\
\qquad\qquad\qquad\qquad\qquad\qquad\qquad \langle m_1, x+y=:z\rangle \ldots
\end{array}
$$

Fig. 1

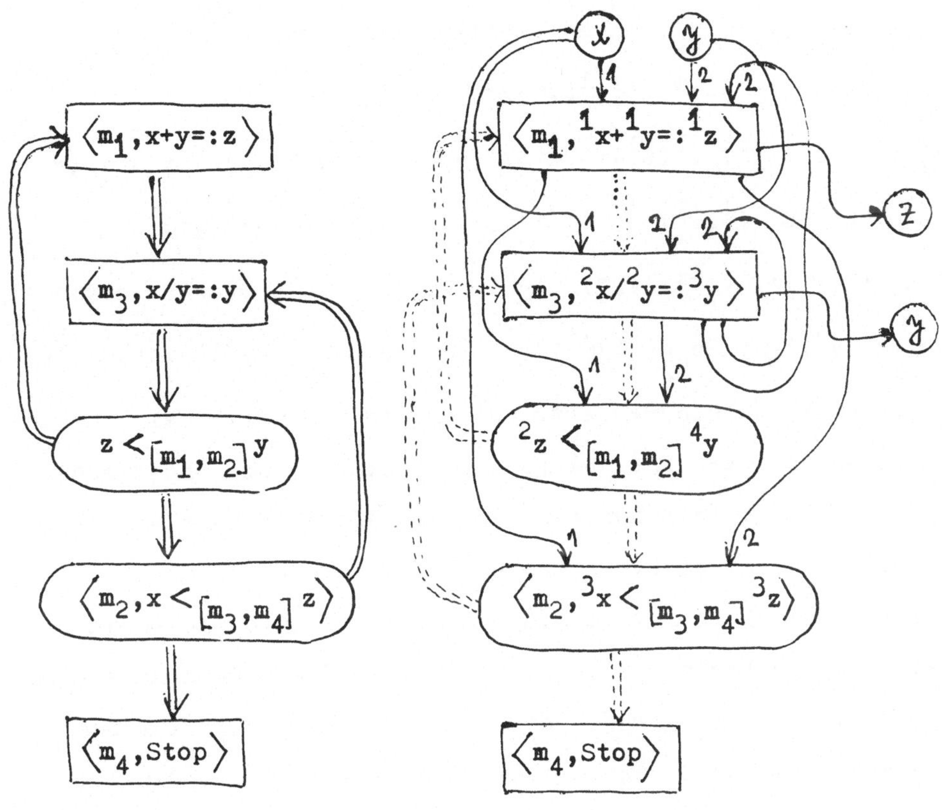

Fig. 2 Fig. 3

It is easy to see that B_1=(x+y=:z;x/y=:y;Stop), B_2= =(x+y=:z;x/y=:y;x/y=:y;Stop), B_3=(x+y=:z;x/y=:y;x+y=:z;x/y=:y; Stop) etc. are examples of branch programs of P where all markers and conditional commands are omitted.

It is clear that $I_{B_1}=I_{B_2}=I_{B_3}=\{x,y\}$ and $O_{B_1}=O_{B_2}=O_{B_3}=\{y,z\}$. Further it can be easily shown that $I_P=\{x,y\}$ and $O_P=\{y,z\}$ and moreover that e.g. $Sc_P({}^0y)=\{{}^1y,{}^2y\}$, $Sc_P({}^0x)=\{{}^1x,{}^2x,{}^3x\}$, $Sc_P({}^1z)=\{{}^2z,{}^3z\}$ and

$Sc_P({}^3y)=\{{}^4y,{}^1y,{}^2y\}$, which easily follows by using

$B_1^*=({}^1(x^1)+{}^1(y^1)=:{}^1(z^1);{}^1(x^2)/{}^1(y^2)=:{}^1(y^3);Stop)$,

$B_2^*=({}^1(x^1)+{}^1(y^1)=:{}^1(z^1);{}^1(x^2)/{}^1(y^2)=:{}^1(y^3);{}^2(x^2)/{}^2(y^2)=:{}^2(y^3);$ $Stop)$ and $B_3^*=({}^1(x^1)+{}^1(y^1)=:{}^1(z^1);{}^1(x^2)/{}^1(y^2)=:{}^1(y^3);$ ${}^2(x^1)+{}^2(y^1)=:{}^2(z^1);{}^2(x^2)/{}^2(y^2)=:{}^2(y^3),Stop)$, because obviously $Sc_{B_1^*}({}^1(y^3))=\emptyset$, $Sc_{B_2^*}({}^1(y^3))=\{{}^2(y^2)\}$ and $Sc_{B_3}({}^1(y^3))=\{{}^2(y^1),{}^2(y^2)\}$ (the remaining occurence ${}^4y$ belongs to a conditional command which was omitted for the reason of clarity and shortness).

In Fig. 4 is shown the corresponding variableless algorithmic diagram of P. In the case that no conditional commands occur in P this diagram is similar to the known switching or logical circuits (with two feed-backs here without any delay elements) where sometimes two inputs in the same place are admitted, which must be generally forbidden. It is easy to see how this variableless diagram may be modified in the way to a markerless diagram (the markers are replaced by "true" and "false" as labels of the flow edges).

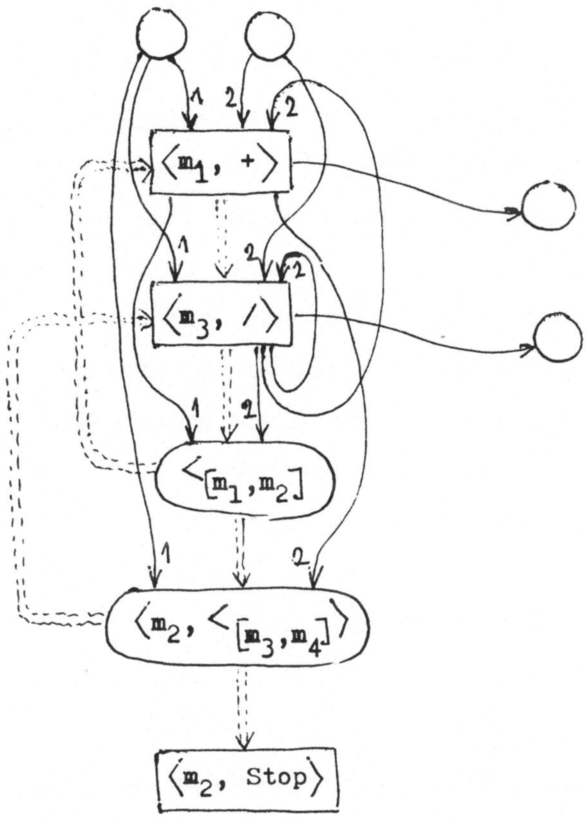

Fig. 4

3. Structural similarities in PLSs

Each program is intended to be a prescription of a computation process and therefore it could itself be considered as an algorithmic method, but this concept of algorithmic method is too week. In [2] there were shown three types of similarities among simple programs (i.e. if no conditional jumping command appears) of a given PLS, which concern either certain changes of varibles (or addresses) called <u>readdressings</u>, or certain changes of the order of command called <u>permutings</u>, or finally certain <u>omittings</u> of superfluous commands. From a point of view of a programmer or of a mathematician all the programs differing only in the used addresses or only in the order of command or only in the fact that some superfluous commands are added or not, are considered as equivalent or similar, or in other words, they are different realisations of one and the same algorithmic method. In the following the elementary steps of these and of some further changes are described without any restriction to the simple programs only.

Everywhere a program $P=(K^{(1)},K^{(2)},\dots,K^{(n)})\in$ Prog is considered where either $K^{(i)}=\langle k^{(i)},C^{(i)}\rangle$ or $K^{(i)}=C^{(i)}$ for $i=1,2,\dots,n$.

An <u>elementary renaming</u> (readdressing) <u>of variables</u> consists in replacing of all occurrences of a variable $x\in \mathrm{VarP}$ which belong to a scope $Sc_P({}^{i}x)$ where ${}^{i}x$ is a defining or zero occurrence of x, by the occurrences of a variable y such that

(1) $\mathrm{CoFaSc}({}^{i}x)\cap \mathrm{CoFaSc}({}^{h}y)=\emptyset$ for each defining or zero occurrence ${}^{h}y$ where $1\leqslant h\leqslant sc_P(y)$, if $y\in \mathrm{VarP}$ (otherwise always).

It should be mentioned that in the case VarP=Var it can happen that no elementary renaming is possible within Var (but there are possible renamings using new variables not contained in the given Var).

An <u>elementary reordering</u> (permuting) <u>of operational commands</u> consists in an exchange of places of two neighbouring commands $K^{(p)}=O^{(p)}$ and $K^{(p+1)}=O^{(p+1)}$ such that

(2) if $O^{(p)}=[f(x_1,\dots,x_n)=:x_o]$ and $O^{(p+1)}=[g(y_1,\dots,y_m)=:y_o]$ then $x_o \neq y_i$ for $i=0,1,\dots,m$ and $y_o \neq x_i$ for $i=1,2,\dots,n$.

Thus one could express this similarity by an equality:

(I) $P=(\dots; O^{(p)}; O^{(p+1)};\dots)=(\dots; O^{(p+1)}; O^{(p)};\dots)=P^*$.

An <u>elementary splitting of an operational command</u> into two branches consists in the following construction: if $K^{(p)}=O^{(p)}$ and $K^{(p+1)}=\langle k^{(p+1)},C^{(p+1)}\rangle$ ($K^{(p+1)}$ need not be marked) where $O^{(p)}=[f(x_1,\dots,x_n)=:x_o]$ and $J^{(p+1)}=[m_1,m_2][g(y_1,\dots,y_m)]$ satisfy (2) and if there are commands $K^{(r)}=\langle k^{(r)},C^{(r)}\rangle$ or $K^{(s)}=\langle k^{(s)},C^{(s)}\rangle$ such that $k^{(r)}=m_1$ or $k^{(s)}=m_2$ respectively, then the command $K^{(p)}$ is omitted, the markers $k^{(r)}$ and $k^{(s)}$ of the commands $K^{(r)}$ and $K^{(s)}$ are omitted too, but immediately on the left of this modified $\bar{K}^{(r)}$ or $\bar{K}^{(s)}$ a new marked command $\langle k^{(r)},O^{(p)}\rangle$ or $\langle k^{(s)},O^{(p)}\rangle$ respectively must be inserted.

This similarity may be expressed by the following equality:

(II) $P=(\dots; \langle k^{(r)},C^{(r)}\rangle;\dots; O^{(p)}; \langle k^{(p+1)},J^{(p+1)}\rangle;\dots$
$\dots; \langle k^{(s)},C^{(s)}\rangle;\dots)=(\dots; \langle k^{(r)}, O^{(p)}\rangle; C^{(r)};\dots; \langle k^{(p+1)},$
$J^{(p+1)}\rangle;\dots; \langle k^{(s)}, O^{(p)}\rangle; C^{(s)};\dots)=P^*$.

Obviously the converse change to the previous one, called an elementary joining of two operational commands splitted into two branches, need not be described here.

The repeating of an operational command consists in the insertion of a new copy of a command $O^{(p)}=[f(x_1,\dots,x_n)=:$ $=:x_o]$ such that $x_o \neq x_i$ for $i=1,2,\dots,n$, immediately on the right of it, which may be visualized by the following equality:

(III) $P=(\dots;\ \langle k^{(p)},\ O^{(p)}\rangle\ ,\dots)=(\dots;\ \langle k^{(p)},\ O^{(p)}\rangle\ ;\ O^{(p)},\dots)=$ $=P^*$.

Again the converse change expressed by this equality by reading from the right to the left, and called an omission of a repeated operational command, need not further be described.

The division of a scope consists in a special renaming of variables defined as follows: if ${}^k x$ and ${}^h x$ are the defining occurrences appearing in operational commands $\langle k^{(p)},\ O^{(p)}\rangle$ and $O^{(p)}$ such that the second of them arised by repetition of the first, then $Sc_P({}^k x)=Sc_P({}^h x)$ and the occurrence ${}^h x$ and some of the occurrences from $Sc_P({}^k x)$ may be replaced by occurrences of a variable y such that if S is the set of new occurrences of y and ${}^{j}y$ is the new defining occurrence arised from ${}^h x$, then the following holds:

(3) $S \cap CoFSc({}^i y)=\emptyset$ for each defining or zero occurrence ${}^i y \neq {}^{j}y$. and therefore $Sc_P({}^{j}y)=S$.

The identification of scopes is a converse change for the previous division of a scope.

The *developing of a cycle* consists in the following construction visualized by a corresponding equality: a sequence of commands $K^{(i)};K^{(i+1)};\dots;K^{(h)}$ is called *cycle* if $i \quad h$, $K^{(h)}=\langle k^{(h)},J^{(h)}\rangle$ where $J^{(h)}=\left[g_{[m_1,m_2]}(y_1,\dots,y_m)\right]$ is a conditional jumping command and either $k^{(i)}=m_1$ or $k^{(i)}=m_2$; if there is a cycle then:

(IV) $P=(\dots;K^{(i-1)};K^{(i)};K^{(i+1)};\dots;K^{(h)};K^{(h+1)};\dots)=$
$=(\dots;K^{(i-1)};C^{(i)};C^{(i+1)};\dots;C^{(h)};K^{(i)};K^{(i+1)};\dots$
$\dots K^{(h)};K^{(h+1)};\dots)=P$.

By reading this equality from the right to the left one gets a *wraping up of a cycle*.

Some further equalities may also be introduced (e.g. if two different conditional jumping commands cause a jump to the same marked command, which is followed by operational or stopping commands, then it is possible to change markers and repeat the mentioned part of the program, etc.) and probably in the future some new ones will be discovered. The question whether or not the set of elementary changes or of the corresponding equalities is complete, and in what sense, will be answered in Sect.5.

4. Programming language of a PLS

In contradistinction to the programming language schemes which correspond to the machine independent languages, the concept of machine dependency may be clarified by the requirement of a particular computer the computations of which are to be determined by such a machine dependent programming language.

All the computers may be classified according to their operational units OU and according to their storages, which are restricted here to one single storage unit, SU being a set of memory cells Adr, in such a way that each class of computers is characterized exactly by one programming language scheme, i.e. by its operational, conditional, variable and marker types in the following way:

$OU=\langle Obj,Fct,\{true,false\},Rel\rangle$ where Obj is a set of <u>basic objects</u> the computer is dealing with, Fct is a set of <u>basic functions=operations</u> in Obj and Rel is a set of <u>basic relations</u> in Obj considered as functions with values in the set $\{true,false\}$ (it is assumed that $Obj\cap\{true,false\}=\emptyset$).

If a set of labels Lab is prescribed, then the following set of functions called <u>conditions</u> $Rel_{[Lab]}=\{b^{(n)}[m_1,m_2];$ $b^{(n)}\in Rel$ is an n-ary function and $m_1,m_2\in Lab$ such that $b^{(n)}[m_1,m_2](o_1,o_2,\dots,o_n)=m_1$ (or m_2) $\Leftrightarrow b^{(n)}(o_1,o_2,\dots,o_n)=$ $=$true (or false) for all $o_i\in Obj$ where $i=1,2,\dots,n\}$. Thus a labelled operational unit is defined as follows: $OU_{[Lab]}=$ $=\langle Obj,Fct,Lab,Rel_{[Lab]}\rangle$.

The <u>interpretation of a</u> $PLS=\langle Opr,Pred,Mar,Var\rangle$ <u>in a computer</u> $OUSU=\langle Obj,Fct,\{true,false\},Rel,Lab,Adr\rangle$ is an one-to-one function int such that

(a) Domain int=Opr $\cup$ Pred, Range int=Fct $\cup$ Rel;

(b) if $f \in Opr^{(n)}$, then $int_{\smile} f \in Fct$ and $int_{\smile} f$ is an n-ary operation for each n=1,2,...,;

(c) if $g \in Pred^{(n)}$, then $int_{\smile} g \in Rel$ and $int_{\smile} g$ is an n-ary relation for each n=1,2,...;

under the assumption that Mar=Lab and Var=Adr (there is no loss of generality and the situation is essentially clearer than if some correspondences between Mar and Lab on the one hand and between Var and Adr on the other hand, were introduced).

The programming language scheme PLS= $\langle$Opr,Pred,Mar,Var$\rangle$ together with one of its interpretations int in a computer CU= $\langle$Obj,Fct,$\{$true,false$\}$,Rel$\rangle$ is called a <u>programming language</u> PL <u>for the computer</u> OU and a <u>programming language</u> PL <u>of the programming language scheme</u> PLS.

Each interpretation int of a PLS may be extended uniquely in such a way that $int_{\smile}(Cond)=Rel_{[Mar]}$ and

(d) if $g[m_1,m_2] \in Cond^{(n)}$ then $int\big(g[m_1,m_2]\big) \in Rel_{[Mar]}$ and $int\big(g[m_1,m_2]\big)$ is an n-ary function for each n=1,2,... .

It is clear that after this extension, the interpretation int remains to be one-to-one mapping.

Further we shall discuss the programming languages of programming languages shemes and therefore we shall accept a usual language convention, i.e. we shall write the name of an operation f but we shall mean the corresponding int$f$, etc.

Therefore we write a command scheme $f(x_1,x_2,\dots,x_n)=:x_o$ but we mean the corresponding actual command int $f(x_1,x_2,\dots,x_n)=:x_o$ and similarly the program schemes, under the interpretation, become actual programs.

By the storage unit SU of the considered computer the set of all <u>states of storage</u> $Sta=\{S;\ S$ is a function such that The Domain $S=Var$ and Range $S\subset Obj\}$ is determined.

If $C=[f(x_1,x_2,\dots,x_n)=:x_o]$ is an operational command and $S\in Sta$ a state of storage, then by application of C to S one gets a new state $S^*=CS$ such that $S^*(x_o)=f(S(x_1),S(x_2),\dots,S(x_n))$ and $S^*(x)=S(x)$ for each $x\in Var$ such that $x\neq x_o$. As f need not be a total function, the new state S need not be always determined; in such a case one says that C <u>is not applicable to S</u> (and similarly it is defined a non-applicability of a conditional command $C=[g[m_1,m_2](y_1,y_2,\dots,y_n)]$ to a state S; if C is applicable to S, then $g(S(y_1),S(y_2),\dots,S(y_n))\in Mar$ and therefore $CS=m_1$ or $=m_2$, i.e. CS is no state).

According to [3] the computing prescription for an activity of the considered computer consists in a consecutive application of the commands of the program $P=(K^{(1)},K^{(2)},\dots,K^{(n)})$ to the intermediate states of storage, if a prescribed initial state $S\in Sta$ is given. This activity is completely described as follows:

One defines $K_1=K^{(1)}$, $S_o=S$ and $C_1=C^{(1)}$ at the beginning and if K_i, S_{i-1} and C_i (contained in K_i) have been defined, where $K_i=K^{(j)}$ for some j, $1 \leq j \leq n$, then the following cases must be distinguished: (i) either C_i=Stop and then the activity is finished and called <u>stopped</u>; the state S_{i-1} is called the <u>resulting state of the state</u> S_o which is called an <u>original state</u>; (ii) or C_i is an operational command which is either not applicable to S_{i-1} or j=n and then the activity is finished (but not stopped), or C_i is applicable to S_{i-1} and $j < n$ and then one defines $K_{i+1}=K^{(j+1)}$, $S_i=C_iS_{i-1}$; (iii) or C_i is a conditional jumping command, which is either not applicable to S_{i-1} and then the activity is finished (but not stopped), or C_i is applicable to S_{i-1} and in this case either there exists h, $1 \leq h \leq n$ such that $k^{(h)}=CS_{i-1}$ and then $K_{i+1}=K^{(h)}$ and $S_i=S_{i-1}$, or $CS_{i-1} \neq k^{(h)}$ for each h=1,2,...,n and then the activity is again finished (but not stopped).

If the activity is stopped at K_{m+1}(i.e. C_{m+1}=Stop) then the sequence $(S_1,S_2,\ldots,S_m)$ or $(S_o,S_1,\ldots,S_m)$ is called <u>computation</u> or <u>complete computation</u> by P for S_o respectively and the sequence $(K_1,K_2,\ldots,K_{m+1})$ is called a <u>course of P for S_o</u> being a branch program according to Sect. 1. By omission of all conditional commands (and of all markers of marked commands) from the course $(K_1,K_2,\ldots,K_{m+1})$ a sequence $(C_{i_1},C_{i_2},\ldots,C_{i_p})$ arises where C_{i_j} is contained in K_{i_j} and $1 \leq i_1 < i_2 < \ldots < i_p=m+1$, which is called <u>operational course of P for S_o</u>. This operational course of P for S_o is proper operational meaning of the program P and it should be stressed that this meaning depends on the original state S_o (this operational meaning may be found among the branches of the program scheme P independentely on any interpretation but in PLS no correspondence between these operational meanings and the original and resulting states may be established). Obviously the operational meaning of P is the set of all courses of P or of all its operational courses, and only in very special cases, i.e. of simple programs without conditional commands, this set contains only one single course.

The function $F_P^* = \{(S_o, S_m);\ S_o \in \text{Sta}$ and there exists a complete computation by P from S_o such that its last element is $S_m \in \text{Sta}\}$ is called a computable (state function) by P in the considered computer QUSU and by partialization original or resulting state concerning the input or output variables of P respectively one gets a p/q variabled function computable by P $f_P = \{(S_o|_{I_P}, S_m|_{O_P});\ (S_o, S_m) \in f_P^*\}$ which is a functional meaning of P in the considered computer QUSU. The dependency of f_P on the variables from Var may be excluded by introduction of an unordered p/q function which, of course, must be represented by any member uf_P of the following class of usual ordered p/q functions: arbitrary but fixed orderings of variables in I_P and O_P are prescribed, e.g. $I_P = \{x_1, x_2, \ldots, x_p\}$ and $O_P = \{y_1, y_2, \ldots \ldots, y_q\}$ and then $uf_P = \{[(\sigma_{i_1}, \sigma_{i_2}, \ldots, \sigma_{i_p}), (\sigma_{j_1}, \sigma_{j_2}, \ldots, \sigma_{j_q})];$

There exist $(S_o,S_m)\in f_P^*$ such that $S_o|_{I_P}=\{(x_1, \sigma_{i_1}),(x_2, \sigma_{i_2}),\ldots$ $\ldots,(x_p, \sigma_{i_p})\}$ and $S_m|_{O_P}=\{(y_1, \sigma_{j_1}),(y_2, \sigma_{j_2}),\ldots,(y_q, \sigma_{j_q})\}$. Thus uf_P is a system of q functions of p variables in Obj and therefore it has very good sense a question whether or not an arbitrary function f of p variables in Obj being prescribed is computable in the given computer OUSU, i.e. whether or not there exists a program P such that $|I_P|=p$ and $|O_P|=q$ and $f=uf_P$ for suitable choice of an ordering of input variables of P.

Then one may say that P and Q are <u>functionaly equivalent</u> and write $f_P=f_Q$ for two programs $P,Q\in$ Prog in the considered programming language PL of PLS, if the following requirement is satisfied; uf_P and uf_Q are <u>permutationally identical</u>, i.e. one of them may be obtained from the other by suitable permutation of its input columns and by suitable permutation of its output columns.

5. Some concepts of algorithmic method in a PLS

In Sec. 3 there was proposed that an algorithmic method in a PLS is a class of all programs which are structurally equivalent or similar each the other. If a PL of the PLS is taken in account then a class of programs in PL may be considered as an algorithmic method only if all these programs are functionaly equivalent, i.e. it seems to us natural to require that by all programs being realisations of the same algorithmic method the same computable function must be determined.

A justification of the above proposed concept of algorithmic method being a class of all similar programs in a PLS may be found in the following theorem which can be proved using several lemmas and auxiliary theorems:

Theorem 1 If P and Q are similar programs of a programming language scheme PLS, i.e. one of them may be obtained from the other by consecutive applications of all the elementary changes listed in Sect. 3, then $f_P=f_Q$ in each programming language PL of the PLS, i.e. in each computer required by any interpretation of the PLS.

On the other hand if $f_P=f_Q$ in a programming language PL of the PLS then P and Q need not be similar at all, which corresponds to the well known fact, that the same problem may be solved by using different algorithmic methods, i.e. the same function may be computed, by essentially different programs, which means by programs which are realizations of two different algorithmic methods.

Using a series of lemmas and auxiliary theorems another theorem may be proved:

Theorem 2 If P and Q are simple programs, i.e. no conditional commands are admitted, of a programming language scheme PLS such that $f_P=f_Q$ holds in each programming language PL of the PLS, then P and Q are similar, i.e. one of them may be obtained from the other by consecutive application of some elementary changes listed in Sect. 3.

Now it is clear that the list of types of elementary changes required in Sect. 3 is complete with respect to the set of simple programs. Generally the question about a complete list of types of changes remains open.

Interesting question about suitable representation of an algorithmic method (i.e. of a similarity classes of programs) leads to the notion of algorithmic diagram defined in Sect. 2 which may be addressless and, noreover, markerless too, and it will be not discussed here further. It should be mentioned, that if some flow-edges are removed from an algorithmic diagram an algorithmic net arises the concept of which probably is sufficient and unique representation of algorithmic method in the above defined sense.

A second concept of algorithmic method can be introduced if the independency on the used conditions, and even on the corresponding relations, is required. This independency may be defined as follows: if $P=(K^{(1)},K^{(2)},\ldots,K^{(n)})$ is a program then an occurrence of an operational command is called essential if either its defining occurrence (of a variable appearing on the right of =:) is an output occurrence or the scope of its defining occurrence contains an applied occurrence (of a variable appearing on the left of =:) in an occurrence of an essential operational command. By definition each occurrence of a stopping command may be considered as essential too. All other occurrences of commands, which are not essential, are called <u>decision occurrences of commands</u>, because they are used for some decision purposes only, i.e. they prepare certain jumps. If in branch programs only all essential occurrences of commands are kept (without markers, because they are superfluous in this case), i.e. all decision occurrences of commands are omitted, then arise their <u>essential branch programs</u> and it is easy to see that each branch program is functionally equivalent to its essential branch program. Finally one may define a <u>decision-free algorithmic method</u> as a class of all weakly similar programs in a PLS where P and Q are said to be <u>weakly similar</u> if there exists an one-to-one correspondence among the sets of their essential branch programs such that the corresponding branches are functionally equivalent, i.e. by Theorem 2 they must be similar too. In a flow-diagram FT_P of P it is possible to define <u>essential</u> and <u>decision subprograms</u> as maximal convex (i.e. with respect to the ordering in branches) sets of essential or decision occurrences of commands respectively, and in a more complicated way (similarly as with scopes in P) may be introduced essential and decision subprograms in P itself. In the example 1 there exist two essential subprograms in P: EP_1=(x+y=:z;x/y=:y; Stop) and EP_2=(x/y=:y;Stop) and also two decision subprograms $DP_1=(z <_{[m_1,m_2]} y)$ and $DP_2=(z <_{[m_1,m_2]} y; \langle m_2, x <_{[m_3,m_4]} z \rangle)$ by which the tree FT_P may be covered completelly.

The above mentioned weak similarity allows to compore programs in such a way that some of their parts are prescribed which need not be similar but only functionally equivalent (in each interpretation). This example of a relativisation of the original concept of algorithmic method shows some further possibilities in this direction . Of course we are who must decide how strong or weak concept of algorithmic method will be useful.

As the third and last concept of algorithmic method will be discussed a possibility to restrict the class of all possible interpretations of a programming language scheme PLS for a computer $\mathfrak{OU}=\langle Obj,Fct,\{true,false\},Rel\rangle$ in the same way as it is usual in logic, i.e. if each algebraic structure $\mathfrak{OU}$ must satisfy certain <u>axioms</u> of $\mathfrak{OU}$ concerning the functions from Fct and relations from Rel. E.g. the following may be required: the commutativity or the associativy or the distributivity of some binary functions or the reflexivity, symmetry, anti-symmetry, transitivity,of some binary relations, etc. Obviously these axioms are expressed using the considered PLS, i.e. using names of functions from Opr and of relations from Pred and the variables from Var.

If the symbol $+\in$ Opr is a name of a binary operation of a PLS (which need not be commutative) then the programs consisting of single operational commands P=(x+y=:y) and Q=(y+x=:y) are not functionally equivalent in all interpretations of the PLS, because if one takes Obj=$\{0,1\}$ and $int_{\smile}+=\{((1,0),1),((1,1),1),$

((0,1),0),((0,0),0)} then for x=1, y=0 one gets x+y=1≠0=y+x, etc. On the other hand if int + is a commutative function then $f_P=f_Q$ is true in each interpretation of PLS satisfying axiom (scheme) X+Y=Y+X. Therefore although P and Q are not similar (by Theorem 2) they could be made similar if some further elementary changes of programs are added. And it is clear that the axiom of commutativity of the operation + is equivalent to the requirement of similarity of all pairs of programs which are obtained by substitution of arbitrary variables from Var in the following similarity scheme:

(commut) (X+Y=:Y)=(Y+X=:Y).

It is clear that using this axiom for similarity much more programs of PLS will be similar than sooner without this axiom. Therefore a larger class of similar programs is determined than before, i.e. concept of algorithmic method is relativised to the prescribed axiomatic system of similarities.

It is easy to see what meanings have the following axioms of similarities:

(assoc) (X+Y=:A;A+Z=:B)=(Y+Z=:A;X+A=:B),

(distrib) (X+Y=:A;A.Z=:B)=(X.Z=:A;Y.Z=:C;A+C=:B).

Now it is quite clear that a programming language scheme is an analogon to a programming theory and all its programming languages are its programming models. In general, if no axioms are required, then a lot of similarities hold (e.g. (I), (II), (III) etc.) which correspond to the tautologies in logic. The similarities, i.e. the equalities, are theorems in the considered theories but the elements are not propositions or formulas but commands or programs. Thus the calculus of propositions is replaced by a calculus of programs and instead of general and existential quantifiers the concepts of defining and applied occurrences and of scope are introduced.

If we take Opr= $\{+, \cdot, /, -\}$, Rel= $\{<, \leq, =, \neq, \text{etc.}\}$ and Obj= {the set of all rational numbers} and if all these operational or relational symbols are interpreted in the usual way as in numerical analysis of rational numbers, i.e. all known axioms of ring of rational numbers are accepted, then the concept of <u>rational arithmetics method</u> is introduced and all the apparatus of the considered PLS and of its choosen PL is a new tool for investigations in theory of rational numbers.

If we take Opr= $\{\wedge, \vee, \neg, \rightarrow, |\}$, Rel= $\{=, \neq\}$, Obj= $\{0,1\}$ and if these symbols are interpreted as usual in the smallest Boolean algebra then it is easy to see that in this case the concept of Boolean method corresponds with the concept of Boolean function itself.

R e f e r e n c e s

[1] A.J.Perlis and K.Samelson, Preliminary report of ACM-GAMM Committee on an International Algebraic Language, Annual review in automatic programming, I, ed. R.Goodman, Pergamon Press, New York-Oxford-London-Paris, 1960, pp.268-290

[2] K.Čulík, On semantics of programming languages, Automatentheorie und formale Sprachen, ed. J.Dörr-G.Hotz, Bibliographisches Institute, Mannheim-Wien-Zurüch, 1970, pp.291-303

[3] K,Čulík, On sequential and non-sequential machines and their relation to the computation in computers (in print)

Lecture Notes in Economics and Mathematical Systems

Vol. 69: S. Ashour, Sequencing Theory. V, 133 pages. 4°. 1972. DM 16,–

Vol. 70: J. P. Brown, The Economic Effects of Floods. Investigations of a Stochastic Model of Rational Investment Behavior in the Face of Floods. V, 87 pages. 4°. 1972. DM 16,–

Vol. 71: R. Henn und O. Opitz, Konsum- und Produktionstheorie II. V, 134 Seiten. 4°. 1972. DM 16,–

Vol. 72: T. P. Bagchi and J. G. C. Templeton, Numerical Methods in Markov Chains and Bulk Queues. XI, 89 pages. 4°. 1972. DM 16,–

Vol. 73: H. Kiendl, Suboptimale Regler mit abschnittweise linearer Struktur. VI, 146 Seiten. 4°. 1971. DM 16,–

Vol. 74: F. Pokropp, Aggregation von Produktionsfunktionen. VI, 107 Seiten. 4°. 1972. DM 16,–

Vol. 75: GI-Gesellschaft für Informatik e.V. Bericht Nr. 3. 1. Fachtagung über Programmiersprachen · München, 9.–11. März 1971. Herausgegeben im Auftrag der Gesellschaft für Informatik von H. Langmaack und M. Paul. VII, 280 Seiten. 4°. 1972. DM 24,–

Vol. 76: G. Fandel, Optimale Entscheidung bei mehrfacher Zielsetzung, VI, 114 Seiten, 1972. DM 16,–.

Vol. 77: A. Auslender, Problèmes de Minimax via l'Analyse Convexe et les Inegalités Variationnelles: Théorie et Algorithmes. VII, 132 Seiten. 1972. DM 16,–

Ökonometrie und Unternehmensforschung
Econometrics and Operations Research

Vol. I — Nichtlineare Programmierung. Von H. P. Künzi und W. Krelle unter Mitwirkung von W. Oettli. – Mit 18 Abbildungen. XV, 221 Seiten. 1962. Geb. DM 38,–

Vol. II — Lineare Programmierung und Erweiterungen. Von G. B. Dantzig. Ins Deutsche übertragen und bearbeitet von A. Jaeger. – Mit 103 Abbildungen. XVI, 712 Seiten. 1966. Geb. DM 68,–

Vol. III — Stochastic Processes. By M. Girault. – With 35 figures. XII, 126 pages. 1966. Cloth DM 28,–

Vol. IV — Methoden der Unternehmensforschung im Versicherungswesen. Von K.-H. Wolff. – Mit 14 Diagrammen. VIII, 266 Seiten. 1966. Geb. DM 49,–

Vol. V — The Theory of Max-Min and its Application to Weapons Allocation Problems. By John M. Danskin. – With 6 figures. X, 126 pages. 1967. Cloth DM 32,–

Vol. VI — Entscheidungskriterien bei Risiko. Von H. Schneeweiss. – Mit 35 Abbildungen. XII, 214 Seiten. 1967. Geb. DM 48,–

Vol. VII — Boolean Methods in Operations Research and Related Areas. By P. L. Hammer (Ivănescu) and S. Rudeanu. With a preface by R. Bellman. – With 25 figures. XVI, 329 pages. 1968. Cloth DM 46,–

Vol. VIII — Strategy for R & D: Studies in the Microeconomics of Development. By Th. Marschak, Th. K. Glennan JR., and R. Summers. – With 44 figures. XIV, 330 pages. 1967. Cloth DM 56,80

Vol. IX — Dynamic Programming of Economic Decisions. By M. J. Beckmann. – With 9 figures XII, 143 pages. 1968. Cloth DM 28,–

Vol. X — Input-Output-Analyse. Von J. Schumann. – Mit 12 Abbildungen. X, 311 Seiten. 1968. Geb. DM 58,–

Vol. XI — Produktionstheorie. Von W. Wittmann. – Mit 54 Abbildungen. VIII, 177 Seiten. 1968. Geb. DM 42,–

Vol. XII — Sensivitätsanalysen und parametrische Programmierung. Von W. Dinkelbach. – Mit 20 Abbildungen. XI, 190 Seiten. 1969. Geb. DM 48,–

Vol. XIII — Graphentheoretische Methoden und ihre Anwendungen. Von W. Knödel. – Mit 24 Abbildungen. VIII, 111 Seiten. 1969. Geb. DM 38,–

Vol. XIV — Praktische Studien zur Unternehmensforschung. Von E. Nievergelt, O. Müller, F. E. Schlaepfer und W. H. Landis. – Mit 82 Abbildungen. XII, 240 Seiten. Geb. DM 58,–

Vol. XV — Optimale Reihenfolgen. Von H. Müller-Merbach. – Mit 43 Abbildungen. IX, 225 Seiten. 1970. Geb. DM 60,–

Vol. XVI — Preispolitik der Mehrproduktenunternehmung in der statischen Theorie. Von R. Selten. – Mit 20 Abbildungen. VIII, 195 Seiten. 1970. Geb. DM 64,–

Vol. XVII — Information Theory for Systems Engineers. By L. P. Hyvärinen. – With 42 figures. VIII, 197 pages. 1970. Cloth DM 44,–

Vol. XVIII — Unternehmensforschung im Bergbau. Von F. L. Wilke. – Mit 29 Abbildungen. VIII, 150 Seiten. 1972. Geb. DM 54,–